American College of Physicians

MKSAP® 15

Medical Knowledge Self-Assessment Program®

Dermatology

Dermatology

Contributors

Kathryn Schwarzenberger, MD, Book Editor[2]
Associate Professor of Medicine (Dermatology)
Associate Chief and Residency Program Director
Division of Dermatology
University of Vermont College of Medicine
Burlington, Vermont

Jack Ende, MD, MACP, Associate Editor[1]
Professor of Medicine
University of Pennsylvania
Chief, Department of Medicine
Penn Presbyterian Medical Center
Philadelphia, Pennsylvania

Jeffrey P. Callen, MD, FACP[2]
Professor of Medicine (Dermatology)
Chief, Division of Dermatology
University of Louisville School of Medicine
Louisville, Kentucky

Dirk Elston, MD[2]
Director, Department of Dermatology
Geisinger Medical Center
Danville, Pennsylvania

Lindy P. Fox, MD[2]
Assistant Professor of Clinical Dermatology
Director, Hospital Consultation Service
Department of Dermatology
University of California, San Francisco
San Francisco, California

William D. James, MD[1]
Paul R. Gross Professor and Vice Chair
Department of Dermatology
University of Pennsylvania
Philadelphia, Pennsylvania

Editor-in-Chief

Patrick C. Alguire, MD, FACP[1]
Director, Education and Career Development
American College of Physicians
Philadelphia, Pennsylvania

Dermatology Reviewers

Richard Fatica, MD[1]
Lisa Inouye, MD, MPH, FACP[1]
Khalid J. Qazi, MD, MACP[1]
Steven F. Reichert, MD, FACP[1]
Leonard H. Sigal, MD, FACP[2]
Laura J. Zakowski, MD[1]

Dermatology ACP Editorial Staff

Katie Idell, Production Administrator/Editor
Sean McKinney, Director, Self-Assessment Programs
Margaret Wells, Managing Editor
Charles Rossi, Senior Associate of Clinical Content
Development
Shannon O'Sullivan, Editorial Coordinator

ACP Principal Staff

Steven E. Weinberger, MD, FACP[2]
Deputy Executive Vice President
Senior Vice President, Medical Education and Publishing

D. Theresa Kanya, MBA[1]
Vice President, Medical Education and Publishing

Sean McKinney[1]
Director, Self-Assessment Programs

Margaret Wells[1]
Managing Editor

Charles Rossi[1]
Senior Associate of Clinical Content Development

Becky Krumm[1]
Senior Staff Editor

Ellen McDonald, PhD[1]
Senior Staff Editor

Amanda Neiley[1]
Staff Editor

Katie Idell[1]
Production Administrator/Editor

Valerie Dangovetsky[1]
Program Administrator

John Murray[1]
Editorial Coordinator

Shannon O'Sullivan[1]
Editorial Coordinator

Developed by the American College of Physicians

---

1. Has no relationships with any entity producing, marketing, re-selling, or distributing health care goods or services consumed by, or used on, patients.

2. Has disclosed relationships with entities producing, marketing, re-selling, or distributing health care goods or services consumed by, or used on, patients. See below.

Conflicts of Interest

The following contributors and ACP staff members have disclosed relationships with commercial companies:

Jeffrey P. Callen, MD, FACP
Honoraria
Stiefel Laboratories
Consultantship
Amgen, Centocor, Abbott, EOS, Genentech, Medicis, VSLT
Royalties
Elsevier
Speakers Bureau
Amgen
Other
Genmab (Safety Monitoring Committee)

Dirk Elston, MD
Consultantship
Abbott, Medicis

Lindy P. Fox, MD
Honoraria
Bristol-Myers Squibb, Galderma, Elsevier

Kathryn Schwarzenberger, MD
Research Grants/Contracts
Galderma, Genentech, Amgen
Honoraria
Abbott

Leonard H. Sigal, MD, FACP
Employment
Bristol-Myers Squibb

Steven E. Weinberger, MD, FACP
Stock Options/Holdings
Abbott, GlaxoSmithKline

Acknowledgments

The American College of Physicians (ACP) gratefully acknowledges the special contributions to the development and production of the 15th edition of the Medical Knowledge Self-Assessment Program® (MKSAP 15) of Scott Thomas Hurd (Senior Systems Analyst/Developer), Ricki Jo Kauffman (Manager, Systems Development), Michael Ripca (Technical Administrator/Graphics Designer), and Lisa Torrieri (Graphic Designer). The Digital version (CD-ROM and Online components) was developed within the ACP's Interactive Product Development Department by Steven Spadt (Director), Christopher Forrest (Senior Software Developer), Ryan Hinkel (Senior Software Developer), John McKnight (Software Developer), Sean O'Donnell (Senior Software Developer), and Brian Sweigard (Senior Software Developer). Computer scoring and reporting are being performed by ACT, Inc., Iowa City, Iowa. The College also wishes to acknowledge that many other persons, too numerous to mention, have contributed to the production of this program. Without their dedicated efforts, this program would not have been possible.

Continuing Medical Education

The American College of Physicians is accredited by the Accreditation Council for Continuing Medical Education (ACCME) to provide continuing medical education for physicians.

The American College of Physicians designates this educational activity for a maximum of 166 *AMA PRA Category 1 Credits*™. Physicians should only claim credit commensurate with the extent of their participation in the activity.

AMA PRA Category 1 Credit™ is available from July 31, 2009, to July 31, 2012.

Learning Objectives

The learning objectives of MKSAP 15 are to:
- Close gaps between actual care in your practice and preferred standards of care, based on best evidence
- Diagnose disease states that are less common and sometimes overlooked and confusing
- Improve management of comorbidities that can complicate patient care
- Determine when to refer patients for surgery or care by subspecialists
- Pass the ABIM certification examination
- Pass the ABIM maintenance of certification examination

Target Audience

- General internists and primary care physicians
- Subspecialists who need to remain up-to-date in internal medicine
- Residents preparing for the certifying examination in internal medicine
- Physicians preparing for maintenance of certification in internal medicine (recertification)

How to Submit for CME Credits

To earn CME credits, complete a MKSAP 15 answer sheet. Use the enclosed, self-addressed envelope to mail your completed answer sheet(s) to the MKSAP Processing Center for scoring. Remember to provide your MKSAP 15 order and ACP ID numbers in the appropriate spaces on the answer sheet. The order and ACP ID numbers are printed on your mailing label. If you have <u>not</u> received these numbers with your MKSAP 15 purchase, you will need to acquire them to earn CME credits. E-mail ACP's customer service center at custserv@acponline.org. In the subject line, write "MKSAP 15 order/ACP ID numbers." In the body of the e-mail, make sure you include your e-mail address as well as your full name, address, city, state, ZIP code, country, and telephone number. Also identify where you have made your MKSAP 15 purchase. You will receive your MKSAP 15 order and ACP ID numbers by e-mail within 72 business hours.

Permission/Consent for Use of Figures Shown in MKSAP 15 Dermatology Multiple-Choice Questions

Figure shown in Self-Assessment Test Item 9 appears courtesy of Dr. Barbara Mathes.

Figure shown in Self-Assessment Test Item 18 appears courtesy of Dr. David Crosby.

Figures shown in Self-Assessment Test Item 25 are reprinted with permission from Shrift K, Wallington CL, Schilling L, Morelli JG, Dellavalle RP. Vitiligo. http://pier.acponline.org/physicians/diseases/d621/diagnosis/d621-s3.html. [Date accessed: 2009 July 27] In: PIER [online database]. Philadelphia, American College of Physicians, 2009.

Disclosure Policy

It is the policy of the American College of Physicians (ACP) to ensure balance, independence, objectivity, and scientific rigor in all its educational activities. To this end, and consistent with the policies of the ACP and the Accreditation Council for Continuing Medical Education (ACCME), contributors to all ACP continuing medical education activities are required to disclose all relevant financial relationships with any entity producing, marketing, re-selling, or distributing health care goods or services consumed by, or used on, patients. Contributors are required to use generic names in the discussion of therapeutic options and are required to identify any unapproved, off-label, or investigative use of commercial products or devices. Where a trade name is used, all available trade names for the same product type are also included. If trade-name products manufactured by companies with whom contributors have relationships are discussed, contributors are asked to provide evidence-based citations in support of the discussion. The information is reviewed by the committee responsible for producing this text. If necessary, adjustments to topics or contributors' roles in content development are made to balance the discussion. Further, all readers of this text are asked to evaluate the content for evidence of commercial bias so that future decisions about content and contributors can be made in light of this information.

Resolution of Conflicts

To resolve all conflicts of interest and influences of vested interests, the ACP precluded members of the content-creation committee from deciding on any content issues that involved generic or trade-name products associated with proprietary entities with which these committee members had relationships. In addition, content was based on best evidence and updated clinical care guidelines, when such evidence and guidelines were available. Contributors' disclosure information can be found with the list of contributors' names and those of ACP principal staff listed in the beginning of this book.

Educational Disclaimer

The editors and publisher of MKSAP 15 recognize that the development of new material offers many opportunities for error. Despite our best efforts, some errors may persist in print. Drug dosage schedules are, we believe, accurate and in accordance with current standards. Readers are advised, however, to ensure that the recommended dosages in MKSAP 15 concur with the information provided in the product information material. This is especially important in cases of new, infrequently used, or highly toxic drugs. Application of the information in MKSAP 15 remains the professional responsibility of the practitioner.

The primary purpose of MKSAP 15 is educational. Information presented, as well as publications, technologies, products, and/or services discussed, is intended to inform subscribers about the knowledge, techniques, and experiences of the contributors. A diversity of professional opinion exists, and the views of the contributors are their own and not those of the ACP. Inclusion of any material in the program does not constitute endorsement or recommendation by the ACP. The ACP does not warrant the safety, reliability, accuracy, completeness, or usefulness of and disclaims any and all liability for damages and claims that may result from the use of information, publications, technologies, products, and/or services discussed in this program.

Publisher's Information

Unauthorized Use of This Book Is Against the Law

MKSAP 15 ISBN: 978-1-934465-25-7
Dermatology ISBN: 978-1-934465-33-2

Printed in the United States of America.

For order information in the U.S. or Canada call 800-523-1546, extension 2600. All other countries call 215-351-2600. Fax inquiries to 215-351-2799 or e-mail to custserv@acponline.org.

Errata and Norm Tables

Errata for MKSAP 15 will be posted at http://mksap.acponline.org/errata as new information becomes known to the editors.

MKSAP 15 Performance Interpretation Guidelines with Norm Tables, available December 31, 2010, will reflect the knowledge of physicians who have completed the self-assessment tests before the program was published. These physicians took the tests without being able to refer to the syllabus, answers, and critiques. For your convenience, the tables are available in a printable PDF file at http://mksap.acponline.org/normtables.

Table of Contents

Dermatology

Approach to the Patient with Dermatologic Disease

The Thorough Dermatologic Examination

Patients with no dermatologic symptoms do not require routine screening for skin cancer according to recommendations by the U.S. Preventive Services Task Force, because there is insufficient evidence showing that such screening by primary care physicians results in reduced morbidity and mortality. However, patients who present with dermatologic symptoms or a significant dermatologic history should undergo a thorough physical examination, beginning with a complete history.

The exhaustive history should include the time of onset and duration of symptoms, associated symptoms, aggravating or relieving factors, prior episodes, and previous therapies. A review of systems is important in determining whether the skin condition is a manifestation of an underlying systemic disease. For example, erythema nodosum in a patient with a productive cough might suggest tuberculosis infection as the cause of the skin lesions. Review of medications (including topical, oral, prescription, over-the-counter, and herbal medications), as well as any alterations to medication regimens and level of adherence to a previously prescribed topical regimen, is important in determining whether the patient's skin complaint is a manifestation of a drug reaction.

Medical, family, and social history also figure prominently in the dermatologic evaluation because certain skin conditions are associated with underlying diseases (such as vitiligo and autoimmune thyroid disease), have a genetic component (such as atopic dermatitis), or are associated with or exacerbated by social habits or exposures (such as palmoplantar psoriasis and smoking).

The most important goals of the dermatologic evaluation are to recognize the primary lesion (**Table 1**) and to identify the distribution or pattern of cutaneous involvement. A complete cutaneous examination includes evaluation of the scalp, hair, mucous membranes, nails, genitalia, palms, and soles. This is important even in patients in whom only one area of involvement is noted, because diagnostic clues may be found at sites other than that of the presenting lesion. For example, in evaluating the relatively common presenting symptom of "nail fungus," physicians should inspect the areas of the body typically affected by psoriasis, such as the scalp, postauricular areas, elbows, knees, umbilicus, and gluteal cleft, which might lead to findings suggestive of psoriatic nail involvement rather than a fungal infection.

To maximize visual inspection of the skin, the physician should ensure that the patient is undressed, the lighting is bright, and the examination table allows maneuvering on all sides. Close attention should be given to the entire skin surface, and each lesion identified during the examination should

TABLE 1 Primary Dermatologic Lesions		
Primary Lesion	**Definition**	**Common Example**
Macule	Nonpalpable lesion <1 cm in diameter	Freckle
Patch	Nonpalpable lesion ≥1 cm in diameter; macules may coalesce into patches	Tinea versicolor
Papule	Palpable lesion <1 cm in diameter	Red bumps of acne
Plaque	Palpable lesion ≥1 cm in diameter; papules may coalesce into plaques	Psoriasis
Pustule	Lesion that contains purulent fluid	Folliculitis
Vesicle	Lesion <1 cm in diameter that contains clear fluid	Chickenpox
Bulla	Lesion ≥1 cm in diameter that contains clear fluid; the bulla may be tense or flaccid and may be on a base of normal or erythematous skin	Poison ivy contact dermatitis
Nodule	Firm papule or plaque that is deeper in the skin; the overlying skin may be erythematous, ulcerated, or normal in appearance; deep nodules may be palpable but not visible at the skin surface	Erythema nodosum

be noted. The primary lesion (the lesion that clinically represents the pathophysiologic changes occurring in the skin) should be identified after the entire skin surface and mucous membranes have been examined. Distinguishing primary from secondary lesions is one of the most important and potentially difficult parts of the skin examination. Secondary lesions are modifications, usually made by the patient, of the primary lesion (**Table 2**). Excoriations around itchy lesions are common secondary changes. In patients with extensive secondary changes, finding a primary lesion may be difficult. Diagnostic details of lesions that should also be noted are color, configuration, and grouping. Definitions of selected dermatologic terms are listed in **Table 3**.

The next step in the complete skin examination is to note the distribution and pattern of dermatologic involvement and the areas of the body that are spared. Identifying the distribution of an eruption is important, as particular dermatologic diseases tend to favor or spare certain areas of the body. For example, erythema multiforme minor and syphilis favor the palms and soles; atopic dermatitis favors flexural areas; pityriasis rosea favors the upper trunk.

KEY POINT

- The most important goals of the dermatologic examination are to recognize the primary lesion and to identify the distribution or pattern of cutaneous involvement.

Diagnostic Tests and Procedures

Laboratory and radiographic tests are typically performed in patients with skin complaints when an association with an underlying systemic disease is suspected (for example, a fasting lipid profile in a patient with a xanthoma) or when a skin condition itself may have systemic manifestations (for example, urinalysis to evaluate for renal disease in a patient with cutaneous signs of systemic lupus erythematosus).

Common bedside diagnostic tests performed on skin scrapings include the potassium hydroxide (KOH) test for fungi or yeast, Tzanck preparation for herpesvirus infection, oil preparation for scabies, Gram stain for bacteria, and cultures for bacterial and viral infections. These tests are easy to perform and have minimal reagent and equipment requirements; however, skill and experience are necessary for accurate and reliable interpretation.

The skin biopsy is perhaps the most useful diagnostic tool available in the evaluation of a dermatologic disease. Clinicopathologic correlation and the ability of the physician performing the biopsy to accurately interpret the pathology report are essential. In general, if there is a reasonable working differential diagnosis for the presenting skin complaint, a skin biopsy will likely yield useful information. Rather than performing an uninformed biopsy, clinicians should refer patients to a dermatologist if a differential diagnosis cannot be generated clinically. It is rare for a skin biopsy to be absolutely contraindicated. An infected site usually should not be biopsied unless the infection is the indication for the procedure. Patients with bleeding disorders or those taking warfarin or clopidogrel should be referred to a specialist for the biopsy.

Selecting the appropriate type of skin biopsy (shave, punch, or excisional), as well as the best site to sample within a particular skin lesion, is one of the most important aspects of the dermatologic evaluation and requires some knowledge of the diagnostic possibilities. A shave biopsy is usually adequate for inflammatory conditions in which the histopathologic findings are in the superficial dermis or epidermis; these types of conditions present as a patch or thin plaque with or without overlying scale and include eczema, psoriasis, cutaneous T-cell lymphoma, basal cell carcinoma, and squamous cell carcinoma. If deeper pathology, whether inflammatory or malignant, is suspected (such as sarcoidosis, granuloma annulare, and metastatic cancer), a punch biopsy is recommended. For annular lesions, biopsy of the lesion's border is of higher yield than a biopsy of the lesion's central area of clearing. An excisional biopsy is usually performed in the evaluation of a

TABLE 2 Secondary Dermatologic Lesions	
Secondary Lesion	**Definition**
Erosion	Superficial defect in the skin surface to the level of the epidermis or superficial dermis; linear erosions are termed "excoriations" and result from the patient scratching the skin surface, either because of pruritus (most common) or psychogenic disease; annular erosions may be the only indication of a primary vesiculobullous disease
Ulcer	Defect in the skin surface that extends to the level of the dermis or deeper
Lichenification	Thickening of the skin with exaggeration of skin markings; suggests chronic rubbing or scratching
Verruca	Lesion with papillomatous or warty changes on the surface
Purpura	Purple, nonblanching lesions caused by hemorrhage into the skin; may be pinpoint (petechiae), macular, papular, vesicular, or pustular; palpable purpura is the classic presentation of small-vessel vasculitis

TABLE 3 Dermatologic Lexicon

Description	Definition
Annular	Ring shaped
Arcuate	Arc shaped
Serpiginous	Wavy or snakelike
Guttate	Drop shaped
Scalloped	Having a curvilinear border like a seashell
Morbilliform	Generalized, 2- to 5-mm, erythematous macules and/or papules; lesions are found more often on the trunk than the extremities; measles-like; preferred term over "maculopapular"
Scarlatiniform	Pinpoint, rough, sandpaper-like papules; classic for scarlet fever
Reticulated	Netlike; may be macular or scaly, erythematous, hyperpigmented, or purpuric
Sclerotic	Thickened (indurated) and firm
Erythrodermic	Erythema of >90% of the skin surface
Follicular	Centered around a hair follicle

pigmented lesion to rule out a melanoma. Because the depth of the lesion is the most important prognostic indicator for a patient with a suspected melanoma, it is best, whenever possible, to completely excise the entire lesion to the level of the fat. Removal of small pigmented lesions by deep shave excision is also acceptable; however, care must be taken to shave deeply enough to clear the inferior margin. If the lesion is too large for complete excision or if it is in a cosmetically sensitive area such as the face, a punch biopsy down to the level of the fat of the most suspicious area can be performed. However, performing a partial biopsy of a suspected melanoma confers a risk of failure to establish the diagnosis. Because the consequences of improper sampling can be dire, dermatologic referral for the evaluation of a pigmented lesion may be the best approach.

KEY POINTS

- The proper selection of a skin biopsy technique and the accurate interpretation of the pathology report are dependent upon the ability to generate an informed pretest differential diagnosis.
- An excisional biopsy is the diagnostic test of choice for a pigmented lesion suspicious for melanoma.

Dermatologic Referral

A stable, chronic, inflammatory condition that fails to respond to first-line therapy (for example, psoriasis that no longer responds to topical corticosteroids) constitutes the need for a referral. A changing nevus, rapidly growing lesion, and any condition that may be associated with systemic involvement may be an indication for referral, particularly if the clinician is unsure of the diagnosis or proper management. Erythroderma, widespread skin pain, purpura, widespread vesicles or bullae, and necrotic eschars in an immunosuppressed patient may be signs of life-threatening conditions necessitating an emergent referral. **Table 4** highlights signs and symptoms that may warrant emergent dermatologic referral.

When requesting a dermatologic consultation, communicating a complete history, delivering an accurate morphologic description of the eruption or lesion, and formulating a specific question are fundamental to facilitating a referral and ensuring that a patient is seen in the appropriate time frame. It is also important to convey whether or not the consultation is routine, urgent, or emergent.

KEY POINT

- Patients who present with erythroderma, skin pain, or widespread purpura, pustules, vesicles, or blisters should receive emergent referral to a dermatologist.

TABLE 4 Symptoms or Signs Suggesting Emergent Dermatologic Referral

Symptom or Sign	Potential Diagnosis
Acute erythroderma	Drug hypersensitivity reaction, Stevens-Johnson syndrome, toxic epidermal necrolysis, toxic shock syndrome, staphylococcal scalded skin syndrome
Widespread skin pain	Stevens-Johnson syndrome, toxic epidermal necrolysis, toxic shock syndrome, staphylococcal scalded skin syndrome
Widespread pustular eruption	Drug eruption, pustular psoriasis
Acute widespread vesicles, bullae, or denudation (rupture of bullae leaving exposed dermis)	Stevens-Johnson syndrome, toxic epidermal necrolysis, pemphigus vulgaris, bullous pemphigoid
Necrotic eschar in an immunosuppressed patient	Deep fungal infection
Widespread purpura in a netlike pattern with central necrosis (retiform purpura)	Acute vascular compromise, disseminated intravascular coagulation

Bibliography

Schwarzenberger K. The essentials of the complete skin examination. Med Clin North Am. 1998;82(5):981-999. [PMID: 9769791]

U.S. Preventive Services Task Force. Screening for skin cancer: recommendations and rationale. Am J Prev Med. 2001;20(3 Suppl):44-46. [PMID: 11306231]

Therapeutic Principles in Dermatology

Topical Medications

When choosing the most appropriate prescription or over-the-counter dermatologic therapy, the diagnosis, location of the skin symptoms, and patient-related factors should be considered. The ideal medication is strong enough to effectively treat the disease but is not so strong as to cause unnecessary or avoidable side effects. Patients should be consulted on their preferred preparation (for example, ointment, cream, lotion), because the medication is unlikely to be used effectively if the patient considers its texture or feel to be disagreeable. Cost should also be considered, as it varies significantly among dermatologic medications depending on the preparation and whether or not a generic version is available.

Treatment failure may occur when an insufficient quantity of a topical medication is prescribed. Approximately 30 g of topical product are needed to cover the average body once; proportionately smaller amounts are needed for localized areas. Most commercially available corticosteroids come in 30- to 60-g tubes; however, triamcinolone acetonide is usually available in larger quantities, including a 0.5-kg (1-lb.) jar. Patient education, use of dosing devices, and prescription of a sufficient amount of medication may improve patient compliance and therapeutic outcomes.

Emollients consist of moisturizers and occlusives and are useful in treating pruritic conditions such as dermatitis and xerosis (dry skin). Moisturizers, such as mineral oil, coconut oil, lactate, and urea, supply water to the skin. Occlusives, such as petroleum jelly, reduce water loss from the skin.

Most topical corticosteroids are available in multiple preparations, including creams, ointments, and lotions; some also are available as solutions or foams, embedded in tape, and in an oil base. Creams are generally the most cosmetically acceptable corticosteroid product for treating most dermatoses because they do not feel greasy and they absorb well. Because corticosteroid creams often contain alcohols, they may sting if applied to open areas of skin. They contain preservatives that can rarely cause allergic contact dermatitis. Some creams are formulated to enhance their emollient effect.

Ointments are usually petrolatum-based. They provide more emollient effect than creams or lotions but may be less cosmetically acceptable because of their greasy texture. Because the vehicle has an occlusive effect, a corticosteroid in ointment form is more potent than the same drug in cream or lotion form. Because ointments usually do not contain alcohols, they are less likely to sting when applied to open areas of skin. They do, however, commonly contain propylene glycol, which can be an irritant and a contact allergen. Ointments are particularly helpful when treating vulvar dermatoses or when the skin is irritated, as the alcohols in creams may sting.

Lotions contain more water than oil and are thus easily absorbed into the skin. They spread easily and are useful when treating large areas of the body. The higher proportion of water to oil also helps dry the skin, which may be helpful in treating weepy, eczematous dermatoses. Gels have a similar drying effect.

Foams spread easily and dry without significant residue. They are useful for treating dermatoses in hair-bearing areas, as are solutions. Their cost, however, may be higher than the equivalent liquid formulations.

Topical corticosteroids are grouped according to potency; there is an approximately 1000-fold difference between the weakest and strongest formulations (**Table 5**). Milligram per milligram, halogenated corticosteroids are more potent (as measured by vasoconstriction ability) than

---

TABLE 5 Potencies of Selected Commonly Prescribed Topical Corticosteroids

Class 1: Superpotent
Clobetasol propionate 0.05%
Betamethasone dipropionate ointment 0.05%
Halobetasol propionate 0.05%

Class 2: High Potency
Augmented betamethasone dipropionate cream 0.05% (in optimized vehicle)
Fluocinonide 0.05%
Desoximetasone 0.25%

Class 3: High Potency
Betamethasone dipropionate cream 0.05%
Betamethasone valerate ointment 0.1%
Triamcinolone acetonide ointment 0.1%
Triamcinolone acetonide cream 0.5%
Fluticasone propionate ointment 0.05%

Class 4: Medium Potency
Triamcinolone acetonide cream 0.1%
Hydrocortisone valerate ointment 0.2%
Fluocinolone acetonide ointment 0.025%
Fluticasone propionate cream 0.05%

Class 5: Medium Potency
Betamethasone valerate cream 0.1%
Hydrocortisone valerate cream 0.2%
Triamcinolone acetonide lotion 0.1%
Fluocinolone acetonide cream 0.025%

Class 6: Low Potency
Betamethasone valerate lotion 0.05%
Desonide cream 0.05%
Fluocinolone acetonide cream 0.01%
Fluocinolone acetonide solution 0.05%

Class 7: Low Potency
Hydrocortisone 0.5-1.0%

nonhalogenated compounds and are associated with increased cutaneous and possibly systemic toxicity.

Topical corticosteroids can be used safely on most areas of the body if the lowest effective dose is used and the duration of use is limited. However, local and systemic absorption of corticosteroids is a potential risk of their use, particularly with ultra–high-potency corticosteroids. Absorption of corticosteroids varies considerably among different body sites, largely due to differences in skin thickness and vascular supply of the area. Penetration is high on the face and scrotum and is low on the palms and soles. Absorption is enhanced on open or abraded skin as well as in the intertriginous skin folds, where natural occlusion enhances absorption. In general, it is recommended that no more than 50 g of an ultra-potent or 100 g of a mid–high-potency corticosteroid be used per week to avoid significant systemic absorption. Because of their greater skin surface area–to-weight ratio, children are at particular risk of systemic absorption from topical application of corticosteroids.

Corticosteroids inhibit collagen production and can thin the skin, resulting in translucent skin, visible veins, and stretch marks (**Figure 1** and **Figure 2**). Because of a loss of supportive structures around the blood vessels, atrophic skin bruises easily and may tear with minimal trauma (**Figure 3**). Areas at high risk for thinning of the skin include the face and intertriginous skin folds, including the axillary and inguinal folds. Use of low-potency, nonhalogenated corticosteroids is generally recommended in these areas.

Hypothalamic-pituitary axis suppression has been reported as a result of topical application of corticosteroids, particularly class I agents. Rarely, use of topical corticosteroids can affect glucose control in patients with diabetes mellitus. Corticosteroids should be used with caution around the eyes, as absorption can potentially increase intraocular pressure.

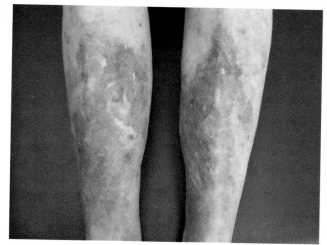

FIGURE 2.
Chronic use of topical corticosteroids can cause marked thinning of the skin, visible veins, and easy bruising and tearing (note scars).

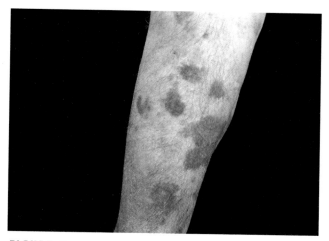

FIGURE 3.
Ecchymoses from minimal trauma in a patient on chronic systemic corticosteroids.

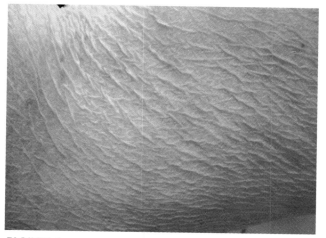

FIGURE 1.
Cutaneous atrophy from chronic systemic corticosteroid use, characterized by thinned skin with "cigarette paper" wrinkling.

Allergic contact sensitization to corticosteroids is well recognized and is more common than was previously appreciated; while the vehicle has often been blamed, it is now clear that allergic reactions to the corticosteroid itself do occur.

Combination corticosteroid-antifungal preparations should be used only when the diagnosis is clear and the use of both agents is indicated. Inflammatory tinea pedis, for example, might benefit from use of both medications simultaneously. They should not be used to compensate for diagnostic uncertainty, as the most readily available combination products contain medium- to high-potency corticosteroids that can cause skin atrophy or striae, even if used only for a short period of time.

Drug Safety in Pregnancy

Women of reproductive age who are being treated for dermatologic conditions should be consulted on their present or future plans for pregnancy. The pregnancy safety category of all medications, both systemic and topical, should be considered when prescribing to women who are pregnant, lactating, or trying to conceive (**Table 6**).

Selected drugs to avoid during pregnancy and lactation are listed in **Table 7**. Isotretinoin, used for the treatment of nodulocystic acne, is extremely teratogenic; to prescribe or receive the drug, providers and patients must participate in a strictly regulated pregnancy prevention program called iPLEDGE. Thalidomide (used to treat chronic cutaneous lupus erythematosus and pyoderma gangrenosum, among other dermatologic conditions) is also teratogenic and has a similar mandatory program, the System for Thalidomide Education and Prescribing Safety (S.T.E.P.S.). Spironolactone (used for the treatment of acne) and oral contraceptives should be avoided in pregnancy because of potential risk to the development of the fetus. Tetracyclines can stain developing teeth and bone and are classified as pregnancy category D drugs. Topical and systemic corticosteroids are category C drugs; while corticosteroids are generally considered safe for use in pregnancy, they may accentuate striae formation. Use of most antihistamines is considered safe during pregnancy; however, use of hydroxyzine during the first trimester is contraindicated by the manufacturer.

Bibliography

Hengge UR, Ruzicka T, Schwartz RA, Cork MJ. Adverse effects of topical glucocorticosteroids. J Am Acad Dermatol. 2006;54(1):1-15. [PMID: 16384751]

Leachman SA, Reed BR. The use of dermatologic drugs in pregnancy and lactation. Dermatol Clin. 2006;24(2):167-197. [PMID: 16677965]

Savary J, Ortonne JP, Aractingi S. The right dose in the right place: an overview of current prescription, instruction and application modalities for topical psoriasis treatments. J Eur Acad Dermatol Venereol. 2005;19 Suppl 3:14-17. [PMID: 16274407]

TABLE 6 U.S. Food and Drug Administration Categories for Drug Use in Pregnancy	
Category	**Description**
A	Adequate, well-controlled studies in pregnant women have not shown an increased risk of fetal abnormalities.
B	Animal studies have revealed no evidence of harm to the fetus; however, there are no adequate and well-controlled studies in pregnant women.
	or
	Animal studies have shown an adverse effect, but adequate and well-controlled studies in pregnant women have failed to demonstrate a risk to the fetus.
C	Animal studies have shown an adverse effect and there are no adequate and well-controlled studies in pregnant women.
	or
	No animal studies have been conducted and there are no adequate and well-controlled studies in pregnant women.
D	Studies, adequate, well-controlled, or observational, in pregnant women have demonstrated a risk to the fetus. However, the benefits of therapy may outweigh the potential risk.
X	Studies, adequate, well-controlled, or observational, in animals or pregnant women have demonstrated positive evidence of fetal abnormalities. The use of the product is contraindicated in women who are or may become pregnant.

TABLE 7 Selected Pregnancy Category X Drugs to Avoid During Pregnancy and Lactation
Acitretin
Danazol
Estrogens
Finasteride
Fluorouracil (5-fluorouracil)
Flutamide
Isotretinoin
Methotrexate
Stanozolol
Tazarotene (topical)
Thalidomide

Common Rashes

Skin Changes from Scratching

Acute and chronic changes in the skin can result from scratching. Linear excoriations are common in acutely itchy skin, and the tops of bumps may be superficially eroded. With repeated scratching, the skin becomes thickened and may be slightly scaly, and skin markings become accentuated (lichenification). Hyperpigmentation is common in dark skin. "Picker's nodules," or prurigo nodularis, are firm, hyperkeratotic, often hyperpigmented nodules that arise in focal areas of repeated picking. Scarring or hypopigmentation from resolved lesions is commonly found in surrounding skin. Areas of skin that cannot be reached (such as the mid back) are usually spared.

Eczemas

Asteatotic Eczema

Also called "winter itch" or "eczema craquelé," asteatotic eczema usually occurs on the anterior shins of older individuals with dry skin. Affected skin is red, dry, and cracked with multiple fine fissures that resemble cracks in porcelain (**Figure 4**). The dermatitis is more common in winter or in dry conditions. Frequent bathing with hot water and drying soaps may contribute to onset. Treatment consists of regular emollient use. Mid- to low-potency topical corticosteroids may minimize itching and facilitate healing.

Contact Dermatitis

Contact dermatitis can be either irritant or allergic in nature, and distinguishing between the two can be difficult. Irritant contact dermatitis is a nonimmunologic, toxic reaction that results from exposure to harsh conditions or chemicals. Examples include chronic hand dermatitis (exacerbated by chronic washing and wet work), frictional dermatitis, and chronic lip licking.

FIGURE 4.
Fine, porcelain-like cracks on eczematous skin in a patient with asteatotic eczema.

Allergic contact dermatitis (ACD) is a delayed-type hypersensitivity reaction that requires initial sensitization. The first reaction to an antigen may occur several weeks after exposure, but subsequent reactions usually develop within 24 to 48 hours of reexposure. Reactions often become more intense with repeated exposure. ACD is usually intensely itchy. In acute reactions, the skin is red, edematous, weepy, and crusted, and there may be vesicles or bullae (**Figure 5**). As the dermatitis becomes chronic, the skin becomes lichenified (thickened, with exaggeration of normal skin markings), scaly, and hyperpigmented (**Figure 6**).

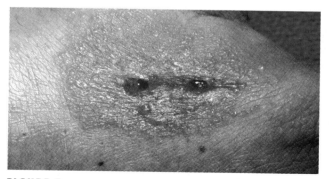

FIGURE 5.
Erythema and vesicles at the site of exposure to bacitracin in a patient with acute allergic contact dermatitis.

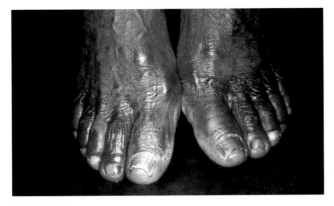

FIGURE 6.
Lichenified and hyperpigmented skin in chronic allergic contact dermatitis.

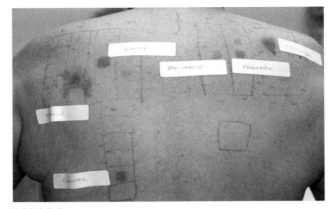

FIGURE 7.
Patch testing, with erythema and induration indicating allergic reactions to test chemicals.

Exposure history and pattern of the rash may provide clues as to the causal allergen. For example, plants often cause linear lesions where they brush against the skin. However, not all rashes occur at the site of contact with the allergen. Eyelid dermatitis, for example, can result from allergen contact on the hands, in the hair, or elsewhere on the body. Because these are delayed-type reactions, exposure to the allergen may have occurred several days prior to onset of the rash, which makes identification of the allergen challenging. Plant allergens, such as urushiol in poison ivy, are the most common cause of ACD; other common allergens include fragrances, preservatives, metals, and chemicals used in the processing of rubber (**Table 8**).

Epicutaneous patch testing is the gold standard for diagnosis of ACD (**Figure 7**). Patch testing should be performed to evaluate recurrent or recalcitrant dermatitis. ACD usually responds to mid- to high-potency topical corticosteroids. The topical immunomodulators tacrolimus and pimecrolimus may also be effective, but they are not U.S. Food and Drug Administration approved for this indication. Severe or widespread reactions may require systemic corticosteroids, which should be tapered over a 2- to 4-week period to prevent rebound reactions that may follow shorter courses. Avoidance of exposure to the offending allergen is essential, as there are no consistently effective desensitization protocols for these allergies. Commercially available barrier creams may help minimize exposure to urushiol in plants.

KEY POINTS

- Epicutaneous patch testing is the gold standard for the diagnosis of allergic contact dermatitis.
- Topical or systemic corticosteroids are used for treatment of acute and chronic allergic contact dermatitis.
- Avoidance of exposure to the allergen is key to treatment and prevention of recurrences of allergic contact dermatitis.

TABLE 8 Allergens with Most Frequently Positive Patch-Test Results

Allergen	Common Route of Patient Exposure
Nickel sulfate	Jewelry
Neomycin	Topical antibiotics
Balsam of Peru (marker for fragrance allergy)	Cologne or perfume
Fragrance mix	Most personal care products; products labeled "unscented" may contain masking fragrances
Thimerosal (frequently positive, but rarely relevant)	Eye-care products (eyedrops, contact lens solutions); preservative in some vaccines
Sodium gold thiosulfate	Jewelry; dental work
Quaternium-15 (formaldehyde-releasing preservative)	Personal care products
Formaldehyde	Personal care products
Bacitracin	Topical antibiotic; may cross-react with neomycin
Cobalt chloride	Blue paint; vitamin B_{12} (cyanocobalamin); may cross-react with other metals, including nickel

Adapted from Pratt MD, Belsito DV, DeLeo VA, et al. North American Contact Dermatitis Group patch-test results, 2001-2002 study period. Dermatitis. 2004;15(4):176-183. [PMID: 15842061]

Venous Stasis Dermatitis

Venous hypertension, chronic inflammation, and microangiopathy are thought to contribute to the development of venous stasis dermatitis. Stasis dermatitis affects the skin on the lower legs, particularly around the medial malleoli. Affected skin is red, warm, and may have eczematous changes (**Figure 8**). Distinguishing stasis dermatitis from bacterial cellulitis can be difficult, but bilateral involvement, absence of fever or leukocytosis, or minimal pain suggests stasis dermatitis. Other findings that support the diagnosis of stasis dermatitis include hyperpigmentation, hemosiderin deposition, and visible varicose veins. Stasis dermatitis can arise acutely; however, if accompanied by swelling and pain in the thigh or calf, the possibility of an associated deep venous thrombosis should be considered. Stasis dermatitis is diagnosed clinically. A biopsy can cause a nonhealing ulcer and therefore should be performed only if necessary to make the diagnosis.

The skin and subcutaneous tissues thicken with chronic stasis dermatitis, resulting in lipodermatosclerosis (**Figure 9**). Ulceration is a potential complication, particularly following trauma (see Leg Ulcers).

Stasis dermatitis is treated with low- to mid-potency topical corticosteroids. Topical antibiotics should be avoided, as allergic sensitization can occur. Leg edema must be minimized by leg elevation and compression therapy to facilitate healing and to help prevent recurrence of the dermatitis. Diuretics offer minimal benefit to patients whose edema results from venous insufficiency. Therapy with Unna boots worn over applied topical corticosteroids is helpful in the treatment of the acute dermatitis, and knee-high compression stockings that provide pressure of 20 to 40 mm Hg should be worn thereafter to help prevent recurrences. Compression should be avoided in patients with arterial insufficiency. Medications should be reviewed, because certain drugs, particularly calcium channel blockers and thiazolidinediones, can cause pedal edema.

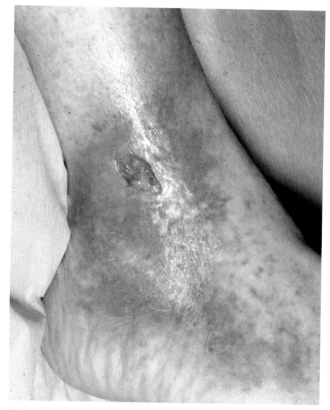

FIGURE 9.
Lipodermatosclerosis with ulcer, resulting from chronic thickening of the skin in chronic venous stasis dermatitis.

KEY POINTS

- Venous stasis dermatitis is characterized by red, warm, potentially eczematous skin on the lower legs, particularly around the medial malleoli, and can clinically resemble cellulitis.

- Chronic venous stasis is a common cause of leg ulcers.

- Venous stasis dermatitis should be treated with topical corticosteroids accompanied by compression therapy to minimize leg edema.

- Topical antibiotics should be avoided in the treatment of venous stasis dermatitis because of the risk for allergic sensitization.

Atopic Dermatitis

Atopic dermatitis (AD) primarily affects children, but it can continue into adulthood as persistent "eczema," sensitive skin, and sometimes hand dermatitis. The pathogenesis of AD is thought to involve interaction of both genetic and environmental factors. AD is common in persons with a personal or family history of allergies, asthma, or allergic rhinitis. Adult AD characteristically involves the antecubital and popliteal fossae and flexural wrists (**Figure 10**). When AD is acute,

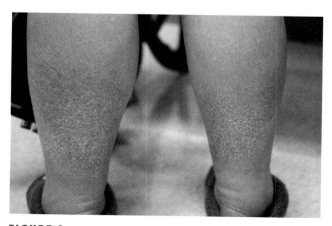

FIGURE 8.
Skin in acute venous stasis dermatitis is red, warm, and scaly.

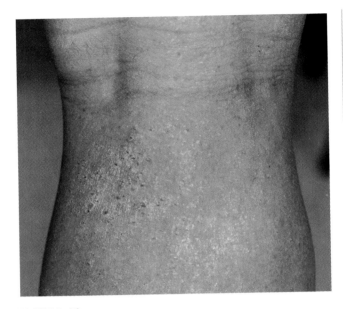

FIGURE 10.
Atopic dermatitis with involvement of the flexures, especially the ante-cubital and popliteal fossae.

the skin is pruritic and red with poorly demarcated, eczematous, crusted, papulovesicular plaques and excoriations. As the dermatitis becomes chronic, skin becomes lichenified with accentuated skin lines (lichen simplex chronicus) and, particularly in dark skin, hyperpigmentation. Many affected persons are intolerant of wool clothing and find clothing labels intolerably itchy.

AD is diagnosed clinically. Elevated serum IgE levels and increased blood eosinophils support the diagnosis, and some patients have evidence of associated IgE-mediated allergies, particularly to dust mites, on radioallergosorbent or prick testing. The role of food allergies remains under investigation; some patients with AD have food allergies, and testing may be appropriate, particularly if patients note any exacerbation of their dermatitis by foods. Allergic contact dermatitis can also complicate the clinical picture. New onset of widespread eczematous dermatitis in an adult with no history of atopy can be caused by a drug eruption or, more rarely, cutaneous T-cell lymphoma. Biopsy may help distinguish between these diagnoses.

Gentle skin care, including daily use of bland emollients, should be routine for all patients with AD. Once-daily topical corticosteroids are first-line drug therapy. The topical macrolide immunomodulators tacrolimus and pimecrolimus do not cause skin atrophy and may be preferred for use on the face (especially around the eyes) and in intertriginous areas, where there is higher risk for thinning of the skin. However, a potential increased risk of lymphoma associated with their use has relegated them to second-line therapy for moderate to severe AD. Sedating antihistamines may improve itching, particularly when used regularly. Anti-staphylococcal antibiotics

may be of benefit if the skin is open and crusted or if there is documented evidence of bacterial superinfection. Patients with recalcitrant AD may require referral for systemic therapy; systemic agents include corticosteroids, mycophenolate mofetil, cyclosporine, and azathioprine.

Community-acquired methicillin-resistant *Staphylococcus aureus* is being isolated with increasing frequency from the skin and nares of patients with atopic dermatitis and should be considered in patients with recalcitrant superinfection. Widespread, localized dissemination of herpes simplex virus infection, known as eczema herpeticum, can be a medical emergency, particularly when the face or eyes are involved.

KEY POINTS

- Atopic dermatitis usually affects persons with a personal or family history of other atopic conditions, such as asthma, allergies, or allergic rhinitis.
- Primarily a disease of childhood, atopic dermatitis can persist into adulthood as "eczema," sensitive skin, or hand dermatitis.
- Skin care with regular use of emollients should be routine for patients with atopic dermatitis.
- Topical corticosteroids are first-line drug therapy for atopic dermatitis.
- Potential complications of atopic dermatitis include staphylococcal superinfection and eczema herpeticum.

Hand Dermatitis

Irritation, allergic reactions, and various dermatoses can cause hand dermatitis. Adults with AD may outgrow their childhood eczema but may subsequently develop hand dermatitis. Contact dermatitis, both allergic and irritant, is a frequent occupational cause of hand dermatitis. Allergic hand dermatitis in health care workers, for example, is often caused by allergy to rubber-related substances; reactions in cosmetologists are more commonly caused by hair dyes or chemicals used in permanent wave solutions. Clinical findings that suggest an allergic cause of hand dermatitis include involvement of the dorsal hands, finger web spaces, and skin on the volar wrists, particularly when the palms are spared. Wet work, chemical exposures, or friction may cause or worsen hand dermatitis, regardless of the underlying diagnosis.

Several dermatoses can cause hand dermatitis, including dyshidrosis (or dyshidrotic eczema) (**Figure 11**), psoriasis, and tinea (dermatophyte) infections of the hands (**Figure 12**). Diagnostic clues are listed in **Table 9**. Scabies should also be considered, particularly in children who present with papules, pustules, and vesicles on the palms, web spaces, and the volar wrists.

Diagnosing hand dermatitis can be difficult, as the results of a skin biopsy may be nonspecific. Patch testing should be considered. Scrapings for potassium hydroxide

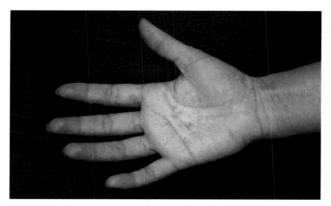

FIGURE 11.
Dyshidrotic hand eczema, characterized by acute episodes of intensely pruritic small vesicles on the palms.

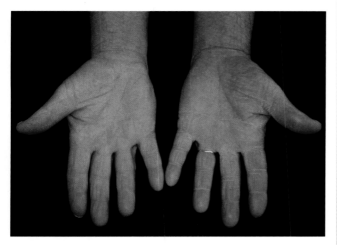

FIGURE 12.
Unilateral tinea manuum, presenting as diffuse hyperkeratosis of the left hand, particularly in the flexural creases.

(KOH) examination and oil preparation for scabies should be performed when considering the diagnoses of fungi, yeast, or scabies.

Treatment of hand dermatitis is similar to that of other eczematous dermatoses and involves the use of mid- to ultra-potent topical corticosteroids. Patients should avoid exposure to known allergens and irritants; protective gloves (preferably nonlatex) should be worn. Regular use of emollients is also essential. Patients with recalcitrant hand dermatitis may require referral and treatment with immunosuppressive medications, such as methotrexate, mycophenolate mofetil, or azathioprine, as well as some of the newer biologic agents.

> **KEY POINTS**
>
> - Wet work, exposure to harsh substances, or frequent hand washing often contributes to hand dermatitis, regardless of the underlying diagnosis.
> - Treatment of hand dermatitis includes mid- to ultra-potent corticosteroids, avoidance of allergens and irritants, and regular use of emollients.

Pigmented Purpuras

The pigmented purpuras are a group of conditions characterized by petechiae, hyperpigmentation, and sometimes eczematous changes that usually appear on the legs (**Figure 13**). While the clinical variants differ slightly, they share a common pathogenesis of capillaritis with minimal inflammation in the superficial dermal vessels. Most pigmented purpuras arise after adolescence or during adulthood. The lesions may be mildly pruritic or asymptomatic. The inflammation resolves over time and may leave behind persistent hyperpigmentation. The presence of petechiae may warrant a search for underlying thrombocytopenia or vasculitis; however, these conditions can usually be distinguished clinically. Rarely, cutaneous T-cell lymphoma can resemble pigmented purpura. A skin biopsy will clarify the diagnosis if it is unclear.

Treatment with low-potency topical corticosteroids may be helpful in resolving symptoms, although development of new lesions is common even when corticosteroids are used. Use of compression stockings may be beneficial if there is associated venous disease and leg edema.

TABLE 9 Clinical Clues to the Diagnosis of Hand Dermatitis	
Diagnosis	**Clinical Clues**
Irritant dermatitis	Skin is red, dry, and hyperkeratotic with fissures; burning or pain is more common than itching; rapid onset after exposure
Allergic contact dermatitis	Erythema, edema, and papulovesicles are common; may involve dorsum of hands and volar wrists; usually very itchy; delayed onset 1 to 3 days after exposure
Dyshidrotic eczema	Involves palms and sides of fingers; recurrent episodes of tense, tapioca-like, fluid-filled vesicles; very itchy
Psoriasis	Well-demarcated plaques on palms, often with discrete 2- to 3-mm pustules, collarettes of scale, and erythema; instep of plantar feet often involved; may have associated nail dystrophy
Tinea manuum	Characteristically involves only one hand (and two feet); dry scale, collarettes may be present; can involve nails if chronic; diagnosis unlikely if feet not involved

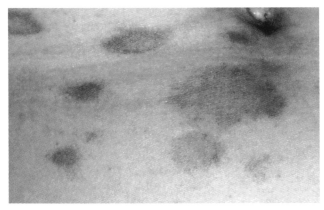

FIGURE 13.
Pigmented purpura with fine "cayenne-pepper" petechiae within pigmented patches of skin, usually appearing on the extremities.

- The pigmented purpuras are a group of conditions characterized by petechiae, hyperpigmentation, occasional eczematous changes, and benign capillaritis in the skin.
- Treatment with low-potency topical corticosteroids may be helpful in resolving symptoms of the pigmented purpuras, although development of new lesions is common.

Lichen Planus

Lichen planus (LP) is an inflammatory skin disorder that can affect the skin, mucous membranes, scalp, and/or nails. LP occurs with increased frequency in patients with liver disease, particularly hepatitis C, although the reasons for this remain unclear. Many drugs can cause lichenoid reactions, particularly angiotensin-converting enzyme inhibitors, thiazide diuretics, furosemide, gold, antimalarials, d-penicillamine, and β-blockers (**Table 10**). Withdrawal of the offending drug usually results in resolution, but it may take weeks or even months. Allergy to dental gold or amalgams has been associated with oral LP, and removal of the offending metal has resulted in disease improvement in some patients. Graft-versus-host disease may manifest with findings similar to those of LP.

The hallmark lesion of LP is the so-called pruritic, purple, polygonal papule; these papules are usually distributed symmetrically on the wrists, flexural aspects of the arms and legs, lower back, and genitalia. The papules are small and may be isolated or grouped together; they often develop along lines of prior trauma (**Figure 14**). A reticulated network of gray-white lines (Wickham striae) may be visible on the surface of the papules. The face, palms, and soles are usually spared; however, mucous membranes, including the lips, mouth, and vulva, are commonly involved. Common clinical findings in mucosal LP are a white-reticulated network on the buccal mucosa; desquamative gingivitis; and chronic, painful erosions on the oral or vulvar mucosa. There is an increased, albeit low, risk of squamous cell carcinoma in chronically affected mucosal lesions. LP in the nails causes dystrophy of some or all nails (known as twenty-nail dystrophy) and must be distinguished from other causes of onychodystrophy such

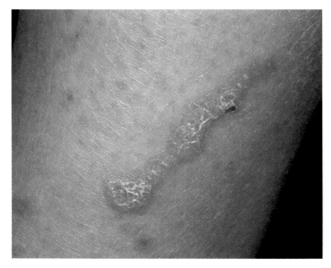

FIGURE 14.
Lichen planus with polygonal, purple papules that group along lines of prior trauma.

TABLE 10 Clues to Distinguishing Between Lichen Planus and Lichenoid Drug Eruption		
Characteristic	**Classic Lichen Planus**	**Lichenoid Drug Eruption**
Location	Wrists, flexor forearms, lower legs, genitalia	Can be generalized like a drug eruption
Morphology	Pruritic, purple-to-violaceous, polygonal papules	More eczematous, psoriasiform, or scaly
Photodistribution	Photodistribution is unusual	Frequently photodistributed
Mucosal involvement	Frequently involves mouth and genital mucosa	Usually does not involve mucosa
Wickham striae	Usually present	Uncommon

Adapted from Shiohara T, Kano Y. Lichen Planus and Lichenoid Dermatoses. In: Bolognia JL, Jorizzo JL, Rapini RP, eds. Dermatology. London: Mosby; 2003:175-198. Copyright © 2003, Elsevier.

as psoriasis and fungal infections. LP of the scalp can cause permanent scarring alopecia.

The course of LP is variable and sometimes will spontaneously remit within 6 to 24 months of onset. The presence of pruritus and/or mucosal erosions usually necessitates treatment; however, the response is variable and often disappointing. Topical corticosteroids and topical immunomodulators are used (off-label) to treat both cutaneous and mucosal LP. Corticosteroids are available in a dental-paste preparation for intraoral application; however, some patients may prefer to use corticosteroid gels or ointments. Systemic corticosteroids effectively treat erosive mucosal disease, but relapse is common following discontinuation. Other systemic immunosuppressants, systemic retinoids, and phototherapy have been used with variable success to treat widespread or recalcitrant disease, and referral to a dermatologist is suggested when the disease fails to respond to treatment with topical therapy or requires prolonged courses of systemic corticosteroids.

Treatment of LP nail involvement is difficult. Intralesional injections of corticosteroids may be effective but are painful. Variable response may be seen from application of ultra-high-potency corticosteroids applied nightly under occlusion. Nail symptoms may also improve with systemic therapy.

KEY POINTS

- Lichen planus is an autoinflammatory condition whose hallmark lesion is the pruritic, purple, polygonal papule.

- Lichen planus is associated with liver disease, particularly hepatitis C.

- Many drugs can cause lichenoid reactions, particularly angiotensin-converting enzyme inhibitors, thiazide diuretics, furosemide, and β-blockers.

- Initial treatment of lichen planus consists mainly of topical corticosteroids and topical immunomodulators (off-label use), but response is variable.

Psoriasis

Epidemiology and Risk Factors

Psoriasis is a lifelong condition that can have a significant negative impact on quality of life. It is one of the most common skin diseases, affecting roughly 2% to 3% of the general population. It most often appears in the second to third decade of life, but onset can occur at any age.

Exacerbating factors include stress, infection, and medications such as lithium and possibly β-blockers. Psoriasis is associated with a higher risk of arthritis, obesity, metabolic syndrome, cardiovascular disease, and lymphoma, particularly in patients with severe disease. Recent reports suggest that weight loss and smoking cessation may lower the risk and/or severity of psoriasis.

Clinical Manifestations

Psoriasis vulgaris most commonly is characterized by sharply marginated, scaly plaques on the elbows (**Figure 15**), knees, presacral skin (**Figure 16**), and scalp. Disease can be limited or widespread. There are several clinical variants of psoriasis: guttate, palmoplantar, and pustular. Guttate psoriasis is characterized by small, droplike, scaly plaques. It most often occurs in children and adolescents and is frequently triggered by prior infection, particularly streptococcal infection. Palmoplantar psoriasis, although localized, may be difficult to manage and may interfere with activities of daily living. Pustular psoriasis has a generalized and localized variant. Generalized pustular psoriasis can be life threatening and frequently occurs following withdrawal of systemic corticosteroids (**Figure 17**). Localized pustular psoriasis is observed on the palms and soles and may be triggered or exacerbated by tumor necrosis factor α (TNF-α) inhibitor therapies (**Figure 18**).

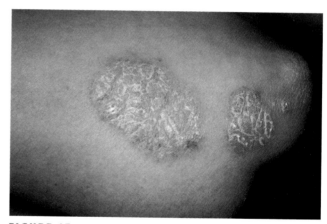

FIGURE 15.
Sharply marginated plaques and micaceous scale on the elbow in a patient with psoriasis.

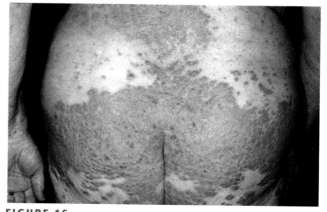

FIGURE 16.
Large, sharply marginated, erythematous plaque on the lower back in a patient with psoriasis.

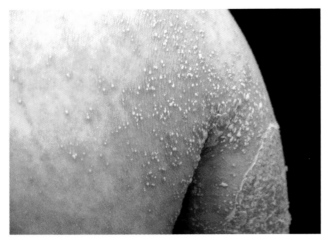

FIGURE 17.
Generalized pustular psoriasis in a patient who had accompanying fever and leukocytosis.

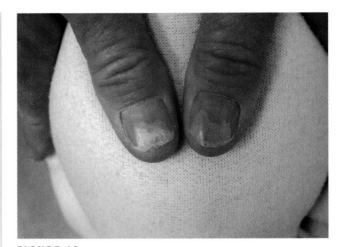

FIGURE 19.
Nail changes in psoriasis, with prominent onycholysis (separation of nail plate from nail bed).

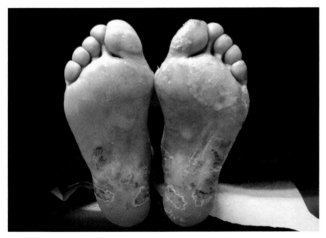

FIGURE 18.
Localized pustular psoriatic lesions in a patient treated with etanercept for rheumatoid arthritis.

The nails are often affected in patients with psoriasis (**Figure 19**). Nail involvement correlates with a greater risk of accompanying psoriatic arthritis. The nail changes must be differentiated from onychomycosis.

Psoriasis on the scalp usually consists of erythematous, scaly plaques. Plaques may be sharply marginated; however, it may be difficult to distinguish psoriasis from seborrheic dermatitis when there is diffuse scaling.

Patients with psoriasis may rarely present with a generalized erythroderma (see Selected Dermatologic Emergencies).

Diagnosis and Management

Psoriasis is diagnosed clinically. Histopathologic examination is rarely, if ever, needed. Psoriasis can be mimicked by chronic dermatitis, lichen planus, the papulosquamous variant of subacute cutaneous lupus erythematosus, and occasionally dermatomyositis. In doubtful cases, the latter three diagnoses can be distinguished from psoriasis on the basis of histopathology.

Patients with mild to moderate disease can generally be managed with topical therapy, while patients with moderate to severe disease may require systemic therapy. Topical therapy should be prescribed even when a systemic therapy is used. For patients who have more widespread disease or who fail to respond to topical therapy, the choice of therapy is phototherapy or a systemic agent. The choice of a systemic therapy should take into consideration all of the patient's characteristics and his or her level of desire for risk.

Topical Therapy

Topical therapies include topical corticosteroids, combination calcipotriene and betamethasone ointment, tazarotene, and anthralin. Topical therapies are impractical if more than 5% of the body surface area is affected or if the patient requires multiple preparations. Calcipotriene with betamethasone ointment may be applied once daily and appears not to result in atrophy; however, long-term therapy should be carefully monitored.

Phototherapy

Phototherapy may be an appropriate choice for patients with widespread or recalcitrant disease who do not desire or are not good candidates for systemic therapy. Because it requires two to three treatments per week in the provider's office and may involve separate patient copayments, it may be too inconvenient or expensive for some patients. Home ultraviolet B (UVB) light units may be appropriate for selected patients. In addition, although remission of the skin disease is possible, phototherapy has little effect on accompanying systemic disease, including arthritis. Narrowband UVB phototherapy appears to be safer than conventional broadband UVB. The combination of the photosensitizing agent psoralen and UVA light (PUVA) is associated with an increased risk of developing both nonmelanoma and melanoma skin cancers. UVA tanning beds are a poor choice for treatment of psoriasis because the wavelength of light is not very effective without a photosensitizing agent.

Systemic Therapy

Systemic therapies for psoriasis include methotrexate, acitretin, cyclosporine, and biologic agents. Methotrexate is a standard therapy for widespread psoriasis and psoriatic arthritis. Its risks include bone marrow toxicity and hepatotoxicity. Bone marrow toxicity is dose related and occurs more frequently in patients with poor renal function or in those treated with drugs that block dihydrofolate reductase (such as trimethoprim) or that decrease renal function (such as indomethacin). The risk of methotrexate-associated hepatotoxicity is greater in patients who drink alcohol, are obese, and/or have diabetes mellitus. Methotrexate is approved for use in combination with etanercept, infliximab, and adalimumab for treatment of psoriatic arthritis; methotrexate is also frequently used in combination to treat psoriasis (off-label). The need for liver biopsy to monitor for methotrexate toxicity remains controversial. Some experts now recommend that liver biopsies may not be indicated or the frequency of liver biopsies may be markedly reduced in patients without risk factors for hepatic fibrosis. However, because patients with psoriasis often have comorbidities that increase the risk of fibrosis, the dermatology community continues to recommend interval liver biopsies in patients receiving methotrexate. Methotrexate is teratogenic and should be stopped at least 3 months prior to conception.

Acitretin is a vitamin A derivative that is approved for treatment of psoriasis. It is particularly useful when combined with phototherapy but may also be used alone. Patients taking acitretin should be monitored monthly for the first 3 months, then quarterly, for hypertriglyceridemia and liver enzyme elevation. Excessive ingestion of vitamin A from other sources must be avoided to prevent hypervitaminosis A. Acitretin does not adequately treat psoriatic arthritis.

Cyclosporine is one of the most effective forms of systemic therapy for psoriasis; however, its long-term use is associated with unacceptable renal toxicity. Its use has therefore been relegated to acute situations in which rapid control of disease is warranted.

Biologic agents target pathogenetic abnormalities that occur in psoriasis, including T-cell activation and trafficking (alefacept), and excess production of TNF-α (etanercept, infliximab, and adalimumab). The TNF inhibitors have multiple potential adverse events that are agent specific, including injection site or infusion reactions, infection (including reactivation tuberculosis, often extrapulmonary), demyelinating disease, heart failure, malignancy, induction of autoimmunity, and increased risk for melanoma. It appears that roughly 45%

to 50% of patients treated with any one of these TNF inhibitors will have continued clinically significant responses at 2 to 3 years. Alefacept has not gained widespread use for the treatment of psoriasis because of its relative poor response rate, and it is not useful for psoriatic arthritis. Alefacept, etanercept, infliximab, and adalimumab are all pregnancy category B.

KEY POINTS

- Psoriasis most commonly is characterized by sharply marginated, scaly plaques on the elbows, knees, presacral skin, and scalp.
- Factors that may exacerbate psoriasis include stress, infection, and medications such as lithium and possibly β-blockers.
- Treatment of psoriasis depends on severity of disease and consists of topical therapy, phototherapy, and/or systemic therapy.

Erythema Multiforme

Erythema multiforme (EM) is an acute, often recurrent mucocutaneous eruption that usually follows an acute infection, most frequently recurrent herpes simplex virus (HSV) infection. It may also be idiopathic or drug related. EM has also been reported to complicate poison ivy dermatitis.

Lesions range in size from several millimeters to several centimeters and consist of erythematous plaques with concentric rings of color (**Figure 20**). The dusky center may become necrotic and can form a discrete blister or eschar. Few to hundreds of lesions develop within several days and are most commonly located on the extensor surfaces of the extremities, particularly the hands and feet. Lesions occur less frequently on the face, trunk, and thighs. Mucosal lesions are present in up to 70% of patients and involve the cutaneous and mucosal lips, gingival sulcus, and the sides of the tongue (**Figure 21**). Mucosal lesions consist of painful erosions or, less commonly, intact bullae. The conjunctival, nasal, and

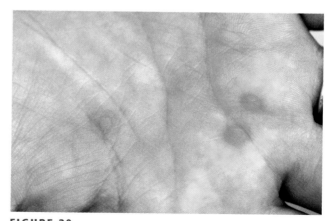

FIGURE 20.
Erythema multiforme, with classic targetoid lesions on the palms, soles, and skin.

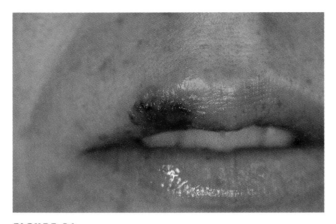

FIGURE 21.
Painful mucosal erosion of the lip in a patient with erythema multiforme.

genital mucosal surfaces can also be affected. Patients may have low-grade fever during an EM outbreak. Lesions usually last 1 to 2 weeks before healing, although hyperpigmentation may persist. Recurrences are common, particularly in HSV-associated cases.

Treatment of EM is primarily symptomatic. Systemic corticosteroids may provide symptomatic improvement but may be associated with complications. Antiviral therapy does not shorten the EM outbreak in HSV-associated cases, but continuous prophylactic antiviral therapy may help prevent further episodes.

KEY POINTS

- Erythema multiforme is an acute, often recurrent, mucocutaneous eruption characterized by targetoid lesions.
- Recurrent episodes of erythema multiforme are often associated with herpes simplex virus infection.
- Treatment of erythema multiforme is primarily symptomatic.

Drug Reactions

Almost all drugs have the potential for cutaneous toxic reactions. Cutaneous drug reactions are common, but most are self-limiting and are not severe. Many patients with drug reactions (particularly those with severe reactions) have a genetic predisposition. Drug eruptions are more likely to occur in patients who are immunosuppressed. Drug reactions have also been linked to an accompanying viral infection, particularly human herpesvirus 6.

Recognition of severe cutaneous adverse reactions (SCAR) is important because these reactions are potentially life threatening and can be treated. Clinical features that are associated with severe drug reactions include confluent erythema, skin pain, facial edema, fever, lymphadenopathy,

mucosal erosions, widespread blistering, purpura, necrosis, dyspnea, and hypotension. In addition, elevated serum aminotransferase levels, lymphocytosis, and/or eosinophilia may occur in association with SCAR.

Drug reactions commonly have an identical presentation to naturally occurring disease; for example, drug-induced cutaneous vasculitis will have identical clinical findings to those of vasculitis that follows an infection. Therefore, skin biopsy is unlikely to identify the eruption as a drug reaction. Skin biopsy is rarely, if ever, useful in confirming that a drug is the cause of an eruption.

The most common reaction patterns include morbilliform reactions (**Figure 22**), urticaria, fixed drug eruptions (**Figure 23**), photosensitivity, and erythema multiforme–like reactions. **Table 11** describes the causes and management of these common drug reaction patterns. Miscellaneous patterns account for roughly 15% to 20% of reactions. **Table 12**

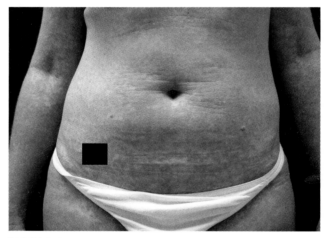

FIGURE 22.
Morbilliform drug eruption consisting of symmetrically arranged erythematous macules and papules, some discrete and others confluent, caused by vancomycin.

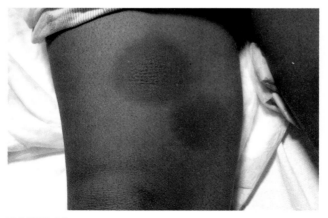

FIGURE 23.
Fixed drug eruption, in which hyperpigmented annular lesions recur in exactly the same location with each reexposure to the offending drug.

TABLE 11 Common Drug Reaction Patterns

Drug Reaction Pattern	Most Common Causative Drugs	Management (Other Than Drug Cessation)	Comments
Morbilliform	Penicillin and other β-lactam antibiotics, carbamazepine, allopurinol, gold	Antihistamines for pruritus and topical corticosteroids	All patients with Epstein-Barr virus or cytomegalovirus infection will develop rash if given ampicillin or amoxicillin
Urticaria	Antibiotics and most classes of other drugs, including radiocontrast agents	Antihistamines and epinephrine; corticosteroids for severe reactions	In some patients, urticaria may be associated with systemic anaphylaxis
Fixed drug eruption	Phenolphthalein, tetracyclines, sulfonamides, metronidazole, anti-inflammatory drugs, barbiturates, oral contraceptives, quinine (including tonic water)	Potent topical corticosteroids	Peas, beans, and lentils have also been implicated
Photosensitivity	Amiodarone, thiazides, tetracyclines, furosemide, phenothiazines, sulfonamides, psoralens	Antihistamines, topical corticosteroids	Can occur with light exposure through windows
Erythema multiforme–like reaction	Sulfonamides, phenytoin, barbiturates, penicillin, allopurinol	Antihistamines; systemic corticosteroids are often used for severe reactions, but effectiveness is not established	Mucous membrane involvement is common; ocular involvement can lead to blindness; severe reactions can be life-threatening

TABLE 12 Selected Newly Described Cutaneous Drug Reactions

Drug Reaction Pattern	Most Common Causative Drugs	Management (Other Than Drug Cessation)	Comments
Acneiform reaction	Epidermal growth factor inhibitors	Topical and/or oral antibiotics	This is not true acne but rather is a follicular reaction; the occurrence and severity of the reaction are predictive of responsiveness to therapy
New-onset psoriasiform eruptions	Tumor necrosis factor inhibitors (primarily in patients with Crohn disease or rheumatoid arthritis)	Potent topical corticosteroids, methotrexate	Reaction pattern is often a pustular reaction of the palms and soles; reaction is likely not classic psoriasis
SCLE	Hydrochlorothiazide, terbinafine, calcium channel blockers, angiotensin-converting enzyme inhibitors	Topical and/or oral corticosteroids, antimalarial agents	Roughly 15% of SCLE cases are potentially caused by a drug; lupus erythematosus may be activated in a patient predestined to develop the disease; patients with this reaction frequently are anti-Ro/SSA positive and rarely have anti-histone antibodies
Dermatomyositis-like eruptions	Hydroxyurea, statins	None	Patients present with Gottron papules more often than other cutaneous manifestations of dermatomyositis; accompanying muscle disease is rare with hydroxyurea but may occur with statins
Sweet syndrome (acute febrile neutrophilic dermatosis)	Imatinib, oral contraceptives, GCSF, all-*trans* retinoic acid	Oral corticosteroids	Drug-induced Sweet syndrome is rare
Eczema-like reactions	Calcium channel blockers	Topical corticosteroids	—

SCLE = subacute cutaneous lupus erythematosus; GCSF = granulocyte colony-stimulating factor.

includes some of the newly described drug reactions. Dermatologic findings in subacute cutaneous lupus erythematosus and eczema-like reactions are shown in **Figure 24** and **Figure 25**, respectively.

Identification of the causative drug is based upon analysis of the patient's drug exposure and the reaction patterns associated with a specific drug or drug class. Drug reactions can occur within days or up to 2 months after exposure to the causative medication. The most common causative drugs are antibiotics (particularly penicillins, β-lactams, and sulfonamides), anticonvulsants, NSAIDs, thiazide diuretics, and allopurinol. Drug eruptions are rarely caused by digitalis, antacids, acetaminophen, diazepam, antihistamines, iron, and insulin.

The reactions that are generally classified within the spectrum of SCAR include acute generalized exanthematous pustulosis (AGEP), Stevens-Johnson syndrome/toxic epidermal necrolysis (see Selected Dermatologic Emergencies), drug reaction with eosinophilia and systemic symptoms (DRESS,

also known as hypersensitivity syndrome), and vasculitis (see Cutaneous Manifestations of Internal Disease).

AGEP is characterized by acute onset of widespread pustules, fever, leukocytosis, and possibly eosinophilia (**Figure 26**). AGEP often resembles pustular psoriasis, but affected patients rarely have a history of psoriasis. The most common causative drugs include β-lactam antibiotics, ampicillin/amoxicillin, fluoroquinolones, antimalarial agents, sulfonamide antibiotics, terbinafine, and diltiazem. AGEP is usually self-limiting and clears without residual sequelae roughly 2 weeks after drug cessation. More serious reactions have been reported but are rare.

DRESS is characterized by a generalized papular eruption (**Figure 27**), facial edema (**Figure 28**), fever, arthralgia, and generalized lymphadenopathy. Patients also commonly have elevated serum aminotransferase levels, eosinophilia, and lymphocytosis. The most common causative drugs include anticonvulsants (reactions are more prevalent in black patients), sulfonamides, minocycline, abacavir, and allopurinol. There

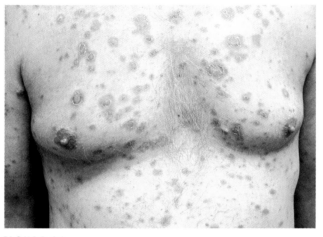

FIGURE 24.
Subacute cutaneous lupus erythematosus, characterized by discrete erythematous papular lesions and scaly plaques, induced by terbinafine.

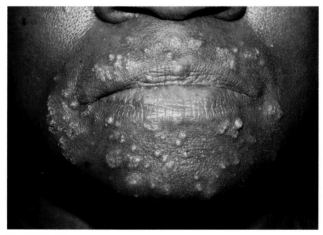

FIGURE 26.
Acute generalized exanthematous pustulosis caused by an antibiotic.

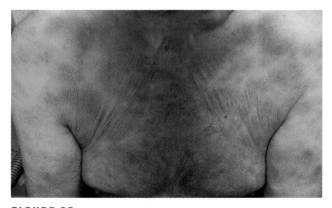

FIGURE 25.
Eczematous drug eruption in a patient taking a calcium channel blocker.

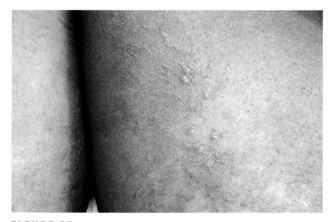

FIGURE 27.
Generalized papular eruption in a patient with drug reaction with eosinophilia and systemic symptoms (DRESS).

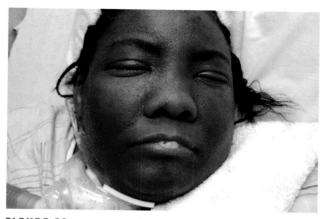

FIGURE 28.
Acute facial edema in a patient with anticonvulsant-induced drug reaction with eosinophilia and systemic symptoms (DRESS).

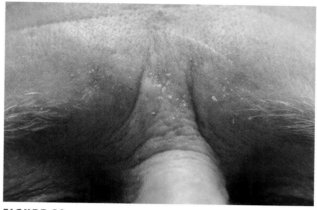

FIGURE 29.
Seborrheic dermatitis, with fine, oily scale around the medial eyebrows and nasolabial folds.

appears to be a genetic predisposition. In addition, there has been a link to concurrent infection with human herpesvirus 6 in patients with DRESS. Treatment with corticosteroids or intravenous immune globulin appears to effectively shorten the disease course. A long-term consequence of DRESS is the development of hypothyroidism.

KEY POINTS

- Drug reactions are most commonly caused by antibiotics (particularly penicillins, β-lactams, and sulfonamides), anticonvulsants, NSAIDs, thiazide diuretics, and allopurinol.

- Clinical features that are associated with severe drug reactions include confluent erythema, skin pain, facial edema, fever, lymphadenopathy, mucosal erosions, widespread blistering, purpura, necrosis, dyspnea, hypotension, elevated serum aminotransferase levels, lymphocytosis, and/or eosinophilia.

Seborrheic Dermatitis

Seborrheic dermatitis is a common inflammatory skin disease that most often affects sebaceous-gland–rich areas of the scalp and face. Seborrheic dermatitis in the scalp resembles severe dandruff. Lesions on the skin are pink to red with greasy scale, crusts, and occasionally small pustules (**Figure 29**). The most common areas of involvement include the nasolabial folds, cheeks, and medial eyebrows; the external auditory canals, skin behind the ears, and mid chest can also be involved. Intertriginous areas and perianal skin are less commonly affected.

Seborrheic dermatitis is more common in persons with neurologic diseases, including Parkinson disease, as well as those with HIV infection; however, most affected persons are healthy. Large amounts of the lipophilic yeast *Malassezia furfur* can be isolated from affected skin and are thought, along

with high sebum levels and individual sensitivity, to contribute to the cause of the dermatitis.

Seborrheic dermatitis responds to low-potency corticosteroids and/or ketoconazole 2% cream. Sulfur-based products are effective but are less acceptable cosmetically. Recalcitrant disease may benefit from off-label use of topical tacrolimus or pimecrolimus. Medicated shampoos containing zinc pyrithione, tar, selenium sulfide, or ketoconazole can be used regularly until the dermatosis is controlled and then can be used several times a week to help prevent recurrences.

KEY POINTS

- Seborrheic dermatitis is characterized by an inflammatory rash on the face and scalp that consists of greasy scale, redness, and sometimes papules and pustules.

- Initial treatment of seborrheic dermatitis consists of low-potency corticosteroids, ketoconazole, sulfur-based products, and/or medicated shampoos.

Pityriasis Rosea

Pityriasis rosea is a common papulosquamous eruption whose cause remains uncertain but has been linked to reactivation of human herpesvirus 6 or 7. Pityriasis rosea most commonly occurs during the spring or fall and classically begins with a single, pink, 2- to 4-cm, thin, oval-shaped plaque with a thin collarette of scale at the periphery (known as the herald patch). Similar but smaller plaques subsequently erupt within days to weeks, usually on the torso along skin cleavage lines, in a Christmas tree–like distribution (**Figure 30**). Lesions can be asymptomatic or mildly itchy. Most affected patients are well, but some have mild flulike symptoms. The eruption usually lasts 4 to 10 weeks but may persist for months. Atypical variants, including vesicobullous lesions and mucosal lesions, occur rarely. Pityriasis rosea must be distinguished from secondary syphilis, drug eruptions, tinea corporis nummular

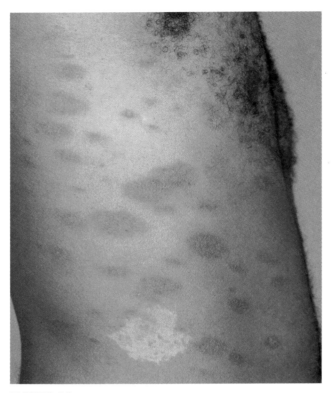

FIGURE 30.
Pityriasis rosea, with oval-shaped patches of fine scale arranged along skin cleavage lines on the torso.

dermatitis, and guttate psoriasis. Because the condition is self-limited, no treatment is needed; however, mid-potency topical corticosteroids, with or without oral antihistamines, may lessen pruritus.

KEY POINTS

- Pityriasis rosea classically begins with a single herald patch before erupting in multiple smaller, scaly plaques on the torso.

- Because pityriasis rosea is self-limited, no treatment is needed; however, mid-potency topical corticosteroids may improve pruritus.

Bibliography

Aurelian L, Ono F, Burnett J. Herpes simplex virus (HSV)-associated erythema multiforme (HAEM): a viral disease with an autoimmune component. Dermatol Online J. 2003;9(1):1. [PMID: 12639459]

Ben m'rad M, Leclerc-Mercier S, Blanche P, et al. Drug-induced hypersensitivity syndrome: clinical and biologic disease patterns in 24 patients. Medicine (Baltimore). 2009;88(3):131-140. [PMID: 19440116]

Broccolo F, Drago F, Careddu AM, et al. Additional evidence that pityriasis rosea is associated with reactivation of human herpesvirus-6 and -7. J Invest Dermatol. 2005;124(6):1234-1240. [PMID: 15955099]

Callen JP. Newly recognized cutaneous drug eruptions. Dermatol Clin. 2007;25(2):255-261. [PMID: 17430762]

DeAngelis YM, Gemmer CM, Kaczvinsky JR, Kenneally DC, Schwartz JR, Dawson TL Jr. Three etiologic facets of dandruff and seborrheic dermatitis: Malassezia fungi, sebaceous lipids, and individual sensitivity. J Invest Dermatol Symp Proc. 2005;10(3):295-297. [PMID: 16382685]

de Gannes GC, Ghoreishi M, Pope J, et al. Psoriasis and pustular dermatitis triggered by TNF-α inhibitors in patients with rheumatologic conditions. Arch Dermatol. 2007;143(2):223-231. [PMID: 17310002]

Griffiths CE, Barker JN. Pathogenesis and clinical features of psoriasis. Lancet. 2007;370(9583):263-271. [PMID: 17658397]

Joly P, Benoit-Corven C, Baricault S, et al. Chronic eczematous eruptions of the elderly are associated with chronic exposure to calcium channel blockers: results from a case-control study. J Invest Dermatol. 2007;127(12):2766-2771. [PMID: 17713574]

Kalb RE, Strober B, Weinstein G, Lebwohl M. Methotrexate and psoriasis: 2009 National Psoriasis Foundation Consensus Conference. J Am Acad Dermatol. 2009;60(5):824-837. [PMID: 19389524]

Lodi B, Scully C, Carrozzo M, Griffiths M, Sugerman PB, Thongprasom K. Current controversies in oral lichen planus: report of an international consensus meeting. Part 1. Viral infections and etiopathogenesis. Oral Surg Oral Med Oral Pathol Oral Radiol Endod. 2005;100(1):40-51. [PMID: 15953916]

Menter A, Griffiths CE. Current and future management of psoriasis. Lancet. 2007;370(9583):272-284. [PMID: 17658398]

Setty AR, Curhan G, Choi HK. Obesity, waist circumference, weight change, and the risk of psoriasis in women: Nurses' Health Study II. Arch Intern Med. 2007;167(15):1670-1675. [PMID: 17698691]

Setty AR, Curhan G, Choi HK. Smoking and the risk of psoriasis in women: Nurses' Health Study II. Am J Med. 2007;120(11):953-959. [PMID: 17976422]

Sidoroff A, Dunant A, Viboud C, et al. Risk factors for acute generalized exanthematous pustulosis (AGEP)-results of a multinational case-control study (EuroSCAR). Br J Dermatol. 2007;157(5):989-996. [PMID: 17854366]

Williams HC. Clinical practice. Atopic dermatitis. N Engl J Med. 2005;352(22):2314-2324. [PMID: 15930422]

Acneiform Lesions

Acne

Epidemiology

Acne vulgaris is a common disease characterized by comedones, pink papules, pustules, and cysts on the face and upper trunk (**Figure 31**). It is a disease of the hair follicles that is caused by excess sebum production, epidermal hyperproliferation, *Propionibacterium acnes*, and inflammation secondary to the interactions of these factors. Adult women may experience disease onset between the ages of 20 and 40 years, when disease is characterized by deep cystic lesions distributed on the lower face and neck (**Figure 32**).

Clinical Manifestations and Diagnosis

The comedo is the primary lesion of acne. In mild and early adolescent disease, facial comedones are the only manifestation (**Figure 33**). Moderate to severe acne is characterized by papules and pustules, which are found predominantly on the face. The most severe form of acne is characterized by

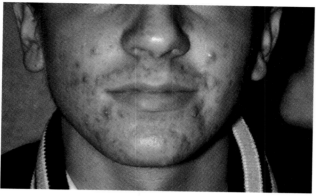

FIGURE 31.
Papules characteristic of inflammatory acne.

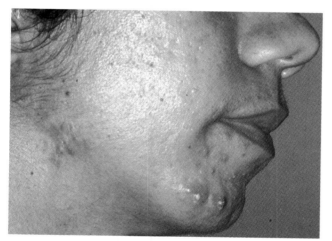

FIGURE 32.
Acne of the lower face with deep cystic lesions in an adult woman.

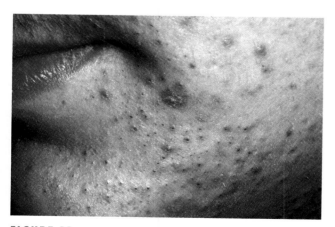

FIGURE 33.
Comedonal acne, with multiple open comedones (blackheads) and a few small inflammatory papules.

nodulocystic lesions on the face and often on the trunk. Scarring may occur with all but the mildest disease.

Routine endocrinologic evaluation is not needed for the majority of patients unless there is evidence of a systemic cause, such as the presence of oligomenorrhea and/or hirsutism (polycystic ovary syndrome) or rapid onset of severe disease with associated virilization (androgen-secreting tumor). **Table 13** describes the differential diagnosis of acne and acneiform skin disorders. Acne that fails to respond after 8 weeks of appropriate therapy, moderate to severe acne, or acneiform lesions in atypical locations may be indications for referral to a dermatologist.

Management

Topical and oral treatments for the varying degrees of acne severity are described in **Table 14**. Mild comedonal acne generally responds best to topical retinoids. As inflammatory components develop but remain localized to the face, other topical preparations such as benzoyl peroxide and/or antibiotics should be added. Once moderate to severe acne is present or significant lesions involve the trunk, oral antibiotics and/or hormonal therapies are required. If severe acne does not respond to these measures, then isotretinoin should be considered. Trimethoprim-sulfamethoxazole and amoxicillin are other treatment options for acne; however, both may produce severe drug eruptions. Patients who take oral antibiotics over many months may develop gram-negative bacterial overgrowth in the anterior nares, and these organisms may infect the acne lesions. Gram-negative folliculitis is characterized by pustules in the perinasal and lower facial skin and requires the use of isotretinoin to reverse the process. If isotretinoin is given for any reason, other acne medications can be discontinued.

KEY POINTS

- Acne vulgaris is characterized by comedones, pink papules, pustules, and cysts on the face and upper trunk.

- Treatment of mild comedonal acne consists of topical therapies such as retinoids, salicylic acid, azelaic acid, and benzoyl peroxide.

- Oral antibiotics are useful in treating moderately severe or severe acne.

- Isotretinoin is extremely effective in treating severe acne; however, it is teratogenic and its use is regulated by the mandatory risk management program iPLEDGE.

Rosacea

Rosacea is characterized by persistent central facial redness that primarily involves the convex surfaces and spares the periocular skin. Telangiectasias, pink papules, small pustules, or ocular disease may also be present, but comedones are not

TABLE 13 Differential Diagnosis of Acne and Acneiform Skin Disorders

Disease	Characteristics
Acne (acne vulgaris)	The microcomedo is the primary lesion; includes noninflammatory and inflammatory types. Very common in adolescents, but also common in preadolescents and adults. Females may have premenstrual flare-ups. Physical examination: coexisting open and closed comedones, papules, pustules, and nodular lesions located primarily on face, neck, and upper trunk.
Rosacea	Not true acne; primary lesion is not a microcomedo but an inflammatory papule; rhinophyma (bulbous, red nose) is a variant. Physical examination: central face erythema, telangiectases, papules, pustules.
Corticosteroid-induced acneiform eruption (steroid acne, steroid folliculitis)	Onset weeks to months after systemic corticosteroids or prolonged topical corticosteroids. Physical examination: hundreds of small follicular papules and pustules in the same stage of evolution, comedones absent; lesions commonly appear on the upper trunk and arms when the cause is systemic corticosteroids; lesions appear on the face when topical agents are implicated.
Bacterial folliculitis	Common in athletes. Physical examination: follicular papules, pustules, occasional furuncles on any hair-bearing area, especially scalp, buttocks, and thighs. Positive culture for pathogenic bacteria. Most common cause is *Staphylococcus aureus*.
Gram-negative folliculitis	Caused by overgrowth of bacteria during prolonged systemic antibiotic treatment for acne, and presents as exacerbation of preexisting acne. Physical examination: many inflamed pustules, most often on the face. Positive culture for gram-negative bacteria, often *Escherichia coli*.
Periorificial dermatitis, idiopathic	More common in females. Physical examination: small (<2 mm) papules and pustules around mouth or eyelids. Similar to acne but without comedones.
Periorificial dermatitis, iatrogenic	Frequent causes are prolonged topical corticosteroid therapy for atopic dermatitis and inappropriate use of these agents to treat acne. Similar in appearance to idiopathic type.

seen. Flushing that lasts longer than 10 minutes in response to a variety of trigger factors such as heat, cold, exercise, embarrassment, red wine, or spicy foods provides supportive historical evidence. Ocular rosacea manifests as redness and irritation caused by blepharitis, conjunctivitis, and/or keratitis that may be present alone or in combination with skin findings. Onset of rosacea typically occurs between the ages of 30 and 50 years and is most often seen in light-skinned women. Men, however, are often the most severely affected; rhinophyma, a dramatic overgrowth of nasal skin, is almost exclusively seen in older men with long-standing uncontrolled disease (**Figure 34**).

The most common differential diagnosis of rosacea is systemic lupus erythematosus (SLE). SLE may cause facial skin findings similar to those of rosacea; however, skin symptoms of SLE are not persistent but rather are sun-induced and transient, and lupus often spares the nasolabial folds. A skin biopsy can help distinguish between SLE and rosacea if clinical and laboratory features are not diagnostic. Chronic application of topical corticosteroids may induce rosacea-like skin symptoms; however, this condition can be distinguished from rosacea by patient history and findings of redness and papules present only at the sites of corticosteroid application.

Treatment with sun avoidance and daily application of sunscreens will limit photodamage. First-line therapies include topical metronidazole or clindamycin, sodium sulfacetamide, and azelaic acid. These therapies are most effective in eliminating erythematous papules and pustules. Failure to respond after 4 to 6 weeks may require oral antibiotics such as tetracyclines. Oral antibiotics are quite useful in ameliorating nodular lesions and eye symptoms. Flushing is often recalcitrant to treatment, but telangiectasias may be treated with laser ablation.

KEY POINTS

- Rosacea is characterized by persistent central facial redness; telangiectasias, pink papules, small pustules, or ocular disease may also be present.

- First-line topical therapy for rosacea consists of metronidazole, sodium sulfacetamide, and azelaic acid.

Hidradenitis Suppurativa

Hidradenitis suppurativa is characterized by painful, recurrent, chronic, sterile abscesses; sinus tract formation; and scarring of the axillary, inguinal, perianal, and inframammary intertriginous areas (**Figure 35**). There is often concomitant acne, scalp folliculitis, or pilonidal cyst formation. This condition is frequently mistaken for furuncles, but the lesions of hidradenitis usually have negative cultures and are centered around the axillae and groin.

Topical treatment options for mild disease include antiseptic washes and antibiotic solutions such as clindamycin. Patients with multiple lesions or associated disability should be referred for specialty care.

TABLE 14 Treatment of Acne

Medication	Indication	Side Effects and Comments
Topical retinoids (tretinoin, adapalene, tazarotene)	Mild comedonal acne; use singly or in combination with other treatments	Skin irritation; may be combined with topical antibiotics; tazarotene is pregnancy category X and requires pregnancy testing prior to prescription
Topical salicylic acid	Mild comedonal acne; use singly or in combination with other treatments	Mainly in patients with retinoid-intolerant skin
Topical azelaic acid	Adjunctive therapy for mild to moderate acne	Local irritation
Topical benzoyl peroxide	First-line therapy for mild to moderate acne; use singly or in combination with other treatments	Local irritation and, rarely, contact sensitivity
Topical antibiotics (clindamycin, erythromycin)	Therapy for mild to moderate inflammatory acne	Local irritation; promotion of antibiotic-resistant bacteria when used singly but not if used in combination with topical benzoyl peroxide
Oral tetracyclines	Moderate to severe inflammatory acne; can be combined with topical agents	Phototoxicity, vaginal yeast infection, dyspepsia, rare hepatotoxicity, staining of teeth in fetuses and children; not for use in children <12 years of age or pregnant women
Oral doxycycline	Moderate to severe inflammatory acne; can be combined with topical agents	Dose-related phototoxicity, vaginal yeast infection, dyspepsia; not for use in children <12 years of age or pregnant women
Oral minocycline	Moderate to severe inflammatory acne; can be combined with topical agents	Dizziness, vertigo, discolored teeth, blue-gray skin staining, rare hepatotoxicity and lupus-like syndrome, mild phototoxicity; not for use in children <12 years of age or pregnant women
Oral erythromycin	Moderate to severe inflammatory acne; can be combined with topical agents	Gastric upset, diarrhea; can be used in children
Oral contraceptives (norethindrone acetate-ethinyl estradiol, norgestimate-ethinyl estradiol)	First-line treatment of moderate to severe acne in adult women or with laboratory evidence of hyperandrogenism	Requires an average of 5 cycles to achieve 50% improvement; adjunctive topical therapy is usually needed
Spironolactone	Moderate to severe acne in adult women	Concurrent oral contraceptives recommended (pregnancy category C, but some experts believe it should be category D)
Isotretinoin	Treatment of choice for severe, recalcitrant nodular acne; prolonged remissions (1-3 years) in 40% of patients	Pregnancy category X; all prescribers, patients, wholesalers, and dispensing pharmacies must be registered in the FDA-approved iPLEDGE program

FDA = U.S. Food and Drug Administration.

NOTE: For specific indications and precautions, please refer to the labeling information of the medications listed.

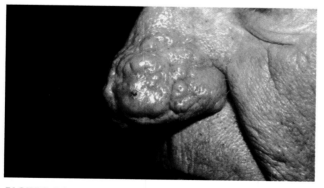

FIGURE 34.
Rhinophyma in a patient with long-standing, uncontrolled rosacea.

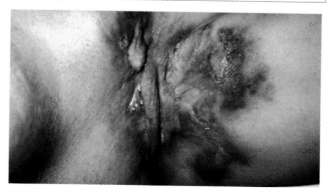

FIGURE 35.
Hidradenitis suppurativa, characterized by painful, recurrent, chronic, sterile abscesses; sinus tract formation; and scarring.

Perioral Dermatitis

Perioral dermatitis is characterized by discrete papules and pustules on an erythematous base that are centered around the mouth (**Figure 36**). The eruption frequently follows the use of topical or inhaled corticosteroids but may occur spontaneously. The dermatitis is usually responsive to discontinuation of the corticosteroid or protecting the skin from the inhaled product. Topical antibiotic solutions or creams and sulfur preparations are usually tried first. Therapy with tacrolimus ointment and oral tetracyclines is usually reserved for patients who fail to respond to initial topical therapy.

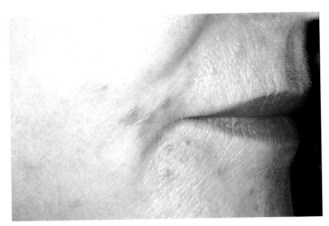

FIGURE 36.
Perioral dermatitis, with discrete papules and pustules on an erythematous base centered around the mouth.

KEY POINT

- Perioral dermatitis is characterized by discrete papules and pustules on an erythematous base.

Bibliography

Crawford GH, Pelle MT, James WD. Rosacea: I. Etiology, pathogenesis, and subtype classification. J Am Acad Dermatol. 2004;51(3):327-341. [PMID: 15337973]

James WD. Clinical practice. Acne. N Engl J Med. 2005;352(14):1463-1472. [PMID: 15814882]

Lee RA, Yoon A, Kist J. Hidradenitis suppurativa: an update. Adv Dermatol. 2007;23:289-306. [PMID: 18159906]

Pelle MT, Crawford GH, James WD. Rosacea: II. Therapy. J Am Acad Dermatol. 2004;51(4):499-512. [PMID: 15389184]

Powell FC. Clinical practice. Rosacea. N Engl J Med. 2005;352(8):793-803. [PMID: 15728812]

Strauss JS, Krowchuk DP, Leyden JJ, et al; American Academy of Dermatology/American Academy of Dermatology Association. Guidelines of care for acne vulgaris management. J Am Acad Dermatol. 2007;56(4):651-663. [PMID: 17276540]

Common Skin and Nail Infections

Superficial Fungal Infections

Fungal infections of the skin, hair, and nails are caused by dermatophyte organisms. The site of infection, rather than the infecting organism, determines the diagnosis.

Dermatophytosis

Risk Factors and Clinical Manifestations

Dermatophytes are the most common fungi that infect skin. Dermatophytes infect the highest level of the epidermis, the stratum corneum, where they cause bothersome, often itchy rashes but not invasive systemic infections. Immunosuppressed patients (such as those with AIDS or those undergoing chemotherapy) are more likely to develop widespread cutaneous disease. The use of topical corticosteroids or topical calcineurin inhibitors may allow overgrowth of the offending organism even in patients with normal immune systems and can make the infection more difficult to diagnose

and eradicate. Hot, humid, occlusive environments favor dermatophyte growth; therefore, hyperhidrosis and occlusive footwear predispose patients to infections of the feet and groin.

An expanding, ringlike lesion with a slightly scaly, erythematous, advancing edge and central clearing suggests a fungal infection; however, the presence of fungus should be confirmed before initiating treatment by scraping the scale, infiltrating it with potassium hydroxide (KOH) solution, and examining it microscopically. It is also reasonable to check any scaly lesion for fungus. Fungal cultures may take weeks to grow, so they tend to be used for patients with atypical presentations, treatment failures, or for research.

Tinea corporis (dermatophyte infection of the body) can occur on any part of the body, including the trunk and extremities, and manifests with the characteristic annular lesion (**Figure 37**).

Tinea capitis mostly affects children. It frequently occurs in small epidemics, in settings such as a day care center. The terminal hairs (thick, pigmented hairs) of adults are more likely to be affected in the beard area rather than the scalp.

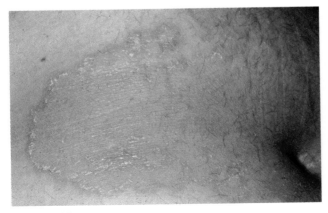

FIGURE 37.
Typical annular patch of tinea corporis with scaly pink edges.

The clinical presentation of tinea capitis ranges from noninflammatory, dry scaling to inflammatory nodules and plaques with superficial crusts. Facial lesions may be misdiagnosed as lupus erythematosus, rosacea, seborrheic dermatitis, or other conditions because they frequently lack the typical annular morphology that characterizes tinea corporis. Diagnosis is made by performing a KOH microscopic examination for fungal elements or by culture.

The most common site of fungal infection is the feet. Tinea pedis may present with silvery scale and dull erythema of the entire foot, characterized by interdigital scaling and maceration or blisters of the plantar arch, sides of the feet, and/or heel (**Figure 38**). It may itch or may be entirely asymptomatic. In the "two feet–one hand syndrome," one hand has a diffuse scaly appearance that is also fungal in nature (**Figure 39**). Tinea pedis can also spread to infect the hair follicles on the legs, causing a deep folliculitis that fails to respond to antibiotic therapy.

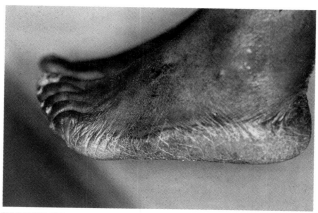

FIGURE 38.
Tinea pedis, with scaling and hyperpigmentation most clearly visible at the edge of the sole.

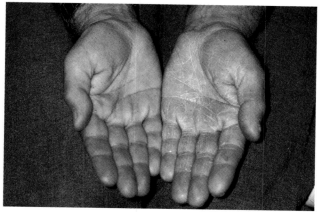

FIGURE 39.
Two feet–one hand syndrome, with scaling of one hand and normal-appearing skin on the other hand. Both of this patient's feet had a potassium hydroxide (KOH)–positive, scaly rash.

Treatment

Topical antifungal creams are usually effective in treating cutaneous fungal infections that do not involve the hair or nails. The over-the-counter products clotrimazole, miconazole, and terbinafine are efficacious and cost-effective. Prescription products such as naftifine, ciclopirox, butenafine, and a variety of azoles are also effective. Combination antifungal and corticosteroid products should be avoided, because the corticosteroid component is of high potency and therefore may diminish treatment efficacy, may convert a superficial fungal infection to a deep inflammatory pustular infection, or may result in striae formation when used in the groin or axilla.

Oral antifungal medication is needed for treatment of widespread tinea corporis, tinea barbae (tinea infection of the beard and moustache areas), or tinea capitis. Griseofulvin, an older drug, is effective and generally safe; however, it has largely been supplanted by newer agents. Itraconazole has good in vitro activity against dermatophytes and concentrates in the skin, hair, and nails. A simple pulse-dosing regimen, where the drug is given daily for 1 week each month, simplifies patient adherence for longer courses of treatment. Ketoconazole, while cheaper than itraconazole, has greater liver and endocrine toxicity and carries the risk for many drug interactions. Terbinafine has few drug interactions and good oral bioavailability; however, severe skin reactions, leukopenia, hepatotoxicity, and taste disturbances can occur.

KEY POINTS

- An expanding annular lesion with a slightly scaly, erythematous, advancing edge and central clearing is suspicious for fungal infection and should be confirmed with a potassium hydroxide (KOH) test.
- Topical antifungal creams are usually effective in treating cutaneous fungal infections.

Onychomycosis

Onychomycosis is usually characterized by a thickened, yellow or white nail with scaling under the elevated distal free edge of the nail plate. Sometimes, however, the infecting organism invades the surface of the toenail or the proximal nail fold (proximal subungual onychomycosis); HIV infection should be suspected in patients with the latter (**Figure 40**).

Nail infections can be diagnosed with KOH examination or culture; however, periodic acid–Schiff staining of a clipping of the nail has proven more sensitive (85%) than either of the former tests. The test is simple to perform and gives results in a few days. Because up to 50% of all nail dystrophies are caused by conditions other than fungal infection, the diagnosis should be confirmed before treatment is initiated. Traumatic nail dystrophy, lichen planus, and psoriasis may have nail involvement that is misdiagnosed as onychomycosis. A nail biopsy may be necessary to clarify the diagnosis.

Most patients with toenail onychomycosis are asymptomatic and do not require treatment. For patients with

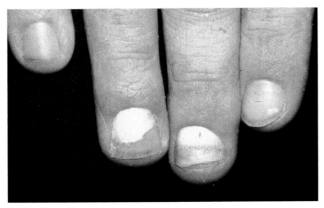

FIGURE 40.
White debris along the proximal nail fold in proximal subungual onychomycosis.

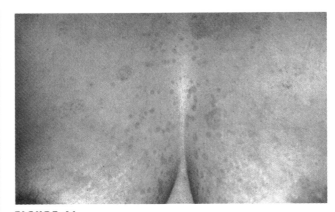

FIGURE 41.
Small, light-brown, coalescing macules on the anterior chest characteristic of tinea versicolor.

fingernail involvement, symptomatic toenail infection, or those with peripheral neuropathy, arterial insufficiency, or diabetes mellitus who are predisposed to complications from onychomycosis (such as cellulitis), oral therapy with terbinafine, itraconazole, or fluconazole is usually necessary for cure (**Table 15**). The topical antifungal lacquers are not often effective.

> **KEY POINTS**
> - Onychomycosis is usually characterized by a thickened, yellow or white nail with scaling under the elevated distal free edge of the nail plate.
> - Because up to 50% of all nail dystrophies are caused by conditions other than fungal infection, the diagnosis should be confirmed before treatment is initiated.

Tinea Versicolor

Slightly scaly hyper- or hypopigmented macules of the trunk and upper arms characterize tinea versicolor (**Figure 41**). The causative yeast organism, *Malassezia furfur*, is a normal inhabitant of the hair follicle; however, when hot and humid environmental conditions favor its growth, disease appears. Diagnosis is confirmed by microscopic evaluation of a KOH preparation made from scrapings of lesions showing the classic appearance of both spores and hyphae in a "spaghetti and meatball" pattern. Selenium sulfide 2.5% lotion, applied either overnight or for 10 to 15 minutes once daily for 1 to 2

weeks, is efficacious and cost-effective. Ketoconazole shampoo and the imidazole or triazole creams are also effective topically. Single-dose oral ketoconazole, 400 mg (may repeat dose in 1 week), is easy and safe oral therapy. Pigmentary alterations will usually take weeks to resolve after successful therapy. If recurrences are problematic, monthly prophylactic treatment may be given.

Candidiasis

Candida albicans is a component of the normal oral and skin flora. *Candida* overgrows and causes disease in immunocompromised patients or when warmth, moisture, maceration, reductions in competing flora due to antibiotic therapy, or increased skin pH occur (panty liners, diapers, and other occlusive garments raise skin pH). Sites that are predisposed to *Candida* overgrowth include the inframammary, axillary, abdominal, periungual, and inguinal creases; the oral and vaginal mucous membranes; and the perianal and interdigital skin. If patients are febrile and unable to ambulate because of other comorbid illnesses, the back and buttocks may be affected.

Cutaneous candidiasis is characterized by red, itchy, inflamed skin. At sites of skin-to-skin contact, lesions have glazed, shiny, and at times eroded surfaces and may be characterized by burning more than pruritus. Satellite pustules (yellow, fluid-filled lesions at the edge of the confluent red eruption) are another key physical finding (**Figure 42**).

TABLE 15 Oral Therapy for Onychomycosis		
Drug	**Dosing for Fingernail Involvement**	**Dosing for Toenail Involvement**
Terbinafine	250 mg/d for 6-8 weeks	250 mg/d for 12-16 weeks
Itraconazole	Pulsed doses of 200 mg twice daily for 1 week of each month for 2 months	Pulsed doses of 200 mg twice daily for 1 week of each month for 3-4 months
Fluconazole	150-300 mg once weekly for 6-12 months	150-300 mg once weekly for 6-12 months

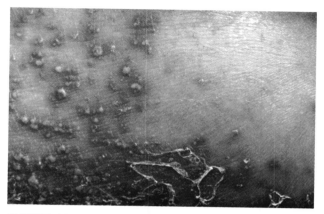

FIGURE 42.
Candidal infection, with satellite pustules at the edge of a pink, moist eruption in the skin folds.

Candidal vulvovaginitis affects the vulvar skin as described above. Risk factors include diabetes, HIV infection, long-term antibiotic or corticosteroid therapy, pregnancy, or long-term tamoxifen treatment. Male sexual partners of affected patients may develop red, moist, painful, or itchy balanitis.

Oropharyngeal candidiasis is characterized by a grayish-white membrane with a red base in the oral mucosa. It is commonly seen in patients with immunosuppression, diabetes, or malnourishment and in patients taking chronic antibiotics or corticosteroids. Immunosuppressed patients with oral candidiasis often have esophageal candidiasis and odynophagia. Erythema, transverse fissuring, and maceration may also occur at the angles of the mouth (perleche) as an associated finding of oral candidiasis, as a complication of ill-fitting dentures, or as a consequence of alveolar ridge atrophy secondary to aging.

The diagnosis of candidiasis may be confirmed by KOH examination, Gram stain, or culture. Candidiasis can often be confused with intertrigo, which is an irritant skin-fold dermatitis that results from moisture and rubbing and is especially prominent in obese patients. Intertrigo usually lacks the same degree of redness and satellite lesions found in candidiasis, and a microscopic examination of a KOH preparation will not demonstrate hyphae and pseudohyphae that are diagnostic of candidiasis.

Treatment of the skin with the topical agents clotrimazole, miconazole, naftifine, ciclopirox, butenafine, and other azoles will usually result in clearance. Terbinafine is less active against *Candida*. Topical imidazoles are useful for uncomplicated oral and vaginal disease. A single dose of 150 mg of fluconazole is also effective. Predisposing factors should be eliminated if possible. When treating immunocompromised patients, fluconazole is often started at 200 mg/d and is increased as needed if there is no response. Duration of therapy is variable. Itraconazole can be substituted when there is concomitant cutaneous dermatophyte disease. Sexual partners of patients with oral or vaginal disease should be screened and treated as necessary.

KEY POINTS

- Cutaneous candidal infection is characterized by red, itchy, inflamed skin with satellite pustules; at sites of skin-to-skin contact, lesions have glazed, shiny, and at times eroded surfaces.
- Oropharyngeal candidiasis is characterized by a grayish-white membrane with a red base in the oral mucosa.

Bacterial Infections

Abscesses

Abscesses are acute, tender, well-delineated, pus-containing lesions that commonly appear on the neck, axilla, and groin but may occur at any skin site (**Figure 43**). Abscesses are nearly always caused by *Staphylococcus aureus*. Exceptions include abscesses that develop in the hospital or in the perianal area of the body. *S. aureus* is persistently and asymptomatically present in the anterior nares of approximately 30% of healthy adults; another 50% are intermittently colonized. This is a significant risk factor for abscess formation. While outbreaks of methicillin-resistant *S. aureus* (MRSA) have been described in many populations, such as prisoners and school athletes, they are so well established in many communities that it may not be productive to look for risk factors. Instead, the focus is on preventing recurrences, a challenge even in highly motivated patients. Strategies that address nasal colonization alone are disappointing, and the best outcomes seem to follow aggressive eradication policies that include topical and systemic treatment, treatment of household contacts (sometimes even pets), and the maintenance of an exceptionally high level of hygiene.

Incision and drainage is the treatment of choice and is effective without concomitant antibiotic therapy in most

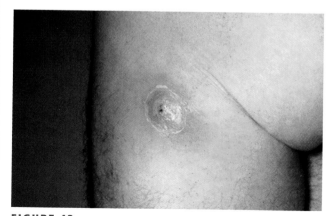

FIGURE 43.
A staphylococcal abscess presenting as a tender, erythematous, fluctuant nodule topped by a central pustule.

patients; however, it is still not known whether concomitant antibiotic treatment may accelerate healing or reduce the risk of recurrence. Cultures can easily distinguish MRSA from methicillin-susceptible *S. aureus* (MSSA); however, antimicrobial treatment, if needed, should begin with medications other than β-lactams. Current choices include tetracyclines, rifampin-containing combinations, and clindamycin (in geographic areas where there is a high rate of susceptibility). Trimethoprim-sulfamethoxazole may be a reasonable alternative if streptococci are not a concern, because it has limited activity against any of the β-hemolytic streptococci. Linezolid has good activity against almost all staphylococci but is much more expensive than the alternatives. Recurrent or refractory infection may be treated by efforts to decrease colonization.

KEY POINTS

- Staphylococcal abscesses are acute, tender, well-delineated, pus-containing lesions that commonly appear on the neck, axillae, and groin but may occur at any skin site.

- Incision and drainage is the treatment of choice for stable patients with staphylococcal abscesses that are not accompanied by systemic toxicity.

Staphylococcal Folliculitis

S. aureus may also cause pustules that are centered on hair follicles (**Figure 44**). The beard, pubic areas, axillae, and thighs are often affected. The infection often resolves spontaneously, but the local application of heat and topical clindamycin or benzoyl peroxide is often effective topical therapy. Patients should avoid shaving in the affected area during active infection. Systemic antibiotics should not be used routinely for treatment of folliculitis, as it generally resolves on its own.

Impetigo

Impetigo is a superficial skin infection characterized by a yellowish, crusted surface that may be caused by staphylococci or streptococci (**Figure 45**). If *S. aureus* is the cause, secretion of exfoliative toxin may result in superficial blister formation. Bullous impetigo is an indication that the lesions are infected with *S. aureus* (**Figure 46**). Systemic spread of the same toxins causes staphylococcal scalded skin syndrome.

Limited disease of the head and neck can usually be effectively treated with topical mupirocin or bacitracin applied after soaking off the crusts. If more extensive disease is present,

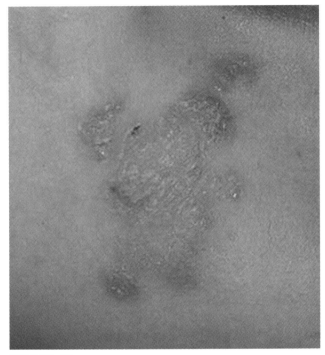

FIGURE 45.
Honey-colored crusts in a patient with impetigo.

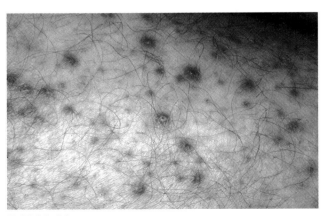

FIGURE 44.
Pink papules and pustules centered around hair follicles, characteristic of folliculitis.

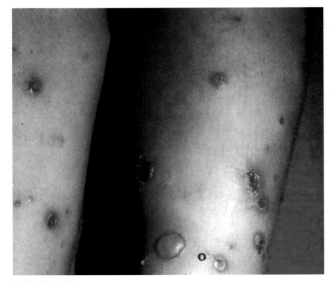

FIGURE 46.
Clear, fluid-filled blisters with surrounding erythema on the legs of a patient with bullous impetigo.

cephalosporin, penicillinase-resistant penicillin, or β-lactam/β-lactamase inhibitor combination therapy added to the topical approach are reasonable initial treatments (**Table 16**). Trimethoprim-sulfamethoxazole is not a first-line drug if streptococcal infection is suspected. Tetracycline is also effective, especially if MRSA is suspected.

Cellulitis

Cellulitis is a rapidly spreading, deep, subcutaneous-based infection characterized by a well-demarcated area of warmth, swelling, tenderness, and erythema that may be accompanied by lymphatic streaking and/or fever and chills (**Figure 47**). Cellulitis can usually be differentiated from contact dermatitis by the absence of pruritus; however, areas of contact and other types of dermatitis can become secondarily impetiginized. Cellulitis is often secondary to streptococcal infection, although staphylococci can also be the cause. Known risk factors for lower-extremity cellulitis include tinea pedis, onychomycosis, chronic leg ulcerations, varicose veins of the leg, phlebitis, obesity, type 2 diabetes mellitus, and heart failure. Cellulitis is a clinical diagnosis; cultures are usually not necessary and are seldom positive (less than 5% of the time). Treatment is based upon the risk of MRSA infection and severity of illness (see Table 16). The role of suppressive antibiotic therapy for recurrent lower-extremity cellulitis is

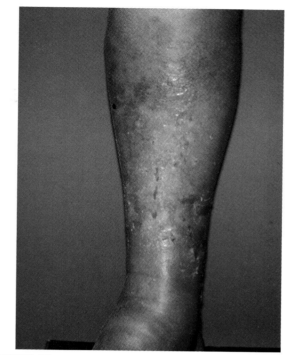

FIGURE 47.
Well-demarcated area of warmth, swelling, tenderness, and erythema in a patient with cellulitis.

TABLE 16 Treatment of Impetigo and Skin and Soft-Tissue Infections

Condition	Drugs	Notes
Impetigo	Dicloxacillin or cephalexin	—
	Erythromycin	Possible resistance in some strains of *Staphylococcus aureus* and *Streptococcus pyogenes* (over 50% of isolates in many communities)
	Clindamycin	—
	Amoxicillin/clavulanate	—
	Mupirocin ointment	Reasonable to treat patients with fewer lesions
MSSA SSTI	Nafcillin or oxacillin	First-line parenteral therapy; not effective against MRSA
	Cefazolin	—
	Clindamycin	Clindamycin resistance is less common than erythromycin resistance, but failures of treatment have been documented
	Dicloxacillin or cephalexin	First-line oral agents for methicillin-susceptible strains
	Doxycycline, minocycline	Recent clinical data is limited
	TMP-SMZ	Efficacy data is limited
MRSA SSTI	Vancomycin	First-line parenteral therapy for treatment of MRSA infection
	Linezolid	Clinical data is limited; no cross-resistance with other antibiotic classes; expensive
	Clindamycin	Clindamycin resistance is less common than erythromycin resistance, but failures of treatment have been documented
	Daptomycin	—
	Doxycycline, minocycline	Recent clinical data is limited
	TMP-SMZ	Efficacy data is limited, but used frequently by dermatology community for treatment of MRSA

MRSA = methicillin-resistant *Staphylococcus aureus*; MSSA = methicillin-susceptible *Staphylococcus aureus*; SSTI = skin and soft-tissue infection; TMP-SMZ = trimethoprim-sulfamethoxazole.

Data from Stevens DL, Bisno AL, Chambers HF, et al; Infectious Diseases Society of America. Practice guidelines for the diagnosis and management of skin and soft-tissue infections. Clin Infect Dis. 2005;41(10):1373-1406. [PMID: 16231249]

unclear, but many experts recommend prolonged prophylactic antibiotic therapy for patients with an underlying predisposing factor for infection that cannot be remedied (such as chronic lymphedema). Acute venous stasis dermatitis can be misdiagnosed as cellulitis. Involvement of both legs, absence of fever and/or leukocytosis, and failure to respond to appropriate antibiotic therapy for staphylococcal/streptococcal infection are more characteristic of venous stasis dermatitis than cellulitis.

KEY POINTS

- Cellulitis is a rapidly spreading, deep, subcutaneous-based infection characterized by a well-demarcated area of warmth, swelling, tenderness, and erythema that may be accompanied by lymphatic streaking and/or fever and chills.
- Cellulitis can be differentiated from contact dermatitis by the absence of pruritus.
- Bilateral leg involvement, absence of fever/leukocytosis, or lack of response to appropriate antibiotics may suggest venous stasis dermatitis rather than cellulitis.

Ecthyma

Superficial, saucer-shaped ulcers with overlying crusts are the classic findings of ecthyma (**Figure 48**). They almost always occur on the legs or feet and are usually caused by streptococci. Injection drug users and patients with AIDS are at increased risk. Cleansing with antibacterial washes followed by topical mupirocin and oral dicloxacillin or a first-generation cephalosporin is effective therapy.

Pseudomonas Folliculitis

Pseudomonas folliculitis is a pruritic eruption that is characterized by follicle-centered erythematous papules and pustules. The trunk, axillae, buttocks, and proximal extremities are most often affected (**Figure 49**). The eruption begins 1 to 4 days after bathing in a hot tub, whirlpool, or, less

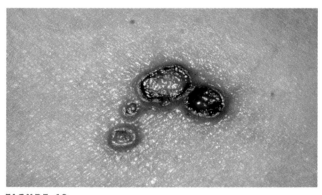

FIGURE 48.
Punched-out ulcer with a yellow eschar on the leg of a patient with ecthyma.

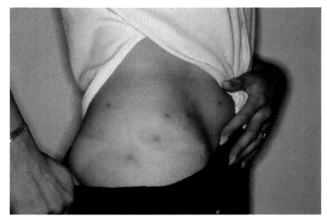

FIGURE 49.
Erythematous papules with flare seen in *Pseudomonas* folliculitis. Skin under the bathing suit is characteristically involved.

commonly, a public swimming pool. Inadequate water chlorination allows proliferation of the causative organism *Pseudomonas aeruginosa*. Fever, external otitis, breast abscess, the "hot foot syndrome" (painful plantar nodules), or bacteremia may infrequently complicate the cutaneous infection. Spontaneous involution without therapy is expected within 7 to 14 days. Severe pruritus, fever, chills, or a prolonged or recurrent course may necessitate therapy with a fluoroquinolone or a third-generation cephalosporin. Treatment should also be considered in immunosuppressed patients. Adequate water filtration and chlorination or bromination of hot tubs and swimming pools will help prevent this condition.

Viral Infections

Herpes Simplex

Two distinct herpes simplex viruses, herpes simplex virus (HSV) types 1 and 2, are recognized. HSV-1 has the highest prevalence; 60% to 85% of U.S. adults are infected with HSV-1 by age 60 years. HSV-2 is the most common sexually transmitted genital ulcer disease, with 500,000 new symptomatic cases occurring each year. The vast majority of initial infections are not clinically apparent. Most clinically recognized first episodes are the result of viral reactivation from its dormant state in the neural ganglia. True primary infection is prolonged, lasting 10 to 14 days, and is often accompanied by fever, lymphadenopathy, and severe pain. Recurrent disease has a prodrome of burning, stinging, or pain occurring approximately 24 hours before onset of vesicles in 60% of patients. Common stressors known to trigger reactivation include ultraviolet light, fatigue, exposure to heat or cold, trauma such as with sexual intercourse or laser surgery, and immunosuppression. When immunosuppression is caused by HIV infection, atypical morphologic features such as nodules or nonhealing ulcers are often present (**Figure 50**).

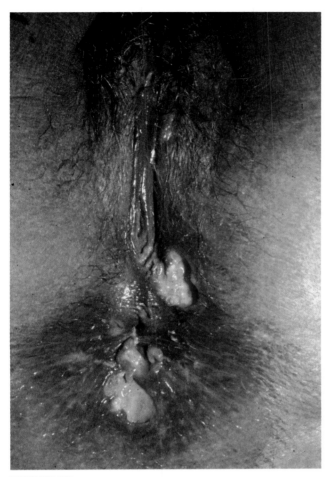

FIGURE 50.
Painful, nonhealing genital ulcers of herpes simplex in a patient with HIV infection.

Classically, both HSV-1 and HSV-2 initially cause a cluster of pink papules that rapidly become vesicular. Grouped vesicles (clear, fluid-filled, small blisters) on an erythematous, edematous base are characteristic. They often become cloudy pustules before rupturing, leaving behind clustered erosions that usually completely involute within 3 to 5 days. Orofacial lesions are most common on the outer edge of the vermilion border, but they may be observed anywhere. Genital recurrences are more common in men, but women are more symptomatic. Beard lesions (resulting from autoinoculation by shaving), facial and neck lesions (contracted by skin-to-skin contact in sporting events such as wrestling or rugby), and finger lesions are less common but are well-recognized sites of involvement. An abnormal skin barrier, as is present in patients with atopic dermatitis, can allow HSV to spread rapidly across large surface areas, causing a disseminated cutaneous infection called eczema herpeticum. Patients with advanced HIV infection or those who have undergone organ transplantation are at risk for more frequent and more severe recurrences of HSV. In extreme cases, the lesions can become

confluent and produce a painful lesion that may be many square centimeters in size.

The diagnosis is usually made clinically, but if the diagnosis is unclear, laboratory confirmation of infection may be helpful. Recommended diagnostic tests include viral culture or the direct fluorescent antibody test, which is the most accurate, sensitive, and rapidly available test. Treatment may be given at the onset of the prodromal symptoms and may be repeated for each occurrence. If recurrences are prolonged, particularly painful, or occur 6 or more times per year, preventive suppressive doses can be prescribed. The oral antiviral agents acyclovir, valacyclovir, and famciclovir are effective and safe treatments. Topical antiviral agents are generally not recommended because of their much-reduced efficacy. In patients with severe immunosuppression, treatment may need to be adjusted in both dose and duration to control disease symptoms. Affected patients should receive preventive education and testing for concurrent sexually transmitted diseases.

KEY POINTS

- Herpes simplex virus type 2 infection is the most common sexually transmitted ulcerative disease.
- A vesicle is the primary lesion of herpes simplex virus infection.
- The oral antiviral agents acyclovir, valacyclovir, and famciclovir are effective and safe treatments for herpes simplex virus infections.

Herpes Zoster

Herpes zoster is a common condition that results from reactivation of the latent varicella-zoster virus, which resides in the nerve ganglia after an initial chickenpox infection (usually during childhood). Over 1 million cases occur in the United States yearly, with more than half affecting individuals over 60 years of age. Immunosuppression increases the risk of disease. In patients with HIV or in those undergoing chemotherapy, the lesions may be bullous; may occur in multiple, widely separated dermatomes; may be disseminated on the skin and internally; or may produce recurrent disease. Recurrent herpes zoster should trigger testing for possible associated HIV infection. Vaccination in healthy adults over 60 years of age reduces the incidence of herpes zoster by over 50% and lessens the severity and chance of complications.

As in herpes simplex, the classic morphology in herpes zoster is grouped vesicles on an erythematous base (**Figure 51**); however, vesicles occur in multiple plaques along one or several contiguous dermatomes in a unilateral configuration. The thoracic region is involved in more than 50% of cases; the first branch of the trigeminal nerve is involved in 10% to 15% of cases. Significantly, involvement of the trigeminal nerve may lead to ocular complications. Pain is the most common associated symptom, and it is frequently present before the skin findings occur. Pain may be debilitating

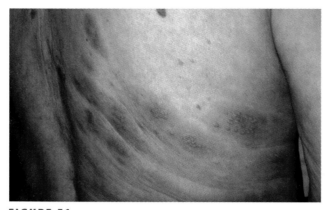

FIGURE 51.
Typical herpes zoster of the trunk, characterized by painful grouped vesicles on an erythematous base in a dermatomal distribution.

throughout the active course of disease, or it may persist indefinitely as postherpetic neuralgia.

Antiviral therapy with acyclovir, valacyclovir, or famciclovir is effective in killing the virus. Benefits of antiviral therapy include faster healing of the skin, lessening of the acute pain, and reduction of the incidence and intensity of postherpetic neuralgia. Postherpetic neuralgia may be improved by treatment with gabapentin, pregabalin, a lidocaine patch, topical capsaicin, tricyclic antidepressants, and opioid analgesics; however, prevention should be emphasized by ensuring that patients over 60 years of age are vaccinated. Urgent ophthalmologic consultation should be sought when the eye or periorbital skin is involved.

KEY POINTS

- Vaccination in patients over the age of 60 years reduces the incidence of herpes zoster by over 50% and lessens the severity and chance of complications.

- Antiviral therapy with acyclovir, valacyclovir, or famciclovir is effective treatment for herpes zoster.

- Recurrent herpes zoster should trigger testing for possible associated HIV infection.

- Urgent ophthalmologic consultation should be sought when herpes zoster involves the eye or periorbital skin.

Molluscum Contagiosum

The majority of patients infected with molluscum contagiosum (poxvirus) are children. Adults may acquire the disease through sexual contact, resulting in genital and pubic lesions. Immunosuppressed patients or patients with active atopic dermatitis may experience widespread, treatment-resistant disease. The infection causes a small, dome-shaped, smooth-surfaced, skin-colored or pink papule that

may have a central umbilication (**Figure 52**). On close inspection, small, white inclusions may be visualized. Molluscum contagiosum normally spontaneously resolves in a few months. Treatment of lesions appearing outside of the genital region is often considered for cosmetic reasons, whereas genital lesions are usually treated to prevent spread by sexual contact. Interventions that have proven successful include destructive methods such as curettage, cautery, or cryotherapy and those topical treatments discussed for warts (see below). Compared with topical therapy, curettage appears to be more efficacious and is associated with the fewest side effects.

Common and Genital Warts

Warts are caused by infection with one or more of the 120 subtypes of the human papillomavirus (HPV). Common warts generally appear as 5- to 10-mm, rough-surfaced, skin-colored papules. The incubation period appears to be approximately 2 to 3 months. The peak age of clinically apparent infection is the teenage and early adult years. The prevalence of common warts is approximately 25%. They can affect any part of the body; however, certain sites warrant special mention. Plantar warts may cause pain, and aggressive therapy (burning, excision, and cryosurgery) may further limit ambulation. Periungual infection is difficult to cure, and pain following destructive treatment is more severe than at other sites of infection. Mucosal infection and genital lesions may particularly predispose patients to cancer formation. Genital HPV infections are the most common sexually transmitted disease, with over 1 million cases diagnosed each year. Condyloma acuminatum is a lobulated growth that usually results from infection with non–cancer-forming types of HPV (**Figure 53**). Infections with HPV type 16 or 18 are the most likely to result in cancer formation; warts caused

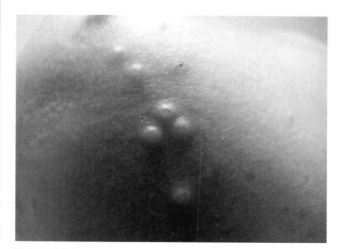

FIGURE 52.
Molluscum contagiosum, with pink papules with a central umbilication.

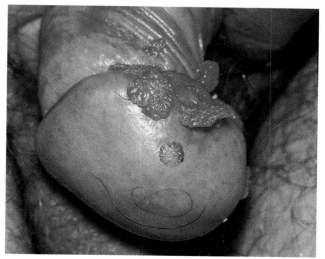

FIGURE 53.
Warty growths on the glans penis typical of condyloma acuminatum.

by these subtypes are usually flat, hyperpigmented macules. In addition to monitoring patients with genital warts for cancer, sexual-partner examination and monitoring are needed, as is vigilance for other sexually transmitted diseases. Flat warts of the face and legs may be numerous and difficult to treat. Such lesions often result from autoinoculation after shaving.

Spontaneous involution of cutaneous warts occurs in 30% of patients within 3 months, 70% within 2 years, and 90% within 3 years. Therapeutic intervention for cutaneous warts should be influenced by the knowledge that spontaneous regression is common and that strong, evidence-based studies showing a definitive highly effective therapy are lacking. Thus, choosing not to treat cutaneous warts is often a reasonable option; however, pain, interference with function, social embarrassment, continual formation of new lesions, and concern for transmission may necessitate treatment. Cost-effective, nonscarring treatment such as topical salicylic acid should be first-line therapy; cryotherapy destruction is a treatment strategy if daily compliance with salicylic acid is problematic.

Genital infections may be observed, but treatment is more often desired and indicated owing to the risk of transmission and predisposition to genital cancer in infected individuals. Podophyllotoxin, imiquimod, cryotherapy, or electrosurgical destruction is often used. HPV vaccination of females between 11 and 26 years of age is recommended. Clinical trials indicate that the vaccine has high efficacy in preventing persistent HPV infection and cervical cancer precursor lesions caused by HPV types 6, 11, 16, or 18 among females who have not already been infected with the respective HPV type.

Bibliography

Crawford F, Hollis S. Topical treatments for fungal infections of the skin and nails of the foot. Cochrane Database Syst Rev. 2007;(3):CD001434. [PMID: 17636672]

de Berker D. Clinical practice. Fungal nail disease. N Engl J Med. 2009;360(20):2108-2116. [PMID: 19439745]

Elston DM. Community-acquired methicillin-resistant *Staphylococcus aureus*. J Am Acad Dermatol. 2007;56(1):1-16. [PMID: 17190619]

Fatahzadeh M, Schwartz RA. Human herpes simplex virus infections: epidemiology, pathogenesis, symptomatology, diagnosis, and management. J Am Acad Dermatol. 2007;57(5):737-763. [PMID: 17939933]

Gibbs S, Harvey I. Topical treatments for cutaneous warts. Cochrane Database Syst Rev. 2006;3:CD001781. [PMID: 16855978]

Stevens DL, Eron LL. Cellulitis and soft-tissue infections. Ann Intern Med. 2009;150(1):ITC11. [PMID: 19124814]

Tyring SK. Management of herpes zoster and postherpetic neuralgia. J Am Acad Dermatol. 2007;57(6 Suppl):S136-42. [PMID: 18021865]

Weinberg JM. Herpes zoster: epidemiology, natural history, and common complications. J Am Acad Dermatol. 2007;57(6 Suppl):S130-5. [PMID: 18021864]

Yu Y, Cheng AS, Wang L, Dunne WM, Bayliss SJ. Hot tub folliculitis or hot hand-foot syndrome caused by *Pseudomonas aeruginosa*. J Am Acad Dermatol. 2007;57(4):596-600. [PMID: 17658195]

Bites and Stings

Overview

Insect bites and stings are a seasonal nuisance and may be significant vectors of disease. On physical examination, look for erythematous papules, sometimes with a central punctum, as well as vesicles, bullae, and impetiginization secondary to scratching. Insect sting–induced anaphylaxis can be life-threatening (see MKSAP 15 Pulmonary and Critical Care Medicine).

Bite and sting reactions are treated symptomatically. Camphor and menthol or pramoxine preparations help to control itch. Topical corticosteroids appropriate for the bite or sting site may be used for up to 2 weeks.

- Camphor and menthol or pramoxine preparations are helpful for the itch associated with insect bites.

Chigger Bites

Chigger bites appear as erythematous, excoriated papules along clothing lines, occasionally with a central punctum. They cluster where tight clothing meets skin. Appropriate therapy consists of a mid-strength topical corticosteroid. Camphor and menthol lotion is helpful for the symptomatic relief of pruritus associated with chigger bites.

- Chigger bites appear as erythematous, excoriated papules along clothing lines, occasionally with a central punctum.

Spider Bites

Spider bites are overdiagnosed. Brown recluse spiders are quite shy (**Figure 54**); houses have been described that contain more than 2000 brown recluse spiders without any bites occurring. In the United States, recluse spiders are limited to Missouri, Oklahoma, Arkansas, Mississippi, Louisiana, and parts of Texas, Alabama, Tennessee, Kentucky, Illinois, Iowa, and Kansas, yet hundreds of "brown recluse spider bites" are reported every year from nonendemic locations. It is unlikely that any of these are true brown recluse spider bites. Rapidly progressive, necrotic skin lesions more commonly represent infections with community-acquired methicillin-resistant *Staphylococcus aureus*. Necrotic lesions with a violaceous, overhanging border are more likely pyoderma gangrenosum.

The diagnosis of brown recluse spider bite can be confirmed by an enzyme immunoassay on a skin biopsy or on plucked hairs or by a passive hemagglutination inhibition test up to 3 days after envenomation.

FIGURE 54.
Brown recluse spiders are quite shy, and brown recluse spider bites are overdiagnosed.

The majority of spider bites require only rest, ice, and elevation.

- Community-acquired methicillin-resistant *Staphylococcus aureus* infections and pyoderma gangrenosum are often misdiagnosed as brown recluse spider bites.

Scabies Infestation

Scabies is spread by direct, personal contact, especially during sex. Acquisition from bedding or clothes is rare. Scabies infestation causes intense itching and a papular or vesicular rash (**Figure 55**). Burrows are visible as short, serpiginous lines. Location in the interdigital webs, flexure surface of the wrists, penis, axillae, nipples, umbilicus, scrotum, and buttocks is diagnostic. Scabies infestation should be suspected whenever a patient and close contacts are itching. Elderly patients may have only scattered excoriations, and web-space involvement is often lacking. Crusted scabies, with widespread scale and heavy crusting on the ears and hands, occurs in debilitated and immunosuppressed patients.

Scabies can be treated with topical permethrin cream, applied overnight to the entire body surface, including the head, neck, scalp, hairline, and face, regardless of the location of the lesion. Efficacy is increased if the treatment is repeated 1 week later. Itching can persist for several weeks after successful treatment; however, the appearance of new lesions may suggest treatment failure or reinfestation. To reduce the potential of reinfestation, clothing, linens, and towels used within the previous week must be washed in hot water and dried at high heat. Patients with crusted scabies often fail to respond to a single application of topical permethrin and may require repeated topical treatments and/or off-label treatment with oral ivermectin.

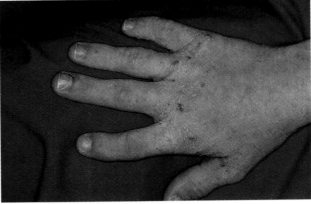

FIGURE 55.
Scabies infestation causes intense itching and a papular or vesicular rash that may be particularly prominent in the interdigital webs. When chronic, such as in this patient, affected skin becomes hyperkeratotic and crusted.

KEY POINTS

- Scabies infestation causes intense itching, a papular or vesicular rash, and burrows that are visible as short, wavy lines.
- Topical permethrin cream is first-line treatment for scabies infestation.

Lice

Head louse infestation is common among school children. Pubic louse infestation is typically a sexually transmitted disease in adults, and affected patients should be screened for other sexually transmitted diseases. Body louse infestation is common among the homeless and is a risk factor for endocarditis caused by *Bartonella quintana*. The diagnosis of lice is established by identifying crawling lice in the scalp or pubic hair. Louse egg cases are called nits and are found sticking to the hair shaft in patients with lice. Nits are generally easier to see than lice.

Topical pediculicides remain the preferred treatment for head and pubic louse infestations. Body louse infestations are treated by disinfecting the clothing. Lindane is considered a second-line treatment by the Centers for Disease Control and Prevention because of its rare association with seizures, but these have almost always been associated with ingestion or gross misuse of the product. Oral ivermectin has been used off-label.

KEY POINTS

- The diagnosis of lice is established by identifying crawling lice in the scalp or pubic hair or nits found sticking to the hair shaft.
- Topical pediculicides remain the preferred treatment for head and pubic louse infestations.

Bedbug Bites

Bedbug infestation is becoming increasingly common. *Cimex lectularius* and *C. hemipterus* (**Figure 56**) are nocturnal, hiding in cracks and crevices during the day and biting at night, often in a series ("breakfast, lunch, and dinner") on exposed sites such as the face, neck, arms, and hands (**Figure 57**). The lesions are painless and appear as pruritic, urticaria-like papules with a central hemorrhagic punctum. Eradication of bedbugs is best done by professionals.

KEY POINT

- Bedbug bites are recognized as painless, pruritic, urticaria-like papules with a central hemorrhagic punctum that appear in a linear distribution.

Bibliography

Brouqui P, Raoult D. Arthropod-borne diseases in homeless. Ann N Y Acad Sci. 2006;1078:223-235. [PMID: 17114713]

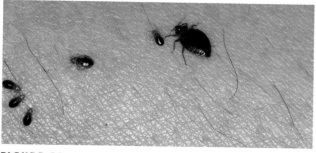

FIGURE 56.
Bedbugs are nocturnal, hiding in cracks and crevices during the day and biting at night.

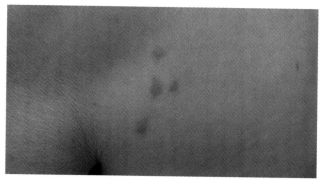

FIGURE 57.
Bedbug bites often occur in a series ("breakfast, lunch, and dinner"); lesions are painless and appear as pruritic, urticaria-like papules.

Lewis FS, Smith LJ. What's eating you? Bees, Part 2: Venom immunotherapy and mastocytosis. Cutis. 2007;80(1):33-37. [PMID: 17725061]

Miller MJ, Gomez HF, Snider RJ, Stephens EL, Czop RM, Warren JS. Detection of Loxosceles venom in lesional hair shafts and skin: application of a specific immunoassay to identify dermonecrotic arachnidism. Am J Emerg Med. 2000;18(5):626-628. [PMID: 10999583]

Partridge ME, Blackwood W, Hamilton RG, Ford J, Young P, Ownby DR. Prevalence of allergic sensitization to imported fire ants in children living in an endemic region of the southeastern United States. Ann Allergy Asthma Immunol. 2008;100(1):54-58. [PMID: 18254483]

Vetter RS, Barger DK. An infestation of 2,055 brown recluse spiders (Araneae: Sicariidae) and no envenomations in a Kansas home: implications for bite diagnoses in nonendemic areas. J Med Entomol. 2002;39(6):948-951. [PMID: 12495200]

Cuts, Scrapes, Burns, and Blisters

Topical Wound Care

Most simple cuts and scrapes heal well with soap, water, and application of white petrolatum. A dressing that provides a moist wound environment is preferred, as it accelerates wound healing time by up to 50%. An inexpensive occlusive dressing can be made using a nonadherent dressing and plain petrolatum. Perforated plastic films, such as those commonly found on adhesive bandages, are inexpensive and readily available. Advanced dressings for larger, complicated wounds can be categorized into five basic types (**Table 17**).

Studies evaluating infection rates following skin biopsy showed no significant differences between prophylactic treatment with petrolatum and bacitracin; treatment with the latter, however, was complicated by allergic contact dermatitis. For this reason, many dermatologists now use only petrolatum following biopsy in noninfected skin.

Oral antibiotic therapy or topical mupirocin is useful for clinically impetiginized (secondarily infected) wounds; however, mupirocin resistance is emerging, with 2% to 50% of isolates demonstrating resistance. There is little evidence of emerging resistance to triple antibiotic ointment (neomycin, polymyxin B, and bacitracin), but neomycin is a frequent contact allergen. Retapamulin is a new pleuromutilin that is effective against staphylococci (including methicillin-resistant *Staphylococcus aureus*) as well as many gram-negative bacteria. How it compares clinically with mupirocin and other older agents remains to be determined.

KEY POINTS
- White petrolatum is the treatment of choice for the care of minor wounds.
- Occlusive, moist (rather than dry) dressings are now recommended for treatment of most wounds.

Burns

Emergency treatment of first-degree burns includes the immediate application of ice or cold compresses until the area is pain free. Dressings are not required, and prophylactic antibiotics are not indicated. Topical anesthetics and oral NSAIDs can reduce pain.

Second-degree burns involving a small amount of body surface area can often be treated in the ambulatory setting. The burn is gently washed with an antiseptic soap and water. Tetanus prophylaxis is indicated in patients who have not been vaccinated within the past 10 years. Liberally applied topical silver sulfadiazine provides prophylaxis against infection but is contraindicated in patients with a sulfa allergy and in pregnant women. Empiric systemic antibiotics are not indicated, but the wound should be monitored for clinical evidence of infection.

KEY POINTS
- First aid for first-degree burns includes the application of ice or cold compresses; a dressing is not indicated.
- Tetanus prophylaxis is indicated for patients with second-degree burns.

Friction Blisters

The incidence of foot blisters can be reduced by the use of closed-cell neoprene insoles, thick acrylic socks, or thin polyester socks combined with thick wool or polypropylene socks. Topical antiperspirants, such as 20% aluminum chloride hexahydrate, applied daily for at least 3 days before a long hike, reduced the incidence of foot blisters from 48% to 21%. However, irritation was commonly reported by those using the antiperspirant.

Topical acrylates have been used to treat friction blisters, but results are mixed, with some studies showing greater discomfort and no improvement in healing time. Treatment of friction blisters remains similar to that for other minor

TABLE 17 Dressing Categories, Indications, Advantages, and Disadvantages

Products	Indications	Advantages	Disadvantages
Hydrogels	Painful wounds, post-dermabrasion, laser wounds, chemical peels, partial-thickness and granulating wounds	Semitransparent, soothing, do not adhere to wounds	Require secondary dressing, frequent dressing changes, difficult to retain in wounds
Alginates	Highly exudative wounds, partial- or full-thickness wounds, cavitary wounds, postoperative wounds	Absorbent, hemostatic, nonadherent, fewer dressing changes	Require secondary dressing, difficult to remove
Hydrocolloids	Partial- or full-thickness wounds, pressure ulcers	Absorbent, bacterial barrier, physical barrier, extended wear time	Opaque, foul-smelling gel, cost
Foams	Moderate to heavy draining wounds to relieve pressure	Absorbent, conform to body contours, act like a cushion	Opaque, require secondary dressing, may adhere to wounds, cost
Films	Donor sites, superficial burns, partial-thickness wounds with minimal exudate	Transparent, bacterial barrier, adherent	May adhere to wounds, can cause fluid collection

Adapted from Chouchair M, Faria D. Dressings and Wound Care. In: Alguire PC, Mathes BM, eds. The Clinics Atlas of Office Procedures: Dermatologic Procedures. Philadelphia, PA: W.B. Saunders Company; 1999: 75-83. Copyright © 1999, Elsevier.

injuries. Removal of the blister roof with application of a thin adherent hydrocolloid dressing can improve function during the healing phase.

KEY POINTS

- The best strategy for the prevention of friction blisters is the use of thick, soft socks.

- Antiperspirants decrease the incidence of blisters but may cause irritant dermatitis.

Bibliography

Acikel C, Oncul O, Ulkur E, Bayram I, Celikoz B, Cavuslu S. Comparison of silver sulfadiazine 1%, mupirocin 2%, and fusidic acid 2% for topical antibacterial effect in methicillin-resistant staphylococci-infected, full-skin thickness rat burn wounds. J Burn Care Rehabil. 2003;24(1):37-41. [PMID: 12543989]

Herring KM, Richie DH Jr. Comparison of cotton and acrylic socks using a generic cushion sole design for runners. J Am Podiatr Med Assoc. 1993;83(9):515-522. [PMID: 8289142]

Knapik JJ, Reynolds K, Barson J. Influence of an antiperspirant on foot blister incidence during cross-country hiking. J Am Acad Dermatol. 1998;39(2 Pt 1):202-206. [PMID: 9704829]

Odou MF, Muller C, Calvet L, Dubreuil L. In vitro activity against anaerobes of retapamulin, a new topical antibiotic for treatment of skin infections. J Antimicrob Chemother. 2007;59(4):646-651. [PMID: 17350985]

Smack DP, Harrington AC, Dunn C, et al. Infection and allergy incidence in ambulatory surgery patients using white petrolatum vs bacitracin ointment. A randomized controlled trial. JAMA. 1996;276(12):972-977. [PMID: 8805732]

Common Neoplasms

Premalignant and Malignant Tumors

Basal Cell Carcinoma

Basal cell carcinoma (BCC) is the most common form of skin cancer. It rarely metastasizes, but its growth and treatment can be a source of morbidity. The most common type of BCC is the nodular type. Nodular lesions are pearly and pink with telangiectatic vessels (**Figure 58**) and may have a central depression; ulceration and crusting can occur. Flecks of melanin pigment may be present. BCC may be clinically difficult to visualize in sun-damaged skin; the diagnosis should be suspected in any area of friable skin that bleeds easily. Superficial multifocal BCC commonly occurs on the trunk or limbs as discrete erythematous patches. A thin, rolled border may be visible. Morpheaform, infiltrative, and micronodular variants are more aggressive and often have ill-defined clinical margins. Morpheaform BCC resembles a scar that gradually expands.

Most often the diagnosis of BCC can be suspected by findings on clinical examination, but diagnosis and selection of the most appropriate therapy require biopsy confirmation. Common biopsy techniques include shave or punch. Most

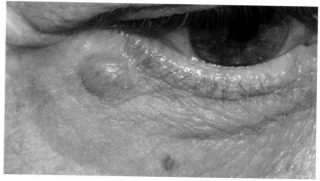

FIGURE 58.
Basal cell carcinomas typically present as pearly papules with telangiectasias.

BCCs will require referral and are treated with excision. Ill-defined lesions, high-risk histologic types, and tumors on the face and hands are often best treated with Mohs micrographic surgery. Selected superficial lesions can be treated with curettage or imiquimod. Radiation therapy is an alternative for patients who are unable to undergo surgery.

KEY POINTS

- Basal cell carcinoma can appear as a translucent nodule with telangiectasia on the face (nodular); pink, scaly, flat lesions with a pearly edge on the trunk or limbs (superficial); or a slowly enlarging, skin-colored "scar" (morpheaform).

- Biopsy of suspected basal cell carcinoma confirms the diagnosis and helps plan the most appropriate therapy.

Invasive Squamous Cell Carcinoma

Cutaneous squamous cell carcinoma (SCC) presents as a slowly evolving, isolated, keratotic or eroded macule, papule, or nodule that commonly appears on the scalp, neck, pinna, or lip (**Figure 59**). There is a higher risk of metastasis in inva-

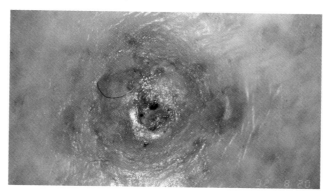

FIGURE 59.
Squamous cell carcinomas present as hyperkeratotic scaly or crateriform lesions.

Courtesy of Barbara Mathes, MD, FACP.

sive carcinoma arising from lesions associated with Bowen disease (see below), scars, and ulcers, as well as those that occur on the lips, ears, and anogenital region. Other risk factors for metastasis include tumors larger than 2 cm or deeper than 4 mm and those that are poorly differentiated or have vascular invasion. SCC of the digits is typically induced by human papillomavirus (HPV) infection. Other risk factors include radiation or arsenic exposure, cigarette smoking, treatment with psoralen and ultraviolet A (PUVA), immunosuppression, xeroderma pigmentosa, and oculocutaneous albinism.

Shave or punch biopsy confirms the diagnosis of SCC, and referral for definitive treatment is recommended. While some shallow lesions can be treated with electrodesiccation and curettage, most lesions require excision. For ill-defined lesions, those with perineural invasion, or those on the face and hands, Mohs micrographic surgery is an excellent choice. Radiation therapy may be appropriate as a primary treatment or as adjuvant therapy in tumors with nodal involvement or a high risk of recurrence.

Bowen Disease

Bowen disease is a form of anaplastic in situ SCC that presents as circumscribed erythematous or pigmented patches that typically have a keratotic surface (**Figure 60**). Invasive carcinoma arising in Bowen disease has a 13% to 33% risk of metastasis. Genital Bowen disease is caused by HPV, and both the patient and sexual partners should be screened for other HPV-induced malignancies, including those of the cervix and anal canal. Bowen disease in nongenital, sun-protected areas may be associated with arsenic ingestion or internal malignancies.

Malignant cells extend along the follicles into the deep dermis, resulting in a significant rate of recurrence after topical therapy. Despite this, many lesions can be "debulked" with topical 5-fluorouracil, imiquimod, photodynamic therapy, or electrodesiccation and curettage. Definitive treatment often requires excision or destruction via cryotherapy.

Keratoacanthoma

Keratoacanthoma is a form of rapidly growing SCC that may undergo terminal differentiation, in which the tumor "keratinizes itself to death" and involutes spontaneously within months. Early lesions present as solitary, round nodules that grow rapidly. As the lesions mature, a central keratotic plug becomes visible and the lesion becomes crater-like (**Figure 61**). Multiple keratoacanthomas can be inherited in an autosomal dominant fashion. Patients who also have sebaceous neoplasms should be screened for Muir-Torre syndrome, which is associated with hereditary nonpolyposis colorectal cancer.

Despite the fact that keratoacanthomas may spontaneously involute, their rapid growth can render them very destructive. Most lesions are best treated with excision.

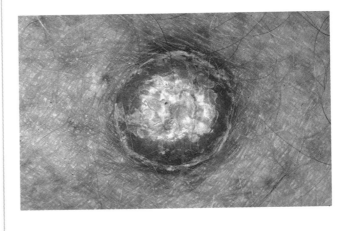

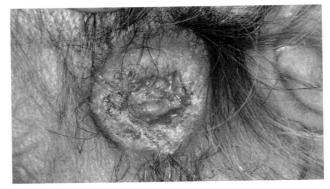

FIGURE 61.
Early keratoacanthoma lesions present as solitary, round nodules that grow rapidly *(top).* Fully developed keratoacanthoma with a visible central keratotic plug *(bottom).*

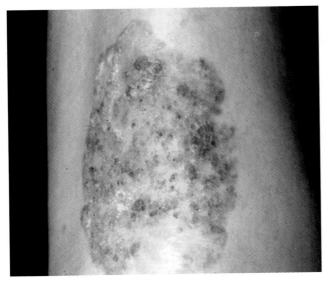

FIGURE 60.
Bowen disease presents with erythematous or hyperpigmented plaques that may have a keratotic surface. The plaques can resemble persistent eczema.

- Cutaneous squamous cell carcinoma presents as a slowly evolving, isolated, keratotic or eroded macule, papule, or nodule that commonly appears on the scalp, neck, pinna, or lip.

- Keratoacanthoma presents as a nodule that grows rapidly and develops a central keratotic plug; most lesions involute within 2 months to 1 year.

Malignant Melanoma

The incidence of malignant melanoma in the United States has increased dramatically in the past several decades. The lifetime risk of melanoma in the United States for persons with light skin is close to 1 in 50. The disease is less common in the Hispanic and black populations. Melanomas occur with increasing frequency in older persons, but younger persons and even children can be affected. Melanoma is now one of the most common malignancies in women between the ages of 25 and 40 years. Patients at greatest risk for melanoma include those with a family history of melanoma, 50 or more moles, atypical moles, fair skin, freckles, blond or red hair, blue eyes, or a history of sunburns.

Lentigo maligna is the most common form of melanoma. It begins as a uniformly pigmented, light-brown patch on the face or upper trunk that is confined to the epidermis. Over time, the lesion expands and becomes more variegated in color (**Figure 62**). Lentigo maligna melanoma is the term applied to a lentigo maligna that has invaded the epidermis. Superficial spreading melanoma is the next most common variant and presents as a well-defined asymmetric patch or plaque with an irregular border, variation in color, and an expanding diameter (**Figure 63**). Most skin cancers occur on exposed skin, but superficial spreading melanoma tends to occur on the back in men and the legs in women (areas that receive intermittent sun and are prone to sunburn). Nodular, acral lentiginous, and mucosal melanomas are less common but are very important because there is often

FIGURE 63.
Superficial spreading melanomas are typically larger than 6 mm with irregular borders and pigmentation.

Courtesy of Dr. David Crosby.

a delay in diagnosis that leads to a poor prognosis (**Figure 64** and **Figure 65**). Amelanotic lesions resemble basal cell carcinoma or appear as nondescript pink macules (**Figure 66**).

Pigmented lesions should be evaluated using the ABCDE method: Examine for Asymmetry, irregular Border, irregular Color, expanding Diameter, and Evolution. Any expanding pigmented nail streak, papule, nodule, or patch should raise suspicion for melanoma.

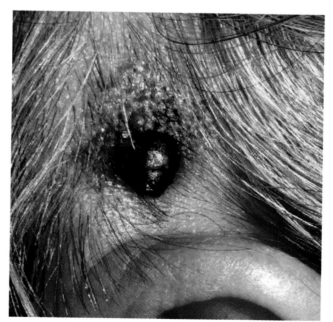

FIGURE 64.
Nodular melanomas often present as uniformly dark blue or black "berry-like" lesions that most commonly originate from normal skin. They can also arise from a preexisting nevus, as did this melanoma. Nodular melanomas expand vertically rather than horizontally.

Robinson JK. Basal Cell Carcinoma.
http://pier.acponline.org/physicians/diseases/d888/d888.html. [Date accessed: 2009 July 9]
In: PIER [online database]. Philadelphia, American College of Physicians, 2003.

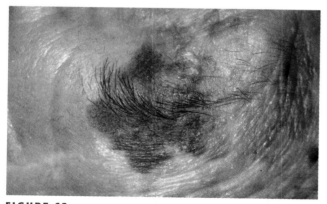

FIGURE 62.
Lentigo maligna presents as a slowly enlarging, variegated, pigmented patch on sun-damaged skin.

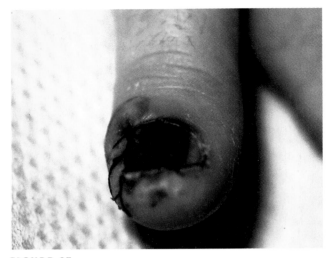

FIGURE 65.
Acral lentiginous melanoma, with pigmentation involving the proximal nail fold and cuticle.

Courtesy of Dr. David Crosby.

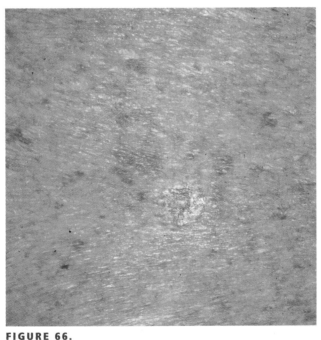

FIGURE 66.
Amelanotic malignant melanoma mimics basal cell carcinoma clinically and can be nonspecific in appearance.

Any suspicious lesion should be biopsied. A complete excisional biopsy is preferred. Lentigo maligna represents an important exception, where a broad, paper-thin shave biopsy offers the highest yield. The biopsy should be performed by an experienced dermatologist. Punch biopsies are to be avoided in the setting of suspected lentigo maligna because the false-negative rate approaches 80%.

Surgery is the mainstay of therapy for patients with melanoma. Because melanoma tumor cells can extend beyond the visible borders of the melanoma, wide excision is necessary to ensure that all melanoma is removed. The extent of surgery depends upon the thickness of the primary melanoma and is best performed by a specialist. Complete excision of thin (less than 1 mm in depth), nonulcerated melanomas is associated with good outcomes, with survival rates greater than 95%. Sentinel lymph node biopsy is generally recommended for patients with tumors greater than 1 mm thick; however, it has not consistently been shown to benefit long-term survival.

The prognosis for metastatic disease remains poor, as melanoma fails to respond to most traditional chemotherapies. Interferon alfa therapy has shown mixed results in clinical trials, and its effect on overall survival remains unclear.

KEY POINTS

- Pigmented lesions should be evaluated using the ABCDE method: Examine for Asymmetry, irregular Border, irregular Color, expanding Diameter, and Evolution.
- All suspicious pigmented lesions should be biopsied; a complete excisional biopsy is generally preferred.
- Surgery is the mainstay of therapy for patients with melanoma; the extent of surgery depends upon the thickness of the primary melanoma.

Actinic Keratosis

Actinic keratoses are precancerous lesions that can develop into invasive SCC. They typically present clinically as erythematous lesions with overlying hyperkeratosis (**Figure 67**).

Actinic keratoses are often easier to feel than to see, making palpation a key element of the physical examination. Actinic keratoses can be treated with liquid nitrogen cryotherapy, topical application of 5-fluorouracil or imiquimod, photodynamic therapy, chemical peels, or dermabrasion.

Sun Protection and Skin Cancer Prevention

Protective clothing, topical sunscreen preparations, and avoidance of midday sun remain the major interventions for the prevention of skin cancer. Regular application of a high–sun-protection-factor sunscreen (at least 15, preferably 30 or greater) that protects against both ultraviolet B and ultraviolet A rays is recommended. Sunscreen has a direct protective effect against acute ultraviolet damage and nonmelanoma skin cancer. Concerns that the use of sunscreen may increase the incidence of melanoma have not been borne out in studies; however, patients who are aggressive about sun protection may be at risk for vitamin D deficiency. Appropriate oral vitamin D supplementation should be considered.

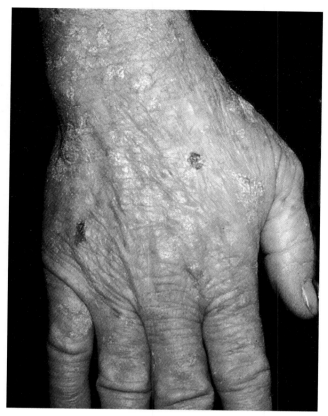

FIGURE 67.
Actinic keratoses present as scaly to gritty macules or flat papules that are often better felt than seen. More hypertrophic lesions may be thickened and may even develop into cutaneous horns.

The U.S. Preventive Services Task Force has not found sufficient evidence to recommend for or against routine screening by clinical examination to prevent skin cancer. Patients at high risk for melanoma should receive annual skin examinations. Patients should be asked if they have noticed any new or changing moles, and patients with atypical moles and a personal or family history of melanoma should be encouraged to perform periodic self-examination.

KEY POINTS

- Protective clothing, use of topical sunscreens, and avoidance of midday sun are the major interventions for the prevention of skin cancer.

- Patients who are aggressive about sun protection may be at risk for vitamin D deficiency; appropriate oral vitamin D supplementation should be considered.

- Patients at high risk for melanoma should receive annual skin examinations and should be counseled to perform self-examination.

- Any new or changing mole should be evaluated for possible biopsy.

Benign Tumors

Seborrheic Keratosis

Seborrheic keratoses are common, benign neoplasms that present as brown to black, well-demarcated, "stuck-on"–appearing papules with waxy surfaces and horn cysts (**Figure 68**). Variants of seborrheic keratosis include stucco keratosis (small, white, superficial keratoses on the lower legs of older individuals) and dermatosis papulosa nigra (dark-brown macules and papules on the cheeks of black patients). Leser-Trélat sign (the sudden appearance of many seborrheic keratoses, typically with pruritus) may be a sign of internal malignancy.

If the diagnosis is questionable, shave biopsy and histologic evaluation should be obtained. No treatment is needed for seborrheic keratoses unless they are inflamed, irritated, or itchy. They can be treated with liquid nitrogen cryotherapy, curettage, or shave excision.

Skin Tags

Skin tags (acrochordons) are soft, pedunculated, fleshy papules that occur on the sides of the neck, axillae, inframammary region, groin, and buttocks. They may be caused by increased concentrations of insulin or insulin-like growth factors and may be a marker for type 2 diabetes mellitus. Treatment with excision, cryosurgery, or electrodesiccation is necessary only if the lesion is irritated or for cosmetic reasons.

Corns

A corn (clavus) is a localized area of hyperkeratosis with a central, translucent, hyperkeratotic core. Corns form in areas of chronic pressure and are typically quite tender; hard corns occur on the external aspects of the foot, and soft corns are found between the toes. Lesions usually respond to paring or salicylic acid plasters. Radiography may be indicated to identify underlying bony abnormalities in the case of persistent or recurrent corns.

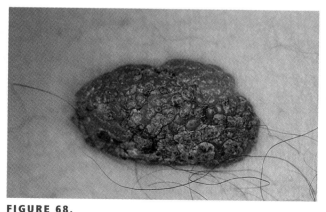

FIGURE 68.
Seborrheic keratoses appear "stuck on" and have a verrucous surface. Pseudo–horn cysts may be visible on the surface.

Epidermoid and Pilar Cysts

Epidermoid cysts (sebaceous cysts) are freely movable, often solitary cysts that have a characteristic central punctum and that occur on the face, neck, upper trunk, and scrotum. Pilar cysts on the scalp usually occur in groups and may be irritated by hair brushing. Although bacteria can commonly be cultured from cysts, the bacterial density is the same in inflamed and noninflamed cysts, which suggests that the inflammation is not related to infection but rather to rupture of the cyst wall and a subsequent intense inflammatory reaction. Inflamed cysts are very painful and respond to incision and drainage or intralesional injection with triamcinolone. Systemic antibiotics are not necessary. In the absence of inflammation, recurrent cysts may be excised.

Benign Melanocytic Nevi

Acquired melanocytic nevi occur in most of the population. Patients with many nevi, atypical nevi, and congenital nevi have a higher risk for malignant melanoma. Suspicious lesions should be removed. Complete excisional biopsy is the preferred method of removal, because a partial biopsy can lead to misdiagnosis.

Halo Nevi

Halo nevi are surrounded by a symmetric halo of depigmentation (**Figure 69**). If the mole is small, evenly pigmented, and symmetric, it does not require a biopsy. Atypical lesions should be removed.

Atypical (Dysplastic) Nevi

Atypical (dysplastic) nevi occur predominantly on the trunk, are usually larger than 6 mm, and have a border that is characteristically fuzzy and ill defined (**Figure 70**). The shape can be round, oval, or asymmetric. The color is usually brown but can be mottled with dark brown, pink, and tan colors. Some of the clinical features of dysplastic nevi are similar to

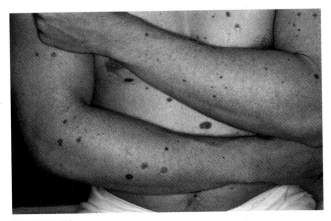

FIGURE 70.
Atypical (dysplastic) nevi are commonly larger than 6 mm with mottled pigment and irregular or blurred margins.

melanoma. Some individuals have only 1 to 5 lesions, whereas others have more than 100 lesions. Multiple atypical moles are a risk factor for melanoma. Changing lesions should be removed. The "ugly duckling" sign refers to the finding of one mole that appears more atypical than those around it; "ugly duckling" moles should also be removed. Excision or scoop saucerization (deep shave that includes the dermis) typically produces the best results.

KEY POINTS

- Patients with many nevi, atypical nevi, and congenital nevi have a higher risk for malignant melanoma.
- Suspicious lesions should be removed, usually with excision or saucerization.

Neurofibromas

Neurofibromas are soft, flesh-colored to hyperpigmented papules and nodules that may resemble benign melanocytic nevi (**Figure 71**). They characteristically demonstrate a

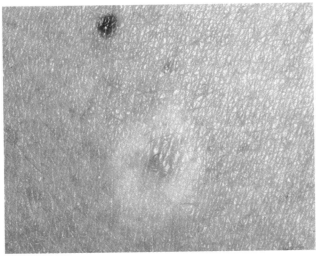

FIGURE 69.
Halo nevus, with a depigmented halo surrounding the lesion.

FIGURE 71.
Neurofibromas present as soft, compressible, flesh-colored to hyperpigmented papules and nodules.

Courtesy of Dr. David Crosby.

"buttonhole sign" (invagination of the lesion with vertical or lateral pressure). Multiple neurofibromas are associated with von Recklinghausen disease; however, many adults have one or two neurofibromas that are not associated with any underlying conditions. Patients with multiple neurofibromas should be examined for other stigmata of von Recklinghausen disease, such as café-au-lait macules and axillary freckling.

Pyogenic Granulomas

Pyogenic granulomas are friable, mushroom-shaped, rapidly growing (a few days to weeks), red papules that bleed easily (**Figure 72**). Despite the name, they are not caused by infection but rather by capillary proliferation. Pyogenic granulomas do not require treatment, but treatment might be considered for cosmetic reasons, if they bleed easily, or if they are painful or otherwise bothersome. Treatment options include shave excision with silver nitrate cauterization and electrodesiccation of the base.

Venous Lakes

Venous lakes are common on sun-damaged skin. They appear as blue-black macules or papules on the ears or lips, where they can be confused with melanoma. They turn red and then disappear when pressure is applied with a glass slide (**Figure 73**). Electrocautery or laser treatment can be used if the lesion causes recurrent bleeding or is cosmetically unacceptable.

Dermatofibromas

Dermatofibromas appear as firm dermal nodules about the size of a pencil eraser; they are associated with a "button hole" or dimple when the lateral sides are pinched together. They

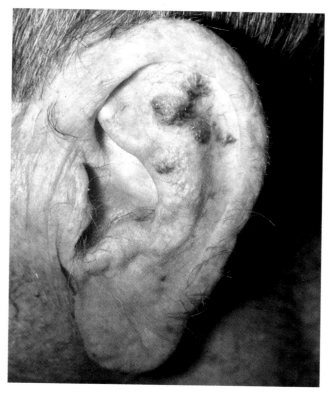
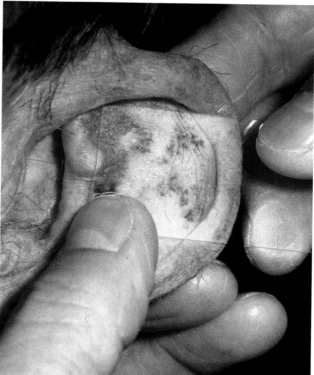

FIGURE 73.
Venous lakes are common on sun-damaged skin and appear as blue-black macules or papules *(top)*. When compressed with a glass slide, venous lakes disappear. This differentiates them from nodular melanoma and blue nevi, which do not disappear with compression *(bottom)*.

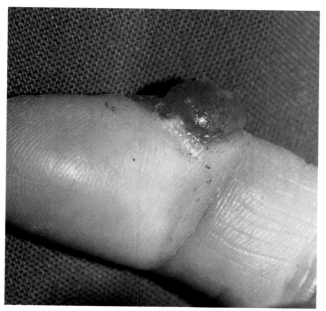

FIGURE 72.
Pyogenic granulomas are red and friable.

are most common on the legs of adult women but also occur on the trunk in both males and females. The surface is often pink or brown (**Figure 74**).

Dermatofibrosarcoma protuberans is a relatively rare form of fibrosarcoma that occurs on the trunk as a plaque studded with nodules. It arises de novo rather than from a benign dermatofibroma.

No treatment for dermatofibroma is necessary unless the lesion is symptomatic, has changed, or is bleeding; in these circumstances, excision is indicated.

Hypertrophic Scars and Keloids

Hypertrophic scars occur at sites of surgery or trauma. They remain confined to the area of the original scar and resolve spontaneously within 2 years. Itchy or troublesome hypertrophic scars respond to intralesional injection with triamcinolone.

In contrast to hypertrophic scars, keloids may occur spontaneously or at sites of trauma. They grow in a clawlike fashion beyond the confines of the original scar (**Figure 75**) and do not resolve spontaneously. They may be treated with intralesional corticosteroids, vascular lasers, and cryotherapy.

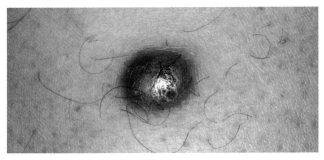

FIGURE 74.
Dermatofibromas appear as firm dermal nodules about the size of a pencil eraser. They are frequently hyperpigmented or may have pigment at the periphery.

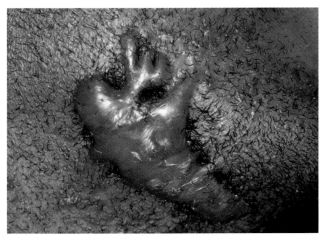

FIGURE 75.
Keloids develop claw-like extensions or dumbbell-shaped ends.

Depigmentation of the overlying skin is the most common complication of therapy. The risk of recurrence after excision can be reduced by intralesional injection of corticosteroids or adjuvant radiation.

Sebaceous Hyperplasia

Sebaceous hyperplasia is a common skin condition that appears as yellow, umbilicated papules on the forehead or cheeks (**Figure 76**). Overlying telangiectasias are common. In black patients, the lesions may occur in parallel rows on the neck and chest. Fordyce spots represent sebaceous hyperplasia of the lips or oral mucosa. Treatment is not necessary.

Digital Mucous Cysts

Digital mucous cysts appear as translucent papules on the distal phalanges of patients with osteoarthritis. Those overlying the nailfolds can cause a corresponding groove in the nail. The lesions form as a result of leakage of joint mucin into the surrounding skin. Digital mucous cysts respond to excision, cryotherapy, or intralesional corticosteroid injection. Because of the possibility of connection to the joint space, therapy should only be attempted by clinicians experienced in treating these lesions.

FIGURE 76.
Sebaceous hyperplasia presents as a yellow to pink papule with a central dimple.

Bibliography

Alam M, Ratner D. Cutaneous squamous-cell carcinoma. N Engl J Med. 2001;344(13):975-983. [PMID: 11274625]

Bath-Hextall F, Leonardi-Bee J, Somchand N, Webster A, Delitt J, Perkins W. Interventions for preventing non-melanoma skin cancers in high-risk groups. Cochrane Database Syst Rev. 2007;(4): CD005414. [PMID: 17943854]

Luba MC, Bangs SA, Mohler AM, Stulberg DL. Common benign skin tumors. Am Fam Physician. 2003;67(4):729-738. [PMID: 12613727]

Naeyaert JM, Brochez L. Clinical practice. Dysplastic nevi. N Engl J Med. 2003;349(23):2233-2240. [PMID: 14657431]

Rubin AI, Chen EH, Ratner D. Basal-cell carcinoma. N Engl J Med. 2005;353(21):2262-2269. [PMID: 16306523]

Wang SQ, Halpern AC. Management of cutaneous melanoma: a public health and individual patient care perspective. Adv Dermatol. 2007;23:81-98. [PMID: 18159897]

Pruritus

Overview

Pruritus is the sensation of itch. Itch can be divided into four categories: pruritoceptive (itch that is generated within the skin), neurogenic (itch caused by a systemic disease or circulating pruritogens), neuropathic (itch caused by an anatomic lesion in the peripheral or central nervous system), and psychogenic.

Evaluation and Diagnosis

Evaluation of pruritus requires a thorough history, including a complete drug history, review of systems, and social history, followed by a detailed physical examination.

Pruritoceptive Pruritus

A history of acute onset, related exposure, recent travel, involvement of household members, or localized itch suggests a cutaneous rather than systemic cause of the itch. The most important features on physical examination are the presence or absence of primary lesions and their distribution. The presence of primary lesions suggests that the cause of pruritus is dermatologic (pruritoceptive itch). The most common causes of this type of itch are primary dermatitis (eczema) and dry skin (xerosis). Other common causes of pruritoceptive itch include urticaria, dermatophyte infections, lice, scabies, lichen simplex chronicus, and psoriasis.

Neurogenic Pruritus

The absence of visible skin lesions or the presence of only secondary lesions (erosions or lichenification) in areas easily reached by the patient (upper shoulders, buttocks, and extensor extremities) and sparing areas that the patient cannot reach (mid back) suggests neurogenic itch (**Figure 77** and **Figure 78**). Neurogenic itch should prompt a thorough evaluation for systemic causes of pruritus. Important underlying causes of neurogenic itch include cholestasis, end-stage renal disease, thyroid disease (hypo- or hyperthyroidism), iron deficiency anemia, malignancy (usually hematologic or lymphoma), medications (opiates), and HIV infection. The suggested evaluation of patients with neurogenic itch is listed in **Table 18**.

Neuropathic Pruritus

A localized and persistent area of pruritus without associated primary skin lesions, usually on the back or forearms, suggests neuropathic itch. The most common forms of neuropathic itch are notalgia paresthetica and brachioradial pruritus. Notalgia paresthetica presents with localized pruritus, most commonly on the medial back around the scapula. Brachioradial pruritus is characterized by burning, itching, or stinging on the extensor arms, forearms, and upper back. The

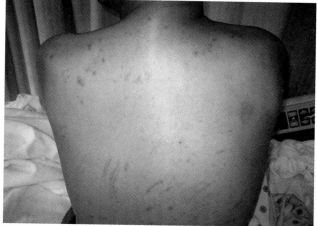

FIGURE 77.
Linear erosions without primary lesions and with an area of sparing in the central back in a patient with cholestatic liver disease.

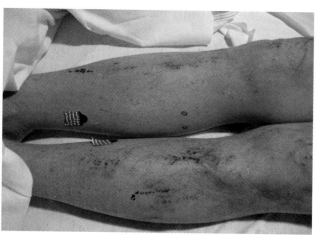

FIGURE 78.
Linear erosions without primary lesions in a patient with cholestatic liver disease.

TABLE 18 Suggested Evaluation of Patients with Neurogenic Pruritus

Complete blood count with differential

Serum iron level, serum ferritin level, total iron-binding capacity

Serum thyroid-stimulating hormone and free thyroxine levels

Renal function tests (blood urea nitrogen and serum creatinine levels)

Liver chemistry tests (serum total and direct bilirubin, alkaline phosphatase, γ-glutamyltransferase, aspartate aminotransferase, alanine aminotransferase, fasting total plasma bile acid levels)

Chest radiograph

Age- and sex-appropriate malignancy screening, with more advanced testing as indicated by symptoms (for example, weight loss, early satiety)

skin in either case may have no visible findings or may have a hyperpigmented patch with a corrugated appearance. Chronic sun damage may also contribute to the cause of brachioradial pruritus. Disease of the cervical and/or thoracic spine, particularly degenerative changes, can be identified in a significant proportion of patients with brachioradial pruritus or notalgia paresthetica. Neurologic examination is appropriate to evaluate for evidence of sensory or motor dysfunction or abnormal reflexes. Spinal imaging can be performed as is clinically indicated; however, in the absence of neurologic dysfunction, studies are unlikely to affect the management and/or outcome of these conditions.

Psychogenic Pruritus

Psychogenic pruritus may be generalized but is most often confined to the extremities, and, like neurogenic and neuropathic pruritus, occurs in the absence of primary skin lesions. Secondary scattered linear excoriations are the most common finding. Most patients with psychogenic pruritus are able to identify a precipitating psychological trigger. Psychogenic pruritus is a diagnosis of exclusion.

KEY POINTS

- Dermatitis (eczema) and dry skin are the most common causes of pruritoceptive pruritus.
- Neurogenic pruritus, generalized itching without evidence of a primary skin disorder, should prompt a thorough evaluation for a systemic cause.
- Intractable neuropathic pruritus is localized itching without evidence of a primary skin disorder and may be the result of degenerative changes or bulging disks.

Treatment

Treatment of pruritus is optimized by identifying the cause and type of itch and addressing the underlying disorder whenever possible. Most patients with pruritus, particularly those with xerosis or atopic dermatitis, should be counseled on gentle skin care, regular use of moisturizers and occlusives, avoiding hot baths and showers, avoiding harsh soap, and use of air humidification. Moisturizers supply water to the skin. Occlusives with petrolatum help to reduce water loss from skin and are appropriate for use in combination with moisturizers.

Topical corticosteroids, often in conjunction with oral antihistamines, are standard treatment for any type of eczema. If a primary skin lesion is present, topical corticosteroids should be used. Topical corticosteroids are usually tried in other causes of itch but have a variable response, particularly for treatment of neuropathic and neurogenic itch.

The following topical and systemic medications are suggestions based on their most efficacious uses, but patient response may be unpredictable. Although marketed for treatment of itch, topical diphenhydramine is rarely used by dermatologists because of its high incidence of contact sensitization. Topical doxepin may be useful but is also a potential sensitizer and may lead to sedation even when applied topically. Topical capsaicin treats itch but often causes itching, stinging, and burning, especially at the beginning of therapy. Topical anesthetics, including pramoxine and a cream containing 2.5% lidocaine and 2.5% prilocaine, may be useful for treating localized itch, but, because of potential systemic absorption, should be used in small areas for a limited duration. Application of cold packs may help relieve the symptoms of neuropathic itch.

Antihistamines are most effective for treatment of histamine-mediated pruritus, such as that occurring in urticaria or mastocytosis. However, they may also be effective in treating other types of itch, in part due possibly to their sedating properties. Doxepin is a tricyclic antidepressant that has potent H_1 and H_2 antihistamine properties. It is particularly useful for treating pruritus associated with anxiety or depression. Paroxetine and mirtazapine have also been used successfully in some patients with pruritus, although the effect is usually short-lived, diminishing after 4 to 6 weeks of therapy.

Targeted therapies are available for some patients with underlying systemic causes of itch. Ultraviolet B light therapy is helpful for most systemic causes of pruritus. Naltrexone, an opioid μ-receptor antagonist, may be of particular help in treating pruritus in end-stage renal disease and cholestasis; systemic antihistamines and topical corticosteroids are often minimally effective in these settings. Butorphanol, a κ-receptor agonist and μ-receptor antagonist, is safe in both renal and liver failure. Gabapentin may be helpful to treat neuropathic pruritus and pruritus associated with renal failure. Mirtazapine is particularly helpful for nocturnal pruritus and may also help treat pruritus associated with renal disease, lymphoma, or liver failure. Notalgia paresthetica or brachioradial pruritus may respond to topical capsaicin, gabapentin, or carbamazepine. Botulinum toxin has been used successfully for treatment of notalgia paresthetica.

KEY POINTS

- Recognition of the cause of pruritus (pruritoceptive, neurogenic, neuropathic, or psychogenic) guides evaluation and treatment.
- Antihistamines are most useful to treat pruritus that is directly mediated by histamine, but they may be a helpful adjunct in the treatment of other types of pruritus.

Bibliography

Goodkin R, Wingard E, Bernhard JD. Brachioradial pruritus: cervical spine disease and neurogenic/neuropathic [corrected] pruritus. J Am Acad Dermatol. 2003;48(4):521-524. [PMID: 12664013]

Greaves MW. Itch in systemic disease: therapeutic options. Dermatol Ther. 2005;18(4):323-327. [PMID: 16297004]

Greaves MW. Recent advances in pathophysiology and current management of itch. Ann Acad Med Singapore. 2007;36(9):788-792. [PMID: 17925991]

Krishnan A, Koo J. Psyche, opioids, and itch: therapeutic consequences. Dermatol Ther. 2005;18(4):314-322. [PMID: 16297003]

O'Donoghue M, Tharp MD. Antihistamines and their role as antipruritics. Dermatol Ther. 2005;18(4):333-340. [PMID: 16297006]

Savk O, Savk E. Investigation of spinal pathology in notalgia paresthetica. J Am Acad Dermatol. 2005;52(6):1085-1087. [PMID: 15928634]

Zirwas MJ, Seraly MP. Pruritus of unknown origin: a retrospective study. J Am Acad Dermatol. 2001;45(6):892-896. [PMID: 11712035]

Urticaria

Causes

Urticaria (hives) is a reaction pattern that may occur in response to an infection, ingested or inhaled allergen, medication, or direct mast cell degranulator. Common causes of urticaria are medications (including penicillin, sulfonamides, aspirin, NSAIDs, opiates, and contrast dye), foods (nuts, fish, eggs, and chocolate), preservatives (sodium benzoate), viral or bacterial infection, latex or other physical contacts (heat, cold, pressure), and stinging insects. Individuals with asthma, nasal polyps, and aspirin sensitivity often react to tartrazine, natural salicylates, and benzoic acid derivatives. About 30% of patients with chronic urticaria report worsening with aspirin.

Clinical Manifestations and Diagnosis

Urticaria presents as episodes of itchy, red wheals with sharp borders that can last from minutes to hours (**Figure 79**). Some urticarial lesions have dusky centers and can be mistaken for the targetoid lesions of erythema multiforme. Wheals can be multiple or isolated and usually involve the

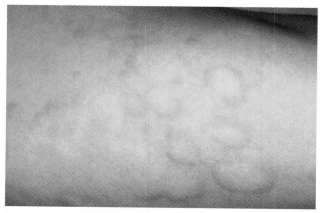

FIGURE 79.
Urticaria, characterized by itchy, red wheals with sharp borders that usually involve the trunk and extremities. Wheals last less than 24 hours.

trunk and extremities, sparing the palms and soles. Those involving the skin around the mouth are considered an emergency, requiring careful observation and investigation for airway obstruction. The clinical classification of urticaria depends on symptom duration and precipitating factors (**Table 19**). Lesions that persist longer than 24 hours, burn, or resolve with purpura are suspicious for urticarial vasculitis and should be biopsied. Dermographism (scratching of skin results in a linear wheal) may be present in any patient with urticaria, but some patients have dermographism alone.

Episodes of urticaria confined to a 6-week period are classified as acute and are commonly caused by an acute infection, medication, food, or pollen. Episodes of urticaria that last longer than 6 weeks are classified as chronic. Many patients with chronic urticaria have an IgG antibody to the IgE receptor; others are reacting to a chronic infection or ingestant. As many as 50% of cases of chronic urticaria have no identifiable cause.

Angioedema, a severe, life-threatening form of urticaria, is characterized by localized edema of the skin or mucosa, usually the lips, face, hands, feet, penis, or scrotum. Concomitant angioedema and urticaria occur in 40% of patients; 40% have hives alone; and 20% have angioedema but no urticaria. Patients with hereditary angioedema (deficiency of C1-esterase) and those with angioedema related to an angiotensin-converting enzyme inhibitor present with angioedema without hives. In patients with

TABLE 19 Clinical Classification of Urticaria and Angioedema	
Classification	**Characteristics**
Ordinary urticaria	Acute: up to 6 weeks of continuous activity
	Chronic: 6 weeks or more of continuous activity
	Episodic: intermittent
Physical urticaria	Reproducibly induced by the same physical stimulus
	Aquagenic urticaria
	Cholinergic urticaria
	Cold urticaria
	Delayed pressure urticaria
	Dermographism
	Localized heat urticaria
	Solar urticaria
	Vibratory angioedema
Angioedema without wheals	—
Contact urticaria	Induced by biologic or chemical skin contact
Urticarial vasculitis	Fixed skin lesions lasting >24 h; vasculitis on skin biopsy

suspected hereditary angioedema, serum complement C2, C4, and C1-esterase inhibitor levels should be measured. The C2 level is depressed during acute attacks of angioedema, and the C4 level is depressed both during and between attacks. Acquired C1-esterase deficiency may be related to lymphoproliferative disease.

Contact urticaria is common in patients with latex and other proteinaceous allergens. The hives occur in areas of direct contact with the allergen. Affected patients often report excessive lacrimation, rhinorrhea, or other signs of histamine release during episodes of contact urticaria and are at risk for severe systemic reactions. Oral allergy syndrome is a form of contact urticaria involving the oropharynx that is related to foods, such as apples, that cross-react with pollen. The oral swelling is rarely associated with systemic symptoms. Variants of urticaria are noted in **Table 20**.

Urticaria is diagnosed clinically and should be accompanied by a careful history and physical examination to determine possible causes. As discussed above, laboratory testing should be dictated by associated signs and symptoms. A complete blood count is reasonable in any patient with chronic idiopathic urticaria. Those with eosinophilia should be evaluated for intestinal parasites. Radioallergosorbent testing (RAST) should be performed when the history suggests food, pollen, or latex allergy. Thyroid antibodies are commonly

found in patients with urticaria, but this finding usually is an epiphenomenon.

Treatment

If a trigger of urticaria can be identified, it should be eliminated. Drugs known to cause mast cell degranulation (such as aspirin and other NSAIDs) should be avoided. A nonsedating antihistamine should be taken on a regular basis, often for weeks to months. Doses higher than those reflected in product labeling are often required. Sedating antihistamines may need to be added, particularly at night. It should be emphasized to patients that the drug should be taken regularly to prevent hives. Patients with severe acute urticaria whose disease is unresponsive to antihistamines (H_1 blockers) should be treated with a 3-week tapered dose of prednisone. Prednisone temporarily suppresses chronic urticaria, but the hives recur as soon as the prednisone is stopped. Therefore, systemic corticosteroids have no role in the management of chronic urticaria.

Not infrequently, treatment with H_1 blockers alone is insufficient to control symptoms, and additional medications are needed. Data regarding the value of adding an H_2 blocker (such as cimetidine or ranitidine) are mixed. Doxepin blocks H_1, H_2, and serotonin receptors; an evening dose of 25-50 mg is often well tolerated. Calcium channel blockers can sometimes be effective. Patients who have chronic autoimmune urticaria commonly may require methotrexate, azathioprine, or cyclosporine. Intravenous immune globulin, omalizumab, and leukotriene inhibitors have produced mixed results. A step approach to treatment of chronic idiopathic urticaria is shown in **Table 21**.

Patients with acquired angioedema should carry epinephrine. Epinephrine is not considered effective for angioedema caused by C1-esterase inhibitory deficiency. Patients with hereditary angioedema related to C1-esterase inhibitor deficiency should receive C1-esterase inhibitor concentrate (or fresh frozen plasma in emergency situations) and antifibrinolytics such as aminocaproic acid or anabolic steroids for maintenance therapy.

TABLE 20 Variants of Urticaria	
Classification	**Characteristics**
Papular urticaria	Associated with insect bites
Cholinergic urticaria	Occurs in response to an increase in core body temperature; lesions present as small papules with a prominent surrounding erythematous flare
Delayed pressure-induced urticaria	Patients often experience systemic symptoms
Exercise-induced urticaria	On a continuum with exercise-induced anaphylaxis; many patients only develop symptoms if primed by an ingested allergen prior to exercise
Solar urticaria	Some patients who appear to have solar urticaria prove to have lupus erythematosus or porphyria
Cold urticaria	Acquired cold urticaria is often related to an underlying infection, whereas familial cold urticaria represents an autoinflammatory syndrome
Vibrational urticaria	—

TABLE 21 Therapeutic Ladder for Chronic Idiopathic Urticaria
Avoidance of triggers
Nonsedating antihistamines
Doxepin, addition of H_2 antagonists, or escalating doses of nonsedating antihistamines
Trial of a calcium channel blocker
Immunosuppressive agents

- Urticaria presents as episodes of itchy, red wheals with sharp borders that can last from minutes to hours.

- Urticarial lesions often have dusky centers and can be misdiagnosed as erythema multiforme.

- Avoidance of triggers and administration of antihistamines are first-line therapy for urticaria.

- Acute urticaria that does not respond to antihistamines can be treated with prednisone; however, there is no role for oral corticosteroids in the management of chronic urticaria.

- Chronic idiopathic urticaria is best managed with avoidance of triggers, adequate doses of a nonsedating antihistamine, a tricyclic agent such as doxepin, a calcium channel blocker, or immunosuppressive therapy.

Bibliography

Frank MM. Hereditary angioedema: the clinical syndrome and its management in the United States. Immunol Allergy Clin North Am. 2006;26(4):653-668. [PMID: 17085283]

Grattan CE, Humphreys F; British Association of Dermatologists Therapy Guidelines and Audit Subcommittee. Guidelines for evaluation and management of urticaria in adults and children. Br J Dermatol. 2007;157(6):1116-1123. [PMID: 18021095]

Greaves MW, Tan KT. Chronic urticaria: recent advances. Clin Rev Allergy Immunol. 2007;33(1-2):134-143. [PMID: 18094952]

Jáuregui I, Ferrer M, Montoro J, et al. Antihistamines in the treatment of chronic urticaria. J Investig Allergol Clin Immunol. 2007;17 Suppl 2:41-52. [PMID: 18228682]

Torchia D, Francalanci S, Bellandi S, Fabbri P. Multiple physical urticarias. Postgrad Med J. 2008;84(987):e1-2. [PMID: 18230741]

Autoimmune Blistering Diseases

Pemphigus Vulgaris and Its Variants

Clinical Manifestations and Diagnosis

Pemphigus vulgaris and its variants are blistering diseases caused by autoantibodies to the keratinocyte adhesion molecules desmoglein 3 and/or desmoglein 1. Pemphigus is characterized by detachment of adhesions between stratified squamous epithelial cells (acantholysis) on skin and mucous membranes. Affected skin has flaccid blisters that generally develop on noninflamed skin, are readily broken, and progress to large, weeping, denuded areas (**Figure 80**).

Oropharyngeal erosions are common and are frequently the presenting manifestation (**Figure 81**). The esophagus and

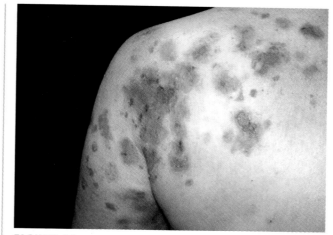

FIGURE 80.
The flaccid, intraepidermal blisters of pemphigus vulgaris are readily broken, leaving behind large, weeping, denuded erosions.

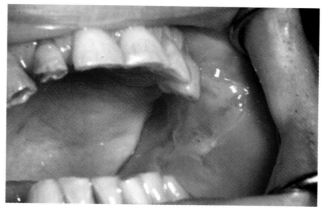

FIGURE 81.
Large superficial erosion on the left buccal membrane characteristic of pemphigus vulgaris.

vulva may be involved, and strictures may develop on these surfaces. Pemphigus has occurred in association with thymoma and myasthenia gravis and may be caused by drugs such as penicillamine and captopril. Variants of pemphigus are listed in **Table 22**.

Paraneoplastic pemphigus is characterized by clinically heterogeneous and somewhat atypical lesions, including lesions that resemble severe erythema multiforme (with targetoid lesions and painful oral lesions), bullous pemphigoid–like lesions, and lichen planus–like lesions. Associated tumors are primarily B-cell lymphoma, chronic lymphocytic leukemia, Waldenström macroglobulinemia, thymoma, and Castleman disease. The skin findings may precede the diagnosis of malignancy or may develop afterwards. In patients with malignancy-associated pemphigus, treatment of the malignancy does not always affect the course of the skin disease.

TABLE 22 Characteristics of Selected Blistering Diseases

Disease	Characteristics
Pemphigus vulgaris	Tender, fragile blisters and erosions seen in oral mucosa and skin; mucous membrane lesions much more common than in bullous pemphigoid; skin biopsy for H&E, DIF, and IIF help to distinguish from bullous pemphigoid; skin biopsy shows suprabasilar clefting compared with subepidermal clefting seen in bullous pemphigoid; Nikolsky sign is positive; autoantibody to desmoglein 3 is a hallmark of disease immunopathology
Pemphigus foliaceus	Scaling and crusted lesions on face and upper trunk, and erythroderma with no mucosal involvement; Nikolsky sign is positive; skin biopsy shows high granular or subcorneal clefting compared with suprabasal clefting seen in PV; autoantibody to desmoglein 1 is a hallmark of this disease
Paraneoplastic pemphigus	Painful oral, conjunctival, esophageal, and laryngeal erosions seen more commonly than in PV; it is a polymorphous skin eruption marked by confluent erythema, bullae, erosions, and intractable stomatitis; patients also have respiratory problems that may be fatal; associated with underlying neoplasms: NHL (42%), CLL (29%), Castleman disease (10%); gold standard for the diagnosis is the demonstration of specific autoantibodies
IgA pemphigus	A vesicopustular eruption with clear blisters that rapidly transform into pustules; trunk and proximal extremities are most commonly involved with relative sparing of the mucous membranes; DIF shows deposition of intercellular IgA at the epidermal surfaces; IIF shows circulating IgA antibodies
Bullous pemphigoid	Tense blisters preceded by intense pruritus or urticarial lesions; most commonly seen in the elderly on the trunk, limbs, and flexures; does not usually present with oral lesions; skin biopsy shows subepidermal bullae without acantholysis and with prominent eosinophils; DIF shows linear IgG deposition at the basement membrane zone; targets of autoantibodies are BP180 and BP230
Cicatricial pemphigoid	Presents with bullae, erosions, milia, and scarring seen on mucous membranes and conjunctivae of middle-aged to elderly patients; oral mucosa is almost always involved; conjunctival lesions are also common; histology is similar to bullous pemphigoid; DIF may reveal patterns similar to BP, linear IgA bullous dermatosis, or epidermolysis bullosa acquisita (CP is a phenotype for a variety of immunologically different patterns)
Dermatitis herpetiformis	Severely pruritic grouped vesicles or erosions on elbows, knees, back, scalp, and buttocks; lesions occur in crops and are symmetrically distributed; often the vesicles are not seen because the process is so itchy that they are almost immediately broken; histology shows neutrophilic infiltrate at the tips of the dermal papillae causing subepidermal separation; DIF shows granular IgA deposition; essentially all patients have celiac disease
Epidermolysis bullosa acquisita	Mechanically induced bullae and erosions mostly on extensor areas that heal with scarring and milia; histology shows subepidermal cleavage without acantholysis; DIF shows IgG deposition at the basement membrane zone that localizes to the base on salt-split skin; antibody reacts with type VII collagen; associated with SLE and inflammatory bowel disease in some patients

BP = bullous pemphigoid; CLL = chronic lymphocytic leukemia; CP = cicatricial pemphigoid; DIF = direct immunofluorescence; H&E = hematoxylin and eosin (stain); IIF = indirect immunofluorescence; NHL = non-Hodgkin lymphoma; PV = pemphigus vulgaris; SLE = systemic lupus erythematosus.

Blistering skin disorders that cannot be easily explained require biopsy. If there is histopathologic acantholysis (loss of cohesion between epidermal cells), biopsy of perilesional skin for direct immunofluorescence should be performed. Deposition of intercellular IgG confirms the diagnosis of pemphigus (**Figure 82**). Indirect immunofluorescence microscopy demonstrating pemphigus antibodies in the serum may also confirm the diagnosis. The quantitative level of pemphigus antibodies, particularly to desmoglein 1 or 3, helps to guide therapy because changes in antibody titer in an individual patient usually correlate with disease activity. Disappearance of the antibody from the serum often precedes clinical remission.

Treatment

Whenever feasible, patients should be referred to a dermatologist for management. Some patients require years of or lifelong immunosuppressive therapy. Treatment of pemphigus and its variants is similar. Initial therapy involves complete

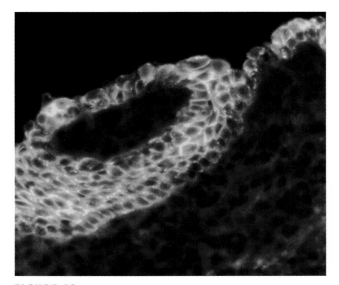

FIGURE 82.
Immunofluorescence stain showing intercellular IgG deposition characteristic of pemphigus vulgaris.

suppression of blistering with prednisone (usually 1 to 2 mg/kg/d). Because therapy may need to be continued for years, corticosteroid side effects become a problem. Adjunctive therapy with other immunosuppressant drugs should be considered in patients who cannot tolerate corticosteroids or in whom the disease is not adequately controlled with corticosteroids. Immunosuppressant drugs should be continued in sufficient doses to suppress blistering until serum antibody titers become negative, at which time tapering of therapy should be attempted.

Although any of the following may be used as a corticosteroid-sparing agent, azathioprine is most frequently utilized. Second-line agents include methotrexate, intravenous cyclophosphamide, and mycophenolate mofetil or chlorambucil. Depending on the agent used, potential side effects include leukopenia, hepatotoxicity, teratogenesis, sterility, oral ulcers, and cystitis. Patients with excessive toxicity from oral corticosteroids or cyclophosphamide may experience decreased side effects with monthly pulse doses.

Additional adjunctive therapies that have been used with varying degrees of success include intramuscular gold therapy, oral dapsone, and oral antimalarial therapy. Dapsone is particularly useful in patients with IgA pemphigus; an antimalarial agent may benefit patients with pemphigus erythematosus or foliaceus.

Intravenous immune globulin therapy is approved by Medicare (but not by the U.S. Food and Drug Administration) as a potential treatment of pemphigus, and reports have documented its effectiveness. The use of biologic agents has been reported to be effective and is being explored in multicenter studies. Additionally, multiple studies document the usefulness of intravenous rituximab. These therapies at present should only be administered to patients who have recalcitrant disease or have intolerable drug-related toxicity.

KEY POINTS

- Pemphigus is characterized by flaccid, fragile blisters that progress to large, weeping, denuded areas; oropharyngeal erosions are common.

- Lesions of paraneoplastic pemphigus may be the first sign of an internal malignancy and should be suspected in patients with ocular and oral blisters and skin lesions that resemble erythema multiforme, bullous pemphigoid, or lichen planus.

- Therapy for pemphigus vulgaris may require years of or lifelong immunosuppression and begins with corticosteroids; a corticosteroid-sparing agent should be used early in the course of treatment.

Bullous Pemphigoid and Other Subepidermal Blistering Diseases

Pathophysiology and Epidemiology

Bullous pemphigoid is a blistering disease associated with autoantibodies; however, it is not clear that these autoantibodies are the direct cause of the disease.

Bullous pemphigoid is more common than pemphigus and is less aggressive; however, most affected patients are elderly, so morbidity is possible, and death from other causes is not uncommon. Although the disease may occur in all age groups, including prepubertal children, its onset is most common in the seventh and eighth decades of life.

Bullous pemphigoid has been associated with psoriasis, diabetes mellitus, systemic lupus erythematosus, pernicious anemia, thyroiditis, polymyositis, and rheumatoid arthritis. Malignancy is not independently associated with bullous pemphigoid; only patients with the anti-epiligrin cicatricial pemphigoid variant need assessment for an associated cancer.

Clinical Manifestations and Diagnosis

Bullous Pemphigoid

Bullous pemphigoid is a chronic, vesiculobullous eruption that predominantly involves nonmucosal surfaces. It is characterized by subepidermal vesicles and blisters that are tense and do not rupture easily (**Figure 83**). Urticarial lesions may precede the onset of blistering. Bullous pemphigoid is usually widespread. Sites of predilection include the lower abdomen, inner thighs, groin, axillae, and flexural aspects of the arms and legs. A localized variant with bullae limited to the pretibial area rarely occurs.

Cicatricial Pemphigoid

Cicatricial pemphigoid is differentiated from bullous pemphigoid in that it primarily involves the mucous membranes

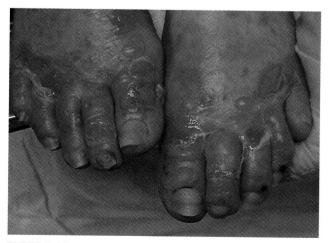

FIGURE 83.
Multiple tense bullae and erosions in a patient with bullous pemphigoid.

and is rarely accompanied by skin disease. Cicatricial pemphigoid is characterized by blistering with eventual scarring. Lesions are found on the conjunctiva (**Figure 84**) but also the nasopharynx, oropharynx, esophagus, larynx, urethra, and anal mucosa. Associated skin lesions occur in the minority of cases. Recurrent lesions cause scarring, and involvement of the eyes can be sight-threatening. The gingivae are commonly involved, and the disease may present as desquamative gingivitis. Esophageal lesions may result in stricture formation that may require repeated dilatations.

Linear IgA Bullous Dermatosis

Linear IgA bullous dermatosis is a subepidermal blistering disease that is associated with tissue-bound and circulating IgA antibodies. Clinically, it can present similarly to bullous pemphigoid, dermatitis herpetiformis (**Figure 85**), or cicatricial pemphigoid with ocular and/or oral involvement. This

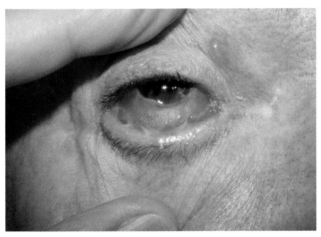

FIGURE 84.
Ocular erythema and symblepharon (adhesion of the eyelid to the globe) in a patient with cicatricial pemphigoid.

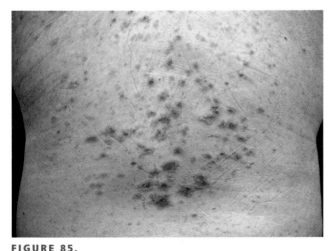

FIGURE 85.
Grouped vesicular lesions on the back in a patient with linear IgA bullous dermatosis. Blisters may be missed because of scratching.

disease may be idiopathic or caused by drugs, most commonly vancomycin. The following agents have also been reported to induce linear IgA bullous dermatosis: captopril, amiodarone, ampicillin, childhood vaccines, diclofenac, interferon gamma, interleukin-2, iodine, lithium, penicillin G, phenytoin, piroxicam, rifampin, somatostatin, and trimethoprim-sulfamethoxazole. In patients with drug-induced disease, withdrawal of the offending agent usually leads to disease resolution. Overall, linear IgA bullous dermatosis is an uncommon cause of drug eruptions.

Epidermolysis Bullosa Acquisita

Epidermolysis bullosa acquisita is an acquired mechanobullous disease that can present with widespread blistering and erosions of the mucosal surfaces; disease may be localized to areas of trauma such as the dorsal hands (**Figure 86**), knees, and elbows. Disease on the dorsal hands may mimic porphyria cutanea tarda or pseudoporphyria. Epidermolysis bullosa acquisita is caused by autoantibodies directed against type VII collagen, which is the major protein in the anchoring fibrils. Epidermolysis bullosa acquisita has been associated with systemic lupus erythematosus and inflammatory bowel disease.

Treatment

Bullous pemphigoid is generally managed with corticosteroid therapy, either with superpotent topical corticosteroids for limited, localized disease or with moderate doses of prednisone for more extensive or recalcitrant disease. Because bullous pemphigoid predominantly occurs in an elderly population, the potential for corticosteroid toxicity may be greater, and, therefore, corticosteroid-sparing agents are regularly considered early in the disease course. Agents used include azathioprine, methotrexate, mycophenolate mofetil, rituximab, and intravenous immune globulin. Cyclophosphamide in combination with corticosteroids has been suggested for patients with ocular pemphigoid. Linear IgA bullous dermatosis is effectively treated with oral dapsone.

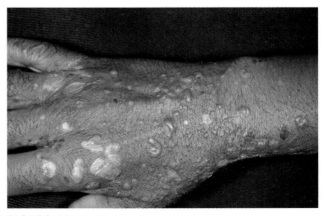

FIGURE 86.
Blisters on the dorsal hands in a patient with epidermolysis bullosa acquisita.

- Bullous pemphigoid predominantly involves nonmucosal surfaces and is characterized by subepidermal vesicles and blisters that are tense and do not rupture easily.

- Cicatricial pemphigoid predominantly involves the mucous membranes and is characterized by blistering with eventual scarring.

- Linear IgA bullous dermatosis can present similarly to bullous pemphigoid, dermatitis herpetiformis, or cicatricial pemphigoid and may be idiopathic or caused by drugs, most commonly vancomycin.

- Treatment of bullous pemphigoid consists of corticosteroid therapy and, usually, corticosteroid-sparing agents such as azathioprine, methotrexate, mycophenolate mofetil, rituximab, and intravenous immune globulin.

Dermatitis Herpetiformis

Dermatitis herpetiformis is characterized by grouped, pruritic, erythematous papulovesicles on the extensor surfaces of the arms, legs, central back, buttocks, and scalp (**Figure 87**). There is a genetic predisposition that is linked to the same genes that are associated with celiac disease. Virtually all patients with dermatitis herpetiformis have celiac disease, but gastrointestinal symptoms occur in only about 25% of patients. Thyroid disorders have been associated with dermatitis herpetiformis. In addition, lymphoma (specifically lymphoma occurring in the gastrointestinal tract, as is also linked to celiac disease) is more common in patients with dermatitis herpetiformis.

Skin biopsy reveals a neutrophil-rich subepidermal blister. The deposition of granular IgA in dermal papillary tips is pathognomonic (**Figure 88**).

FIGURE 88.
Immunofluorescence stain demonstrating granular deposition of IgA in the papillary dermis characteristic of dermatitis herpetiformis.

Treatment with a gluten-free diet is successful in greater than 70% of patients with dermatitis herpetiformis if the diet is adhered to for a minimum of 3 to 12 months. In such patients, initial suppression of symptoms with dapsone is usually necessary. When gluten restriction allows a decrease in dapsone, the patient can gradually taper the dosage and often can discontinue it. A gluten-free diet treats the cause rather than the symptoms of the disease. The primary disadvantage of gluten-free-diet therapy is its inconvenience and difficulty with adherence. Most major cities have celiac disease support groups, which can also provide useful support for patients with dermatitis herpetiformis.

Treatment with oral dapsone usually improves itching within 24 to 48 hours in adults. Dapsone treatment requires continued monitoring and may be associated with significant potential adverse effects. Hemolysis is the most common side effect of treatment and is expected in most patients. It may be severe in patients with glucose-6-phosphate dehydrogenase (G6PD) deficiency, and pretesting for this condition prior to starting therapy is generally recommended. Methemoglobinemia is common but is not usually a severe problem. Additional adverse reactions include toxic hepatitis, cholestatic jaundice, psychosis, and both motor and sensory neuropathy. Hypoalbuminemia may occur after chronic use. Rarely, infectious mononucleosis syndrome with fever and lymphadenopathy occurs.

- Dermatitis herpetiformis is characterized by grouped, pruritic, erythematous papulovesicles on the extensor surfaces of the arms, legs, central back, buttocks, and scalp.

- Dermatitis herpetiformis is associated with celiac disease.

- Management of dermatitis herpetiformis includes a gluten-free diet and dapsone.

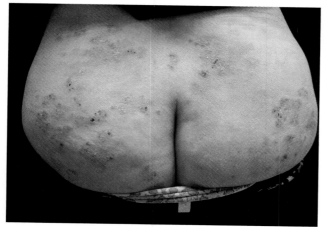

FIGURE 87.
Grouped vesicles and excoriations in a patient with dermatitis herpetiformis.

Bibliography

Amagai M, Ikeda S, Shimizu H, et al; Pemphigus Study Group. A randomized double-blind trial of intravenous immunoglobulin for pemphigus. J Am Acad Dermatol. 2009;60(4):595-603. [PMID: 19293008]

Di Zenzo G, Marazza G, Borradori L. Bullous pemphigoid: physiopathology, clinical features and management. Adv Dermatol. 2007;23:257-288. [PMID: 18159905]

Egan CA, Lazarova Z, Darling TN, Yee C, Coté T, Yancey KB. Anti-epiligrin cicatricial pemphigoid and relative risk for cancer. Lancet. 2001;357(9271):1850-1851. [PMID: 11410196]

Hervonen K, Vornanen M, Kautiainen H, Collin P, Reunala T. Lymphoma in patients with dermatitis herpetiformis and their first-degree relatives. Br J Dermatol. 2005;152(1):82-86. [PMID: 15656805]

Nousari HC, Kimyai-Asadi A, Caeiro JP, Anhalt GJ. Clinical, demographic, and immunohistologic features of vancomycin-induced linear IgA bullous disease of the skin. Report of 2 cases and review of the literature. Medicine (Baltimore). 1999;78(1):1-8. [PMID: 9990350]

Woodley DT, Remington J, Chen M. Autoimmunity to type VII collagen: epidermolysis bullosa acquisita. Clin Rev Allergy Immunol. 2007;33(1-2):78-84. [PMID: 18058258]

Zone JJ. Skin manifestations of celiac disease. Gastroenterology. 2005;128(4 Suppl 1):S87-91. [PMID: 15825132]

Cutaneous Manifestations of Internal Disease

Skin Diseases Associated with Hepatitis C Virus

Mixed Cryoglobulinemia

Mixed cryoglobulinemia is present in up to 50% of patients infected with hepatitis C virus (HCV) but is symptomatic in less than 15% of infected patients. Greater than 90% of cases of mixed cryoglobulinemia are associated with HCV infection. It is recommended that all patients with mixed cryoglobulinemia be screened for hepatitis C, and it is reasonable to screen all patients with hepatitis C for mixed cryoglobulinemia, particularly if compatible symptoms are present.

Mixed cryoglobulinemia consists of circulating immune complexes made up of polyclonal IgG directed against either monoclonal or polyclonal IgM. These immune complexes, derived from cryoglobulin-producing B cells, deposit in postcapillary venules and induce inflammation and vessel damage that present clinically as palpable purpura (**Figure 89**). Associated signs and symptoms may include weakness, arthralgia, peripheral neuropathy, and glomerulonephritis. A skin biopsy will demonstrate leukocytoclastic vasculitis. The diagnosis of mixed cryoglobulinemia is confirmed by identifying elevated serum cryoglobulins. Other supportive laboratory findings include a low serum C4 level and elevated rheumatoid factor. HCV antigens are found in the skin lesions in 40% of cases.

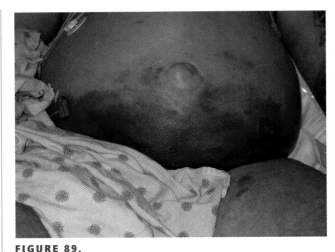

FIGURE 89.
Hepatitis C–associated cryoglobulinemia presenting as abdominal purpura.

Therapy with interferon alfa and ribavirin is aimed at treating the underlying HCV infection. New studies suggest a potential role for rituximab in eliminating the B cells that produce the cryoglobulins.

Porphyria Cutanea Tarda

Porphyria cutanea tarda (PCT) is a hereditary or acquired blistering disease caused by excess circulating porphyrins due to deficiency or reduced activity of the enzyme uroporphyrinogen decarboxylase. Iron overload, as seen with hemochromatosis, leads to decreased activity of this enzyme, resulting in elevations of uroporphyrins.

Up to 50% of patients with sporadic PCT have HCV infection. Clinically, patients present with vesicles and bullae on sun-exposed skin, most commonly on the face, dorsal hands, and scalp (**Figure 90**). Skin fragility (tearing with minimal trauma) is common. Other features include hyperpigmentation, milia (tiny inclusion cysts), hypertrichosis, and alopecia (**Figure 91**). The diagnosis of PCT is strongly suggested by the physical examination. Urine fluoresces coral

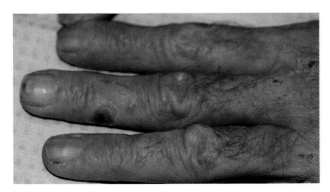

FIGURE 90.
Porphyria cutanea tarda, characterized by erosions and milia (small white pearly cysts).

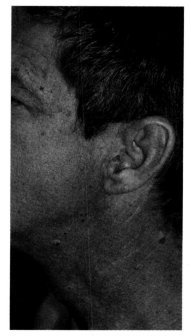

FIGURE 91.
Hyperpigmentation and erosions in a patient with porphyria cutanea tarda.

pink when examined with a Wood lamp. Skin biopsy of a vesicle demonstrates a pauci-inflammatory subepidermal bulla with characteristic festooning of the dermal papillae. The best test for PCT is a 24-hour urine porphyrin determination, which demonstrates elevated levels of uroporphyrin in patients with PCT.

Treatment for PCT includes phlebotomy, low-dose antimalarials, and erythropoietin. In patients with underlying HCV infection, treatment with interferon alfa and ribavirin is indicated.

KEY POINTS

- The most common cutaneous manifestations of infection with hepatitis C virus are mixed cryoglobulinemia and porphyria cutanea tarda.

- Greater than 90% of cases of mixed cryoglobulinemia are associated with hepatitis C virus infection.

- Mixed cryoglobulinemia presents as palpable purpura that may be accompanied by arthralgia, peripheral neuropathy, and glomerulonephritis.

- Porphyria cutanea tarda presents with vesicles and bullae on sun-exposed skin, most commonly on the face, dorsal hands, and scalp.

Livedo Reticularis, Purpura, and Vasculitis

Livedo Reticularis

Livedo reticularis is a cutaneous reaction pattern that produces a pink, red, or bluish-red, mottled, netlike pattern on

the skin (**Figure 92**). It is caused by slowed blood flow through the superficial cutaneous vasculature. It most commonly affects the lower extremities but may also affect the upper extremities and trunk in more severe cases. Idiopathic livedo reticularis is typically transient and asymptomatic, but tingling, numbness, aching, or paresthesias may be present. Lesions are accentuated when exposed to cold and resolve with warming. Fixed livedo reticularis (**Figure 93**) does not resolve with warming and should prompt an evaluation for conditions listed in **Table 23**. Ulceration is rare but is more likely to complicate fixed livedo reticularis than transient, idiopathic livedo reticularis.

Purpura and Vasculitis

Purpura is caused by hemorrhage into the skin. The differential diagnosis of purpura is very broad. The size and distribution of the lesions and whether or not the lesions are palpable are important. Petechial and macular (nonpalpable)

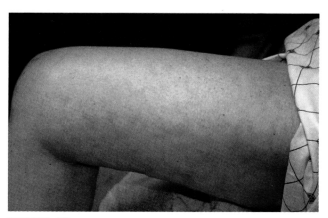

FIGURE 92.
Livedo reticularis, characterized by a pink, red, or bluish-red, mottled, netlike pattern on the skin.

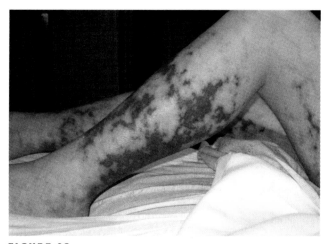

FIGURE 93.
Fixed livedo reticularis with central purpura as the presenting sign of antiphospholipid antibody syndrome.

TABLE 23 Selected Diseases and Conditions Associated with Livedo Reticularis

Disease/Condition	Example
Neurohumoral diseases	Pheochromocytoma, carcinoid syndrome
Hematologic diseases	Polycythemia vera, leukemia, thrombocytosis
Hypercoagulable states	Antiphospholipid antibody syndrome
Paraproteinemias	Multiple myeloma and associated type 1 cryoglobulinemia
Autoimmune diseases	Systemic lupus erythematosus, dermatomyositis, scleroderma, Sjögren syndrome, Still disease, rheumatoid arthritis, Felty syndrome
Infections	Parvovirus B-19, hepatitis C, syphilis, meningococcemia, pneumococcal sepsis, tuberculosis
Drug reactions	Amantadine, quinidine, warfarin, minocycline
Vasculitides	Polyarteritis nodosa, Wegener granulomatosis, microscopic polyarteritis, Churg-Strauss syndrome, Takayasu disease, temporal arteritis
Calciphylaxis	—
Cholesterol emboli	—
Endocarditis	—
Microvascular occlusion syndromes	Hemolytic-uremic syndrome, thrombotic thrombocytopenic purpura, disseminated intravascular coagulation, heparin necrosis, paroxysmal nocturnal hemoglobinuria
Cryoglobulinemia	—
Livedoid vasculopathy	—

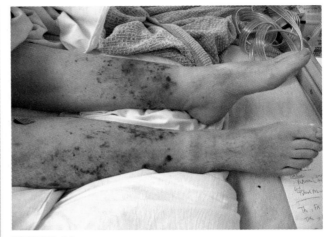

FIGURE 94.
Macular purpura, which may be caused by chronic sun damage, systemic corticosteroids, or trauma from a pneumatic compression device.

of the skin. Cutaneous small vessel vasculitis is idiopathic in 50% of cases, but it can be associated with an underlying condition such as infection, inflammatory disease, medication, or malignancy (**Table 24**).

Palpable purpura from cutaneous small vessel vasculitis is usually accentuated in dependent areas (lower extremities in mobile patients, buttocks and back in supine patients) (**Figure 95**). Lesions may be asymptomatic or may itch, sting, or burn. Patients may have concomitant fever, myalgia, arthralgia, and anorexia. Occasionally, cutaneous small vessel vasculitis may present as urticaria, and is known as urticarial vasculitis (see Urticaria). Definitive diagnosis of cutaneous small vessel vasculitis is made by skin biopsy. Choosing the appropriate lesion to biopsy is critical. Ideally, a lesion between 12 and 48 hours old should be selected, because the classic histologic findings may not be present in very early or late lesions.

Treatment of cutaneous small vessel vasculitis involves excluding systemic vasculitides and removing or treating any underlying cause. First-line treatment includes rest, warming, reducing activity, and leg elevation. Antihistamines and NSAIDs are first-line oral therapies. Colchicine and dapsone, utilized for their antineutrophilic properties, are common second-line therapeutic options. Patients with chronic and/or severe disease may require treatment with systemic immunosuppressants.

The prognosis for cutaneous small vessel vasculitis is generally good. Patients with cutaneous vasculitis caused by a medication or infection tend to have a single, self-limited episode. Those with Henoch-Schönlein purpura or an underlying connective tissue disease may relapse and remit. Patients with cryoglobulinemic vasculitis or an underlying malignancy tend to have chronic, unremitting disease.

purpura (**Figure 94**) usually result from abnormal platelet number or function, coagulation abnormalities, or poor support of dermal vasculature (chronic sun damage, amyloidosis, corticosteroid use, vitamin C deficiency, Ehlers-Danlos syndrome). Actinic or senile purpura is one of the most common types of benign purpura. Senile purpura occurs in the setting of chronic sun damage and presents as painless purpuric macules on the extensor forearms and anterior shins. Minimal, often unrecognized trauma is sufficient to produce the lesion. Lesions resolve slowly, leaving behind hyperpigmentation from hemosiderin deposition in the dermis.

Palpable purpura implies an inflammatory process, most classically cutaneous small vessel vasculitis. Leukocytoclastic vasculitis, or cutaneous small vessel vasculitis, results from immune complex deposition in the small postcapillary venules

TABLE 24 Selected Conditions Associated with Cutaneous Small Vessel Vasculitis
Idiopathic (50%)
Infection (15%-20%)
Group A β-hemolytic streptococci
Hepatitis B virus
Hepatitis C virus (cryoglobulinemia)
Septic vasculitis
Inflammatory Diseases (15%-20%)
Henoch-Schönlein purpura
Systemic vasculitis
Polyarteritis nodosa
Wegener granulomatosis
Microscopic polyangiitis
Churg-Strauss syndrome
Connective tissue disease
Systemic lupus erythematosus
Rheumatoid arthritis
Sjögren syndrome
Behçet syndrome
Inflammatory bowel disease
Medications (10%-15%)
Sulfonamides
Penicillins
Allopurinol
Phenytoin
Thiazides
Fluoroquinolones
Malignancy (<5%)
Paraproteinemia
Lymphoproliferative disease

Data from Fiorentino DF. J Am Acad Dermatol. 2003;48(3):311-340. [PMID: 12637912]

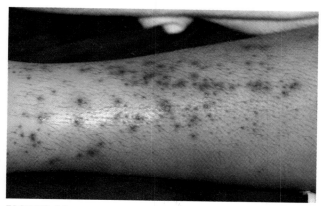

FIGURE 95.
Palpable purpura as a clinical sign of biopsy-proven leukocytoclastic vasculitis.

Neutrophilic Dermatoses

Neutrophilic dermatoses are disorders in which the predominant effector cell is the neutrophil. They include Sweet syndrome, pyoderma gangrenosum, erythema elevatum diutinum, subcorneal pustular dermatosis, and neutrophilic eccrine hidradenitis. Sweet syndrome and pyoderma gangrenosum will be discussed here, as they are the most common.

Sweet Syndrome

Sweet syndrome, or acute febrile neutrophilic dermatitis, most commonly affects middle-aged women after an upper respiratory tract infection. Sweet syndrome may be idiopathic or may be associated with an underlying condition. Twenty percent of cases are associated with an underlying malignancy, most commonly hematologic malignancies, especially acute myeloid leukemia; however, solid-organ malignancies (breast, gastrointestinal, genitourinary) have also been associated. Sweet syndrome can present before, during, or after the diagnosis of malignancy. Inflammatory bowel disease, upper respiratory tract infections, gastrointestinal infections, and medications (granulocyte-colony stimulating factor, all-*trans*-retinoic acid, vaccines, and minocycline) are also associated with Sweet syndrome. It may occur in conjunction with other neutrophilic diseases such as pyoderma gangrenosum.

Patients with Sweet syndrome present with the abrupt onset of fever, arthralgia, myalgia, and cutaneous lesions. Individual lesions are tender, nonpruritic, brightly erythematous, well-demarcated papules and plaques that appear on the neck, upper trunk, and extremities (**Figure 96**). Pathergy, the development of lesions in areas of minor trauma, is characteristic. Lesions heal without scarring. Extracutaneous involvement of the pulmonary, musculoskeletal, hepatic, renal, pancreatic, cardiac, ophthalmologic, and central nervous systems may occur. Leukocytosis with a polymorphonuclear cell predominance is typical but may be absent in patients with an underlying hematologic malignancy.

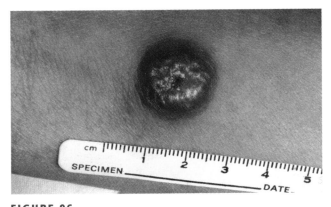

FIGURE 96.
Typical, tender nodule of Sweet syndrome with erythema and "juicy" appearance.

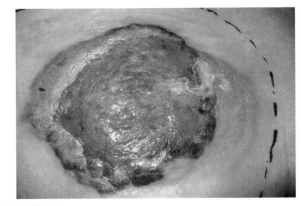

FIGURE 97.
Pyoderma gangrenosum, presenting as a painful ulcer with a purulent base and ragged, violaceous border in a patient with underlying myelodysplasia.

Prednisone leads to rapid improvement and is the initial treatment of choice. When associated with an underlying condition or medication, treatment for that condition or stopping the inciting medication will result in remission. In patients with persistent or severe disease, corticosteroid-sparing agents such as potassium iodide, dapsone, colchicine, NSAIDs, cyclosporine, mycophenolate mofetil, and tumor necrosis factor α inhibitors may be required.

Pyoderma Gangrenosum

Pyoderma gangrenosum (PG) is associated with an underlying systemic disease in 50% to 78% of patients and can present before, concurrently with, or after the development of the underlying condition. Diseases most commonly associated with PG are inflammatory bowel disease (either ulcerative colitis or Crohn disease), rheumatoid arthritis, seronegative spondyloarthritis, and a hematologic disease or malignancy, most commonly acute myeloid leukemia.

PG is an uncommon, neutrophilic, ulcerative skin disease. Lesions tend to be multiple and tend to appear on the lower extremities. They begin as tender papules, pustules, or vesicles that spontaneously ulcerate and progress to painful ulcers with a purulent base and undermined, ragged, violaceous borders (**Figure 97**). Atrophic, cribriform scarring is characteristic of healed lesions. Pathergy is observed in 20% to 30% of patients with PG and can initiate or aggravate PG.

There are no pathognomonic histologic findings for PG, and laboratory tests are nonspecific. The diagnosis requires recognition of the clinical morphology, clinicopathologic correlation, and the exclusion of other disorders that mimic PG. A list of suggested evaluations for patients presenting with skin lesions suggestive of PG is presented in **Table 25**.

Treatment of PG usually requires either local or systemic immunosuppression. Because of pathergy, surgical therapy is almost always contraindicated. Superpotent topical corticosteroids applied under occlusion, intralesional triamcinolone, or topical immunomodulators (tacrolimus ointment) may be appropriate for single lesions. First-line systemic therapy

TABLE 25 Suggested Evaluation for Patients with Skin Lesions Suggestive of Pyoderma Gangrenosum

Skin Biopsy from Inflamed Peripheral Border

Routine histology

Special stains of the tissue to exclude infection (fungal, bacterial, viral, mycobacterial) and/or neoplastic process (immunohistochemical stains)

Tissue culture to exclude infection (fungal, bacterial, viral, mycobacterial)

Laboratory and Other Diagnostic Tests

Suggested for all patients:
  Complete blood count with differential
  Erythrocyte sedimentation rate
  Serum chemistry studies (renal and liver panels)

Based on history, clinical presentation, associated symptoms, and histology:
  Chest radiograph
  Gastrointestinal evaluation (upper endoscopy, colonoscopy)
  Hematologic laboratory tests and evaluation:
    Serum and urine protein electrophoresis
    Serum immunofixation or immunoelectrophoresis
    Hypercoagulability panel (especially antiphospholipid antibody)
    Bone marrow biopsy
  Rheumatologic laboratory tests:
    Rheumatoid factor
    Antinuclear antibody
    Antineutrophil cytoplasmic antibodies
  Cryoglobulins
  Venous and arterial flow studies
  Other:
    Serum iodine levels
    Serum bromide levels

Data from Weenig RH, Davis MD, Dahl PR, Su WP. Skin ulcers misdiagnosed as pyoderma gangrenosum. N Engl J Med. 2002;347(18):1412-1418 [PMID: 12409543] and Bennett ML, Jackson JM, Jorizzo JL, Fleischer AB Jr, White WL, Callen JP. Pyoderma gangrenosum. A comparison of typical and atypical forms with an emphasis on time to remission. Case review of 86 patients from 2 institutions. Medicine (Baltimore). 2000;79(1):37-46. [PMID: 10670408]

includes prednisone or cyclosporine, either alone or in combination. For patients with PG associated with Crohn disease, first-line treatment should include a tumor necrosis factor α inhibitor. Other corticosteroid-sparing agents of potential benefit include thalidomide, mycophenolate mofetil, azathioprine, methotrexate, tacrolimus, dapsone, cyclophosphamide, and intravenous immune globulin. Nearly 70% of lesions will heal within 1 year of treatment, and 95% of patients will achieve remission at 3 years. Despite appropriate therapy, relapse occurs in up to 46% of affected patients.

KEY POINTS

- Neutrophilic diseases are often associated with underlying hematologic malignancies (especially acute myeloid leukemia), inflammatory bowel disease, and rheumatoid arthritis.

- Patients with Sweet syndrome present with abrupt onset of fever, arthralgia, myalgia, and cutaneous lesions; individual lesions are tender, nonpruritic, brightly erythematous, well-demarcated papules and plaques that appear on the neck, upper trunk, and extremities.

- Pyoderma gangrenosum is a diagnosis of exclusion.

- Sweet syndrome and pyoderma gangrenosum respond to immunosuppression with corticosteroids.

Skin Signs of Lipid Disorders

Xanthomas are the characteristic skin conditions associated with primary (due to genetic defects) or secondary hyperlipidemias. Xanthomas are yellow, orange, reddish, or yellow-brown papules, plaques, or nodules (**Figure 98**). If the infiltration is deep, the xanthoma may be nodular and have normal-appearing overlying skin. The type of xanthoma closely correlates with the type of lipoprotein that is elevated. **Table 26**

FIGURE 98.
Tuberous xanthoma in a patient with sitosterolemia (an autosomal recessive disorder characterized by hyperabsorption of cholesterol and plant sterols).

TABLE 26 Xanthomas, Associated Dyslipidemia, and Associated Diseases

Type of Xanthoma	Clinical Presentation	Associated Dyslipidemia	Important Associated Diseases
Xanthelasma	Asymptomatic, flat, yellow-to-orange papules or plaques around eyelids	LDL cholesterol; 50% of patients have no dyslipidemia	Familial hypercholesterolemia
Eruptive xanthomas	Yellow or yellow-orange papules appearing suddenly in crops over buttocks, thighs, arms, forearms, back, or chest; may be pruritic	Triglycerides	Familial lipoprotein deficiency; apoprotein CII deficiency; familial hypertriglyceridemia
Tendon xanthomas	Lipid deposition within tendons, ligaments, and fasciae; smooth, firm, lobulated nodules over extensor tendons of hands, elbows, knees, and Achilles tendon	LDL cholesterol	Familial hypercholesterolemia; cerebrotendinous xanthomatosis; sitosterolemia
Tuberous xanthomas	Small, soft, yellow, orange, or red papules or nodules over extensor surfaces, especially the elbows, knees, and buttocks; often coalesce to form large, lobular masses	LDL cholesterol or triglycerides	Familial hypercholesterolemia
Plane xanthomas	Flat, yellow plaques that most commonly involve the skin folds	—	—
	Diffuse plane xanthomas (neck, face, upper trunk, arms)	Normolipemic	Multiple myeloma; paraproteinemia; leukemia; lymphoma
	Intertriginous areas	LDL cholesterol	Homozygous familial hypercholesterolemia
	Palmar xanthomas	LDL cholesterol or triglycerides	Dysbetalipoproteinemia

outlines the type of xanthoma, clinical presentation, underlying lipid abnormality, and important associated diseases.

Paraneoplastic Dermatoses

Paraneoplastic dermatoses are disorders in which a skin condition may be associated with or serve as a marker for an internal malignancy. A wide spectrum of cutaneous findings and diseases has been diagnosed in relationship to an underlying malignancy, and there are multiple hereditary syndromes with skin manifestations and increased risk of cancer (**Table 27**). Also see **Figure 99**, **Figure 100**, and **Figure 101**.

There are several criteria that point to a relationship between a specific cutaneous disease and internal malignancy. Strongly supporting this link are the following: when the dermatosis occurs concurrently with discovery of the malignancy; when the course of the dermatosis follows that of the cancer; or when a specific tumor cell type, organ, or site of cancer is associated with the dermatosis. While some paraneoplastic skin diseases are highly specific and only occur in the presence of malignancies (for example, paraneoplastic pemphigus), others can also occur in the absence of an underlying cancer (for example, dermatomyositis), but are of importance to the internist because they indicate the potential for an otherwise undiagnosed malignancy.

The evaluation of a patient with a skin condition that may be associated with an internal malignancy must be individualized. All patients should receive age- and sex-appropriate screening tests. Particular care must be taken in reviewing symptoms and performing appropriate physical examination maneuvers of the organ system or systems with which the paraneoplastic dermatosis is associated. Additional testing must be guided by these findings as well as additional risk factors for malignancy, presence of comorbid conditions, and the patient's age.

KEY POINTS

- Skin lesions may serve as markers of internal malignancy.
- The strongest support for a link between a skin condition and an internal malignancy is when the dermatosis occurs concurrently with discovery of the malignancy, there is a distinct type or site of cancer associated with the dermatosis, or the course of the dermatosis follows that of the cancer.

Erythema Nodosum

Erythema nodosum (EN) is relatively common and is most often acute and self-limited. The typical clinical presentation is the sudden onset of one or more tender, erythematous nodules on the anterior legs that are more easily palpated than

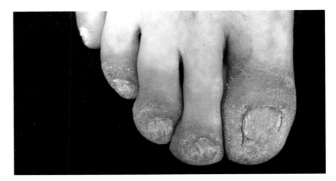

FIGURE 99.
Bazex syndrome (acrokeratosis paraneoplastica) in a patient with squamous cell carcinoma of the tonsillar pillar.

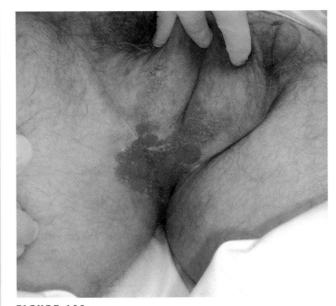

FIGURE 100.
An irregularly shaped erythematous plaque in extramammary Paget disease.

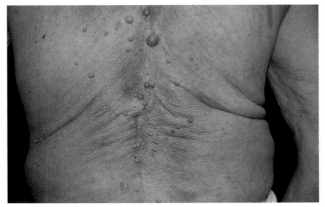

FIGURE 101.
Multiple neurofibromas in a patient with neurofibromatosis type 1.

TABLE 27 Paraneoplastic Disorders

Disease	Clinical Findings	Associated Malignancy/Comments
Conditions That Are Strongly Linked to Internal Malignancy		
Acanthosis nigricans	Velvety or verrucous hyperpigmentation of intertriginous areas, weight loss, glossitis	Adenocarcinoma, usually GI or GU, most commonly stomach; occurs also in patients with endocrinopathy
Leser-Trélat sign	Rapid appearance or inflammation of multiple seborrheic keratoses; often occurs in conjunction with acanthosis nigricans	Same cancer association as acanthosis nigricans; seborrheic keratoses are common lesions; Leser-Trélat sign is very rare
Tripe palms	Rugose folds on the palms and soles; may occur with or without acanthosis nigricans	If occurring with acanthosis nigricans, same cancer association; if occurring without acanthosis nigricans, squamous cell carcinoma of the head and neck or lungs
Bazex syndrome (also known as acrokeratosis paraneoplastica)	Psoriasiform, violaceous scaling on the acral surfaces (fingers, toes, nose, and ears) (**Figure 99**); keratoderma may also be present	Squamous cell carcinoma in the upper respiratory tract or upper GI tract; effective therapy of an associated cancer is followed by resolution of the dermatosis
Carcinoid syndrome	Episodic flushing, often accompanied by diarrhea and bronchospasm; can eventually result in telangiectasia or permanent ruddiness	Pulmonary carcinoid tumors or carcinoid metastatic to the liver; screen with urine for 5-HIAA; tumor removal is followed by resolution of the skin and systemic findings
Ectopic ACTH syndrome	Generalized hyperpigmentation	Small cell lung carcinoma; tumor removal can result in some reversion of the pigmentation
Glucagonoma syndrome	Intertriginous erythema, scales, and erosions known as necrolytic migratory erythema; glossitis and angular cheilitis are common	Glucagon-secreting tumor of the pancreas; rare patients with necrolytic migratory erythema who do not have malignancy have been reported
Neutrophilic dermatoses	Sweet syndrome; atypical pyoderma gangrenosum (bullous lesions with a blue-gray border, often on the hands, arms, or face)	Myeloid leukemia, myelofibrosis, and refractory anemias; these disorders also occur without malignancy in 80% to 90% of patients
Paget disease of the breast	Erythematous, irregularly bordered plaque on the nipple	Represents an extension of a ductal adenocarcinoma of the breast
Extramammary Paget disease	Erythematous scaly patch or plaque on the perineal skin, scrotum, or perianal area (**Figure 100**)	Cancer is present in 25% of patients and is in the GI or GU tract; it is not contiguous with the dermatosis; the dermatosis is a malignancy and needs appropriate excision or destruction
Paraneoplastic pemphigus	Severe mucosal erosions, tense and flaccid bullae that may be widespread	Non-Hodgkin B-cell lymphoma, Castleman disease, chronic lymphocytic leukemia
Conditions with Statistical Evidence of Internal Malignancy Association or Sporadic Association		
Dermatomyositis	Heliotrope rash, Gottron papules and sign, photodistributed violaceous erythema; scaly erythema of the scalp with diffuse alopecia; periungual telangiectasia and cuticular overgrowth	20% of patients with dermatomyositis had, have, or will have a malignancy; ovarian cancer is overrepresented; paraneoplastic course is possible but unusual
Mycosis fungoides	Bizarrely configured, erythematous, scaly plaques, or erythroderma	This is a cutaneous T-cell lymphoma; some patients will develop a second malignancy, but this is uncommon
Porphyria cutanea tarda	Erosions, crusts with or without blisters on photo-exposed areas, particularly the dorsa of the hands; hyperpigmentation and hypertrichosis are often also present	Hepatoma; associated with hepatitis C; treatment of hepatitis C may lessen the risk of hepatoma

(Continued on next page)

TABLE 27 Paraneoplastic Disorders *(continued)*

Disease	Clinical Findings	Associated Malignancy/Comments
Hereditary Syndromes with Prominent Cutaneous Findings and Potential Internal Malignancy		
Neurofibromatosis type I (NF1)	Café-au-lait macules, axillary freckling, neurofibromas (**Figure 101**); Lisch nodules on eye examination	Neurofibrosarcoma, pheochromocytoma, and astrocytoma; autosomal dominant inheritance
Tuberous sclerosis complex	Shagreen patch, ash leaf macules, angiofibromas, periungual and subungual fibromas	Renal angiomyolipoma, renal cysts, and renal cancer; cardiac rhabdomyoma; autosomal dominant disorder
Familial atypical multiple mole melanoma-pancreatic syndrome	Atypical moles (dysplastic nevi), multiple melanomas	Pancreatic carcinoma is more prevalent in these families
Birt-Hogg-Dube syndrome	Flesh-colored central facial papules known as fibrofolliculomas; patients may also have trichodiscomas and multiple acrochordons	Renal cancer; some families may also have medullary cancer of the thyroid; spontaneous pneumothorax is frequent in these patients
Hereditary leiomyomatosis and renal cell carcinoma syndrome	Flesh-colored to erythematous dermal tumors	Renal cell carcinoma and multiple uterine leiomyomas; autosomal dominant
Gardner syndrome	Multiple epidermal cysts, desmoid tumors	Colonic polyposis (adenomatous polyposis coli) with a high frequency of malignant degeneration; autosomal dominant
Cowden syndrome (multiple hamartoma syndrome)	Multiple flesh-colored central facial papules, cobblestoning of the oral mucosa, acral keratoses	Breast cancer; thyroid hamartomas and carcinoma; multiple hamartomatous polyps throughout the GI tract; autosomal dominant

ACTH = adrenocorticotropin; ENT = ear, nose, and throat; GI = gastrointestinal; GU = genitourinary; 5-HIAA = 5-hydroxyindoleacetic acid.

visualized (**Figure 102**). The eruption is often preceded by a prodrome of fever, malaise, and/or arthralgia. A residual ecchymotic appearance is common as the lesions age. Over a 4- to 6-week period, the lesions heal without scar formation. Ulceration is rare. Chronic or recurrent EN most commonly occurs in middle-aged women and is often present for several years.

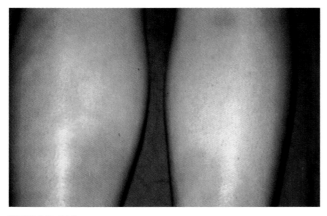

FIGURE 102.
Erythematous, tender nodules of erythema nodosum on the pretibial surface of the legs.

At least half of cases of EN are idiopathic. Causes of EN fall into three broad categories: infections, drugs, and systemic diseases (usually inflammatory disorders). The most common association is a recent streptococcal infection. A partial list of the known associations appears in **Table 28**. The infectious organisms associated with EN tend to primarily affect the respiratory or gastrointestinal tract. Pregnancy, particularly in its second trimester, is a known association, and EN will recur with subsequent pregnancies or with the administration of oral contraceptives. A specific variant of sarcoidosis associated with EN is known as Löfgren syndrome. This is an acute, self-resolving process in which EN occurs with bilateral hilar lymphadenopathy, arthritis of the lower extremities, and anterior uveitis. In patients with inflammatory bowel disease, EN parallels the activity of the bowel disease.

EN is self-limited or resolves with treatment of the underlying disorder. Symptomatic treatment includes NSAIDs or potassium iodide; systemic corticosteroids are rarely needed. Recurrent or chronic EN in the absence of an associated disorder may require therapy with corticosteroids and/or immunosuppressive agents. If the condition is persistent or the presentation is atypical, a skin biopsy should be considered to confirm the diagnosis and rule out the possibility of another form of panniculitis.

TABLE 28 Selected Causes of Erythema Nodosum
Infections
Streptococcal pharyngitis
Tuberculosis
Valley fever (coccidioidomycosis)
Blastomycosis
Histoplasmosis
Psittacosis
Yersinia colitis
Salmonella gastroenteritis
Cat scratch fever
Leprosy
Drugs
Antibiotics (penicillin, sulfonamides)
Oral contraceptives
Systemic Conditions
Pregnancy
Sarcoidosis
Inflammatory bowel disease
Collagen vascular disorders (dermatomyositis, systemic lupus erythematosus, scleroderma)
Malignancy (rare)
Sweet syndrome
Behçet disease

KEY POINTS

- Erythema nodosum is characterized by the sudden onset of one or more tender, erythematous nodules on the anterior legs that are more easily palpated than visualized.

- At least half of cases of erythema nodosum are idiopathic, but the disease may be associated with infections, drugs, and systemic diseases (usually inflammatory disorders).

- The most common secondary cause of erythema nodosum is a recent streptococcal infection.

Cutaneous Lupus Erythematosus

Lupus erythematosus (LE) is a multisystem disorder whose spectrum ranges from a relatively benign cutaneous eruption to a severe, potentially fatal systemic disease. Cutaneous LE is classified into types with LE-specific histology and types with LE-nonspecific histology (in which lesions do not demonstrate the characteristic histopathology). Examples of lesions with nonspecific histopathology are vasculitis, urticarial

lesions, livedo reticularis, mucosal ulcers, and nonscarring alopecia. Bullous LE (**Figure 103**) is a variant associated with antibodies to type VII collagen. LE-specific lesions are further categorized as chronic (usually associated with scarring and/or atrophy), subacute, and acute. The importance of this classification is its ability to predict systemic manifestations of LE.

Acute cutaneous LE is found almost exclusively in patients with systemic lupus erythematosus (SLE) and is typically precipitated by sunlight. Acute cutaneous LE can present as the classic "butterfly rash," characterized by confluent malar erythema (**Figure 104**), or as generalized, red, papular or urticarial lesions on the sun-exposed skin.

Chronic cutaneous LE consists of chronic, slowly progressive, scaly, infiltrative papules and plaques or atrophic red plaques (also known as discoid lupus) on sun-exposed skin

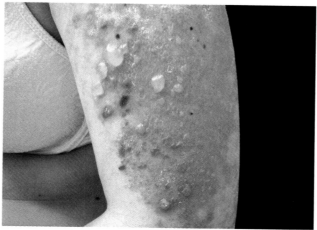

FIGURE 103.
Bullous lupus erythematosus, characterized by tense, subepidermal blisters on an erythematous base. Erosions are present where blisters have ruptured.

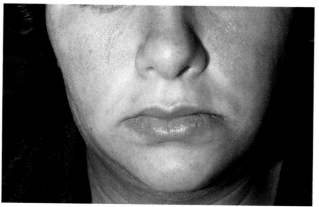

FIGURE 104.
"Butterfly rash," characterized by violaceous erythema on the malar aspects of the face in a patient with systemic lupus erythematosus.

surfaces (**Figure 105**). Other chronic lesions may be hypertrophic or verrucous appearing (**Figure 106**). Most patients with chronic cutaneous LE do not have systemic disease.

Patients with subacute cutaneous LE have annular or papulosquamous (psoriasis-like) lesions that are typically light induced. Unlike chronic cutaneous LE, there is little induration, scarring, or atrophy. The annular lesions are bright red with central clearing (**Figure 107**). The papulosquamous lesions are bright red plaques with sharp borders and fine scaling (**Figure 108**). Subacute cutaneous LE may be associated with medications (hydrochlorothiazide, calcium channel blockers, angiotensin-converting enzyme inhibitors, and terbinafine) and may be associated with some of the less serious SLE manifestations (arthralgia, photosensitivity, serositis) and anti-Ro/SS-A and anti-La/SS-B antibodies.

The diagnosis of cutaneous LE is based upon correlating the clinical lesions with the histopathologic findings on skin biopsy.

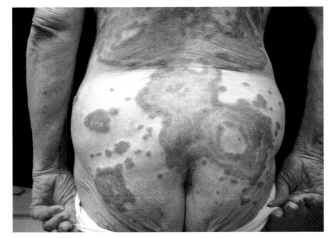

FIGURE 107.
Annular lesions of subacute cutaneous lupus erythematosus.

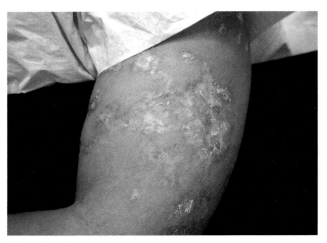

FIGURE 105.
Discoid lupus erythematosus, characterized by erythematous and hypopigmented, scarred, atrophic, discoid plaques with raised borders.

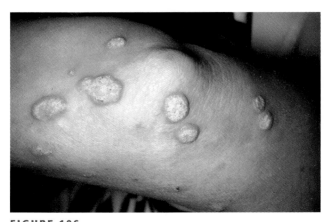

FIGURE 106.
Hypertrophic, verrucous lesions of chronic cutaneous lupus erythematosus.

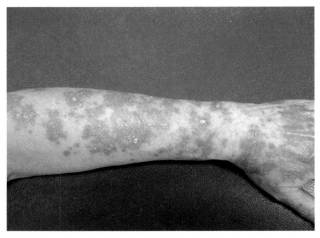

FIGURE 108.
Papulosquamous lesions of subacute cutaneous lupus erythematosus.

Therapy for cutaneous LE is needed to prevent scarring and development of additional lesions. Because sunlight and artificial light sources may exacerbate cutaneous and systemic disease in patients with LE, patients are advised to avoid sun exposure, wear sun-protective clothing, and frequently apply broad-spectrum sunblock with a high sun protective factor. While topical corticosteroids are the initial treatment for all LE lesions, the response is often disappointing. Patients with a poor response to the above measures are usually treated with an antimalarial agent, most often hydroxychloroquine. Patients who smoke seem to respond less well to antimalarial therapy and may have more active disease than nonsmokers; patients who stop smoking may improve. Further escalation in therapy is needed for patients with disease that does not respond to these standard therapies. Thalidomide is recommended for patients with discoid LE or subacute cutaneous LE that is refractory to antimalarial therapy. Additional alternative agents include methotrexate, mycophenolate mofetil, and efalizumab. Except for antimalarial agents, use of these alternative therapies is off label and few have been tested in placebo-controlled trials.

KEY POINTS

- Acute cutaneous lupus erythematosus is characterized by a confluent malar erythema or generalized red papular or urticarial lesions on sun-exposed skin and is usually associated with systemic disease.

- Chronic cutaneous lupus erythematosus consists of chronic, slowly progressive, scaly, infiltrated papules and atrophic red plaques (discoid lupus) on sun-exposed skin surfaces and is not associated with systemic disease.

- Patients with subacute cutaneous lupus erythematosus have annular or papulosquamous (psoriasis-like) lesions that may be associated with the more benign manifestations of systemic lupus erythematosus.

- Drugs may cause subacute cutaneous lupus erythematosus.

- Initial management of cutaneous lupus erythematosus includes sun protection, topical corticosteroids, and antimalarial agents.

Dermatomyositis

Dermatomyositis is a condition with characteristic cutaneous manifestations combined with proximal inflammatory myopathy. Cutaneous disease may occur prior to muscle disease, or cutaneous disease may be the only manifestation. There are patients whose muscle disease becomes inactive with therapy but whose skin disease continues. This discussion will only address the cutaneous disease.

The distinctive cutaneous features of dermatomyositis are the heliotrope rash and Gottron papules. The heliotrope rash consists of a violaceous to dusky erythematous rash with or without edema in a symmetric distribution involving periorbital skin (**Figure 109**). Sometimes this sign is quite subtle and may cause only a mild discoloration along the eyelid margin. At other times there may be massive edema (**Figure 110**). Gottron papules arise over bony prominences, particularly the metacarpophalangeal joints, the proximal interphalangeal joints, and/or the distal interphalangeal joints (**Figure 111**). They may also be found overlying the elbows, knees, and/or feet. The lesions consist of slightly elevated, slightly scaly, violaceous papules and plaques.

Several other cutaneous features are characteristic, although not pathognomonic, of dermatomyositis. They include malar erythema, poikiloderma in a photosensitive distribution, violaceous erythema on the extensor surfaces, periungual and cuticular changes, and a diffuse, scaly, erythematous alopecia. Poikiloderma (the combination of atrophy, dyspigmentation, and telangiectasia) may occur on exposed

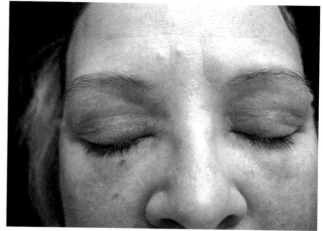

FIGURE 109.
Heliotrope rash in a patient with dermatomyositis.

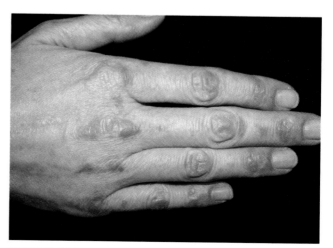

FIGURE 110.
Massive edema accompanied by a heliotrope eruption in a patient with dermatomyositis.

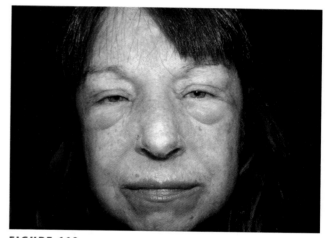

FIGURE 111.
Gottron papules are violaceous, slightly scaly plaques over the bony prominences on the hands.

skin such as the extensor surfaces of the arms, the V of the neck (**Figure 112**), the upper back ("shawl sign"), and/or the upper-lateral thighs ("holster sign") (**Figure 113**). Patients rarely complain of photosensitivity despite the prominent photodistribution of the rash. Nail-fold changes consist of periungual telangiectasia and/or a characteristic cuticular change with hypertrophy of the cuticle and small, hemorrhagic infarcts within this hypertrophic area (**Figure 114**). Scalp involvement in dermatomyositis is relatively common and is manifested by an erythematous to violaceous, psoriasiform dermatitis that is often extremely itchy (**Figure 115**). Nonscarring, diffuse hair loss is common.

Dermatomyositis-sine myositis, also known as amyopathic dermatomyositis, is diagnosed in patients with typical cutaneous disease in whom there is no evidence of muscle weakness and who repeatedly have normal serum muscle enzyme levels. Some patients with amyopathic dermatomyositis will have abnormal imaging studies of muscle.

The association between malignancy and the inflammatory myopathies is well established. Patients with dermatomyositis have a sixfold increase in the development of malignancies. The types of malignancies that develop in patients with inflammatory myopathy correlate with those that develop in an age-matched population, except that ovarian

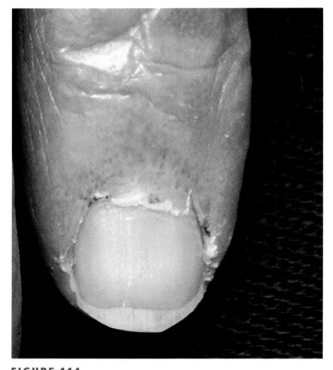

FIGURE 114.
Nail-fold telangiectasia along with cuticular overgrowth in a patient with dermatomyositis.

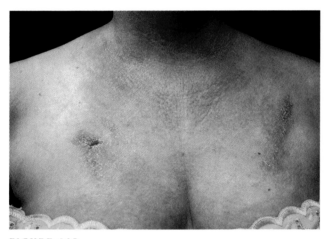

FIGURE 112.
Poikiloderma on the anterior chest in a patient with dermatomyositis.

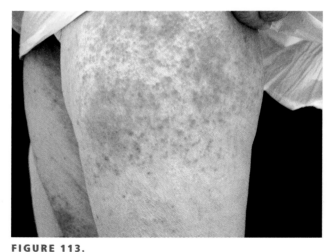

FIGURE 113.
Poikiloderma on the lateral thigh (also known as the "holster sign") in a patient with dermatomyositis.

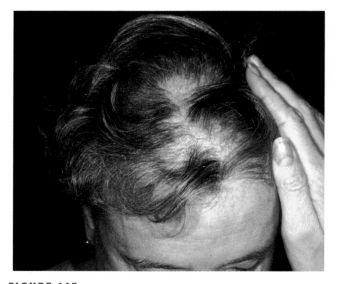

FIGURE 115.
Diffuse alopecia with slight erythema and slight scale in a patient with dermatomyositis.

cancer is more common in patients with inflammatory myopathy. Currently, no generally accepted guidelines exist for malignancy screening in patients with myositis. At minimum, age- and sex-appropriate malignancy screening and chest radiography are recommended for all patients.

Therapy for cutaneous disease in patients with dermatomyositis is often difficult because even though the myositis may respond to treatment with corticosteroids and/or immunosuppressive drugs, the cutaneous lesions often persist.

Most patients with cutaneous lesions are photosensitive; thus, sun avoidance, protective clothing, and the daily use of a broad-spectrum sunscreen with a high sun protective factor are recommended. Topical therapy with a corticosteroid or a nonsteroidal immunomodulator such as tacrolimus ointment or pimecrolimus cream may be useful adjunctive therapy.

Systemic therapies for dermatomyositis that does not respond to first-line topical therapies and sun avoidance consist of hydroxychloroquine, chloroquine, quinacrine, methotrexate, and mycophenolate mofetil. Patients with dermatomyositis have a greater frequency of drug eruptions from antimalarial agents, and patients should be warned about this possibility.

KEY POINTS

- The distinctive cutaneous features of dermatomyositis are the heliotrope rash and Gottron papules.

- Additional cutaneous findings associated with dermatomyositis include malar erythema, poikiloderma in a photosensitive distribution, violaceous erythema on the extensor surfaces, periungual and cuticular changes, and a diffuse, scaly, erythematous alopecia.

- Patients with dermatomyositis have a sixfold increase in the development of malignancies.

- First-line therapy for cutaneous dermatomyositis consists of sun avoidance and sun protection, topical corticosteroids, and topical immunomodulators.

Bibliography

Callen JP. Management of "refractory" skin disease in patients with lupus erythematosus. Best Pract Res Clin Rheumatol. 2005;19(5):767-784. [PMID: 16150402]

Callen JP, Wortmann RL. Dermatomyositis. Clin Dermatol. 2006;24(5):363-373. [PMID: 16966018]

Carlson JA, Cavaliere LF, Grant-Kels JM. Cutaneous vasculitis: diagnosis and management. Clin Dermatol. 2006;24(5):414-429. [PMID: 16966021]

Galossi A, Guarisco R, Bellis L, Puoti C. Extrahepatic manifestations of chronic HCV infection. J Gastrointestin Liver Dis. 2007;16(1):65-73. [PMID: 17410291]

Kasteler JS, Callen JP. Scalp involvement in dermatomyositis. Often overlooked or misdiagnosed. JAMA. 1994;272(24):1939-1941. [PMID: 7990247]

Mert A, Kumbasar H, Ozaras R, et al. Erythema nodosum: an evaluation of 100 cases. Clin Exp Rheumatol. 2007;25(4):563-570. [PMID: 17888212]

Miot HA, Bartoli Miot LD, Haddad GR. Association between discoid lupus erythematosus and cigarette smoking. Dermatology. 2005;211(2):118-122. [PMID: 16088157]

Pitambe HV, Schulz EJ. Life-threatening dermatoses due to metabolic and endocrine disorders. Clin Dermatol. 2005;23(3):258-266. [PMID: 15896541]

Reichrath J, Bens G, Bonowitz A, Tilgen W. Treatment recommendations for pyoderma gangrenosum: an evidence-based review of the literature based on more than 350 patients. J Am Acad Dermatol. 2005;53(2):273-283. [PMID: 16021123]

Saadoun D, Delluc A, Piette JC, Cacoub P. Treatment of hepatitis C-associated mixed cryoglobulinemia vasculitis. Curr Opin Rheumatol. 2008;20(1):23-28. [PMID: 18281853]

Saavedra AP, Kovacs SC, Moschella SL. Neutrophilic dermatoses. Clin Dermatol. 2006;24(6):470-481 [PMID: 17113964]

Thiers BH, Sahn RE, Callen JP. Cutaneous manifestations of internal malignancy. CA Cancer J Clin. 2009;59(2):73-98. [PMID: 19258446]

Selected Dermatologic Emergencies

Stevens-Johnson Syndrome and Toxic Epidermal Necrolysis

Stevens-Johnson syndrome (SJS) and toxic epidermal necrolysis (TEN) are related clinical syndromes that are characterized by acute epidermal necrosis. The classification of SJS and TEN is determined by the percent of body surface area with epidermal detachment: SJS involves less than 10%, SJS/TEN overlap involves 10% to 30%, and TEN involves greater than 30% detachment. Patients may present with SJS that remains localized and is relatively mild, SJS that evolves into TEN, or frank TEN.

Causes

Up to 50% of cases of SJS and up to 80% of cases of TEN are drug related. Drug-associated SJS or TEN typically occurs within 4 to 28 days after initial exposure. The medications most closely associated with SJS and TEN include allopurinol, anticonvulsants (carbamazepine, phenytoin, phenobarbital, and lamotrigine), sulfasalazine, sulfonamide antibiotics, NSAIDs, and nevirapine. Importantly, sulfonamide-related diuretics and sulfonylureas are not significant risk factors for SJS or TEN. Genetic polymorphisms may predispose certain patients to SJS. SJS has also been associated with bacterial, fungal, and viral infections as well as radiation exposure, inflammatory bowel disease, and vaccines. *Mycoplasma pneumoniae* is the most common bacterial cause of SJS, especially in children and young adults, in whom it may cause severe mucosal disease without skin lesions. TEN is rarely associated with infectious causes.

Clinical Manifestations

SJS begins with a prodrome that may include fever, respiratory symptoms, headache, vomiting, and/or diarrhea, followed 1 to 14 days later by the onset of cutaneous lesions and involvement of two or more mucous membranes. Patients often have both skin and mucosal involvement, but mucosa alone may be affected. Individual skin lesions appear as annular erythematous macules or papules, often with a dusky center and rim of bright erythema (targetoid lesions), that may progress to papules or plaques with central bullae (**Figure 116**). The level of skin involvement in patients with SJS can range from a few discrete lesions to multiple coalescing lesions that rapidly progress to epidermal necrosis and sloughing, leaving behind moist, erythematous, exposed dermis. Erythema, crusting, or erosions can occur on any mucosal surface, including nasal, oral, tracheal, conjunctival, urethral, and anal mucosa. Hemorrhagic crusting of the oral mucosa is particularly characteristic of SJS (**Figure 117**). Patients typically are febrile and toxic appearing, and lymphadenopathy is often present. Arthralgia, hepatitis, myocarditis, nephritis, and

pneumonia may occur. The course of SJS ranges from 4 to 6 weeks, and the mortality rate ranges from 1% to 5%.

TEN typically begins with a prodrome of fever, sore throat, or a burning sensation in the eyes 1 to 3 days before skin lesions appear. Skin findings may be characterized by flat, atypical, purpuric, targetoid lesions that coalesce into dusky, poorly demarcated, confluent patches (TEN "with spots") or may consist of confluent, tender erythema without identifiable individual lesions (TEN "without spots"). The involved epidermis blisters and sloughs, leaving behind denuded dermis (**Figure 118**). The Nikolsky sign, in which lateral pressure on erythematous skin shears off the skin, is often present but is not pathognomonic for TEN. The mucous membranes are often involved, but this is not required to make the diagnosis. The prognosis for TEN can be determined by a severity-of-illness score called the SCORTEN (**Table 29**). The mortality rate of patients with TEN ranges from 25% to 35%.

Diagnosis and Management

The evaluation of patients with suspected SJS or TEN begins with a thorough history, which includes medications (including over-the-counter NSAIDs), allergies, and family history of adverse cutaneous drug eruptions. A complete examination of the skin and mucous membranes should be performed. Abnormal laboratory findings may include an elevated erythrocyte sedimentation rate, electrolyte abnormalities, elevated serum aminotransferase levels, leukocytosis, eosinophilia, anemia, proteinuria, and microscopic hematuria.

The diagnosis of SJS or TEN is usually made clinically, but a skin biopsy, possibly with frozen sections, can confirm the diagnosis. The prognosis of patients with SJS or TEN improves with early diagnosis and removal of the offending agent.

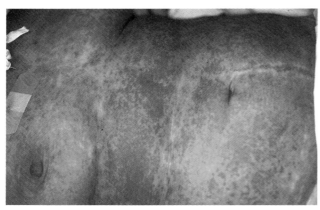

FIGURE 116.
Confluent, targetoid, erythematous papules and plaques with dusky centers in a patient with Stevens-Johnson syndrome.

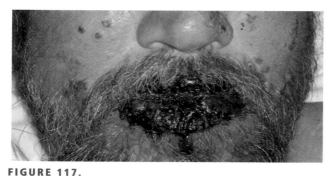

FIGURE 117.
Hemorrhagic crusting of the lips in a patient with Stevens-Johnson syndrome. Similar crusting was also found on the eyes.

Courtesy of Dr. Toby Maurer and Dr. Kieron Leslie.

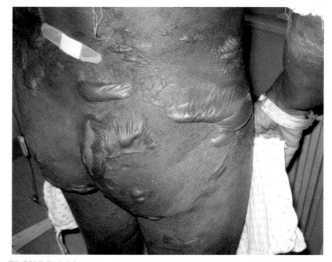

FIGURE 118.
Confluent erythema, bullae, and full-thickness epidermal sloughing of skin (note pink dermis) in a patient with toxic epidermal necrolysis.

Courtesy of Dr. Toby Maurer and Dr. Kieron Leslie.

TABLE 29 SCORTEN Severity-of-Illness Score for the Prognosis of Toxic Epidermal Necrolysis

Criteria*	
1. Age >40 years	
2. Presence of malignancy	
3. Blood urea nitrogen >27 mg/dL (9.64 mmol/L)	
4. Plasma glucose >252 mg/dL (13.99 mmol/L)	
5. Pulse rate >120/min	
6. Serum bicarbonate <20 meq/L (20 mmol/L)	
7. Involvement of >10% body surface area	

Points	Mortality Rate
0-1	3.2%
2	12.1%
3	35.3%
4	58.3%
≥5	90.0%

*One point is assigned for each criterion.

Data from Bastuji-Garin S, Fouchard N, Bertocchi M, Roujeau JC, Revuz J, Wolkenstein P. SCORTEN: a severity-of-illness score for toxic epidermal necrolysis. J Invest Dermatol. 2000;115(2):149-153. [PMID: 10951229]

The appropriate management for SJS/TEN consists of prompt discontinuation of suspected causative medications and supportive care. Many patients with SJS and all patients with TEN should be managed in a hospital setting, ideally an intensive care burn unit. Patients should receive meticulous wound care, management of fluids and electrolytes, nutritional support, and monitoring and treatment of superinfections. Because the epidermal barrier is severely compromised, death in patients with SJS or TEN usually is caused by infection. Appropriate antibiotics should be administered when infection is suspected; however, there is no role for prophylactic antibiotics in SJS or TEN because the goal is to minimize medication exposures. Because ocular involvement can be a source of major morbidity, patients with SJS and TEN should be monitored by an ophthalmologist. Gynecologic evaluation is also appropriate for women, who may experience sloughing of the vulvar and vaginal mucosa. No controlled randomized clinical trials have identified an ideal therapy for SJS or TEN. The use of corticosteroids in SJS/TEN is controversial, as their use may be associated with an increased risk of infection; however, many practicing dermatologists use corticosteroids as part of the management of SJS or TEN. Accumulating data suggest that intravenous immune globulin may halt epidermal necrosis and decrease overall mortality, especially in the setting of TEN, when administered early in the course of the disease and in adequate doses (greater than 2 g/kg total dose).

KEY POINTS

- Stevens-Johnson syndrome and toxic epidermal necrolysis are related clinical syndromes that are characterized by acute epidermal necrosis and are most often caused by reaction to a medication.

- The medications most closely associated with Stevens-Johnson syndrome and toxic epidermal necrolysis include allopurinol, anticonvulsants (carbamazepine, phenytoin, phenobarbital, and lamotrigine), sulfasalazine, sulfonamide antibiotics, NSAIDs, and nevirapine.

- An intensive care burn unit is the ideal setting for the management of many patients with Stevens-Johnson syndrome and all patients with toxic epidermal necrolysis.

- The treatment of Stevens-Johnson syndrome and toxic epidermal necrolysis is primarily supportive; the role of corticosteroids and intravenous immune globulin is controversial, and there is no role for prophylactic antibiotics.

Erythroderma

Erythroderma is defined as redness and scaling of more than 90% of the body surface area. It primarily affects middle-aged men. In at least 50% of affected patients, erythroderma is the result of slow (months to years) evolution, often of a known cutaneous disease such as atopic dermatitis, psoriasis, or cutaneous T-cell lymphoma. Evolution over a shorter (days- to weeks-long) period may occur as a result of drug eruptions, pityriasis rubra pilaris, pemphigus foliaceus, and pustular psoriasis.

Causes

The most common causes of erythroderma are drug eruptions, psoriasis, atopic dermatitis, and cutaneous T-cell lymphoma; up to 47% of cases are idiopathic (**Figure 119**). The diagnosis of idiopathic erythroderma is one of exclusion. Adult onset of atopic dermatitis in a person without a personal or family history of atopy is rare; caution should be used when making this diagnosis because cutaneous T-cell lymphoma can also present with a similar widespread dermatitis or erythroderma. Patients with a history of psoriasis who are treated with systemic corticosteroids, often for another condition, may develop a widespread erythrodermic or pustular flare when the corticosteroids are discontinued. This is considered a medical emergency.

Included in the differential diagnosis of erythroderma are conditions that cause widespread erythema without diffuse scaling, such as staphylococcal scalded skin syndrome, staphylococcal toxic shock syndrome, streptococcal toxic shock syndrome, Kawasaki disease, and early toxic epidermal necrolysis.

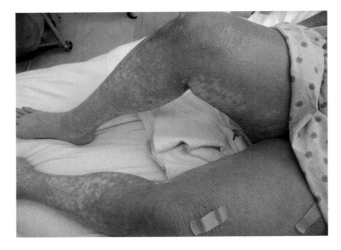

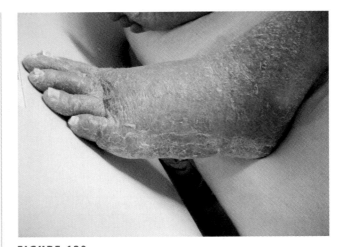

FIGURE 120.
Typical erythema and scale with overlying honey-crusting in a patient with erythroderma and *Staphylococcus aureus* secondary infection.

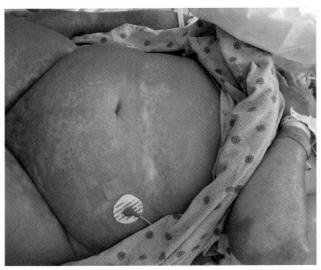

FIGURE 119.
Erythroderma due to drug hypersensitivity.

Diagnosis and Management

Most patients with erythroderma experience severe pruritus, and approximately 50% of patients will have lymphadenopathy. All patients with erythroderma have the potential for systemic complications including hypo- or hyperthermia, edema, intravascular fluid loss, tachycardia, high-output heart failure, and bacterial superinfection, primarily with *Staphylococcus aureus* (**Figure 120**).

It is often difficult to determine the underlying cause of erythroderma during the acute phase. Clinical clues to the diagnosis of the most common causes of erythroderma appear in **Table 30**. Alopecia, nail dystrophy, ectropion, and thickening of the palms and soles suggest that the erythroderma is longstanding. The presence of lymphadenopathy should prompt an excisional lymph node biopsy if lymphoma is suspected.

Laboratory findings are nonspecific but may demonstrate leukocytosis, anemia, eosinophilia, lymphocytosis, an increased erythrocyte sedimentation rate, an elevated serum creatinine level, and a low serum protein level. Imaging of the chest, abdomen, and pelvis is often performed when the underlying cause of erythroderma is not obvious and lymphoma is suspected. Skin biopsy with routine hematoxylin and eosin staining should be performed in every patient with erythroderma; however, histopathologic findings diagnostic of the underlying cause are present in only 50% of patients. If the initial biopsy is negative, repeated biopsies may be useful and are recommended.

All patients with erythroderma should receive supportive hospital care, which includes close monitoring of fluids and electrolytes, nutrition, hypothermia, and bacterial superinfection. Intensive topical care with emollients, topical corticosteroids, and oral antihistamines is often used to control pruritus. Systemic corticosteroids or other immunosuppressants may be required, but these should be used with caution under the supervision of a dermatologist. Treatment should be aimed at the underlying disease, once identified.

KEY POINTS

- Erythroderma is characterized by redness and scaling of more than 90% of the body surface area; approximately 50% of affected patients will have lymphadenopathy.

- The most common causes of erythroderma are drug eruptions, psoriasis, atopic dermatitis, and cutaneous T-cell lymphoma; up to 47% of cases are idiopathic.

- Treatment of erythroderma is aimed at the underlying disease once it is identified.

- Patients with a history of psoriasis who are treated with systemic corticosteroids may develop a widespread pustular flare when the corticosteroids are discontinued.

TABLE 30 Clinical Clues to the Diagnosis of Selected Causes of Erythroderma

Cause	History	Physical Examination Findings	Laboratory Findings
Atopic dermatitis	Personal or family history of atopic dermatitis, allergic rhinitis, or asthma; preexisting skin lesions; severe pruritus	Lichenification	Eosinophilia; elevated serum IgE level
Psoriasis	Personal or family history of psoriasis; preexisting psoriatic skin lesions; history of corticosteroid withdrawal	Nail pitting, oil droplet sign, onycholysis; psoriatic arthritis	Skin biopsy may be diagnostic
Cutaneous T-cell lymphoma/Sézary syndrome	Slowly progressive; extreme, intractable pruritus	Lymphadenopathy; painful, fissured keratoderma; alopecia; leonine facies	Peripheral blood smear with >20% Sézary cells; clonal T-cell population in skin, blood, and/or lymph node
Hypersensitivity drug eruption	Onset 3-6 weeks after start of a new medication; most common causative medications are allopurinol, aromatic anticonvulsants, dapsone, NSAIDs, sulfonamides, lamotrigine	Facial edema; cervical lymphadenopathy; fine scale around nose; hepatosplenomegaly	Leukocytosis with eosinophilia or atypical lymphocytosis; elevated serum aminotransferases; elevated blood urea nitrogen or serum creatinine levels

Bibliography

Akhyani M, Ghodsi ZS, Toosi S, Dabbaghian H. Erythroderma: a clinical study of 97 cases. BMC Dermatol. 2005;5:5. [PMID: 15882451]

French LE. Toxic epidermal necrolysis and Stevens Johnson syndrome: our current understanding. Allergol Int. 2006;55(1):9-16. [PMID: 17075281]

Mockenhaupt M, Viboud C, Dunant A, et al. Stevens-Johnson syndrome and toxic epidermal necrolysis: assessment of medication risks with emphasis on recently marketed drugs. The EuroSCAR study. J Invest Dermatol. 2008;128(1):35-44. [PMID: 17805350]

Rothe MJ, Bernstein ML, Grant-Kels JM. Life-threatening erythroderma: diagnosing and treating the "red man." Clin Dermatol. 2005;23(2):206-217. [PMID: 15802214]

Alopecia

Overview

Alopecia consists of generalized or patchy hair loss, usually from the scalp, but it occurs at other sites as well. The initial step in the evaluation is to determine if hair loss is scarring or nonscarring. In nonscarring alopecia, the follicular openings are preserved, whereas they are lost in scarring alopecia.

Nonscarring Alopecia

Patient history and physical examination are sufficient to establish the cause of most cases of nonscarring alopecia. A few inexpensive laboratory tests, such as thyroid-stimulating hormone measurement and iron studies, may be necessary, but extensive panels of endocrine studies are seldom of any clinical value. The most common causes of nonscarring alopecia are alopecia areata, trichorrhexis nodosa, pattern alopecia, telogen effluvium, and tinea capitis (see Common Skin and Nail Infections).

Alopecia Areata

Patients with alopecia areata have well-defined, round, smooth areas of hair loss (**Figure 121**). Short, fractured, exclamation-point hairs may be visible at the periphery. Easily extracted hairs at the periphery demonstrate a tapered "pencil-point" fracture. Nail pitting is often present.

Alopecia areata is an autoimmune disorder, but screening for other autoimmune disorders is only necessary in the presence of suggestive signs or symptoms. The major differential diagnosis is syphilis, which commonly presents with

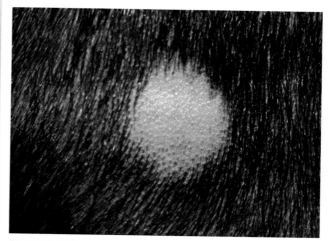

FIGURE 121.
A well-defined, round, smooth area of hair loss with preserved follicular openings in a patient with alopecia areata.

patchy, "moth-eaten" alopecia and a generalized papulosquamous rash that also involves the palms and soles.

Local patches of alopecia areata respond to intralesional injections of triamcinolone. An occasional patient will respond to potent topical corticosteroids, but scalp atrophy and depigmentation may result. Further information is available from the National Alopecia Areata Foundation (www.naaf.org).

Trichorrhexis Nodosa

Trichorrhexis nodosa (fracture of the hair shaft) is common in black patients who straighten their hair. A hair with a broomlike, pigmented end is diagnostic of trichorrhexis nodosa. Patches of dense, short hairs with normal follicular density are typical of trichorrhexis nodosa.

Patients with trichorrhexis nodosa will regrow healthy hair if gentle hair-care practices are adopted.

Pattern Alopecia

Pattern alopecia presents with hair thinning on the crown or recession in the area of the temples. In men, pattern alopecia may be treated with 2% to 5% topical minoxidil or oral finasteride.

Women with pattern alopecia present with hair thinning of the crown, a frontal hairline that is preserved, and a part that is distinctly wider anteriorly (**Figure 122**). They respond best to topical minoxidil. Finasteride is of no benefit to the majority of women with pattern alopecia and is a pregnancy risk category X drug. Oral antiandrogens such as spironolactone may be effective. Women with temporal recession or frank virilization require an endocrine evaluation for polycystic ovary syndrome.

Telogen Effluvium

Telogen effluvium presents as a sudden increase in shedding of hairs with white bulbs, usually 3 to 5 months after a period of stress, such as a crash diet, serious illness, surgery, or childbirth. Seborrheic dermatitis, psoriasis, iron deficiency, and thyroid disease may also cause telogen effluvium.

KEY POINTS

- Alopecia areata typically presents with round patches of smooth alopecia without scarring, with exclamation-point hairs and tapered fractures.
- Trichorrhexis nodosa is characterized by hairs with broomlike, pigmented ends and patches of dense, short hairs with normal follicular density.
- Pattern alopecia in men presents with hair thinning on the crown or recession in the area of the temples; women with pattern alopecia present with hair thinning of the crown, a frontal hairline that is preserved, and a part that is distinctly wider anteriorly.

Scarring Alopecia

Scarring alopecia is characterized by patches of hair loss with no visible follicular openings (**Figure 123**). Scarring alopecia begins with erythema at the base of the hairs and evolves to clusters of hairs ("doll's hair") emerging from an inflammatory base. It results in permanent hair loss. Progression is often slow but without appropriate treatment will result in permanent scarring. A scalp biopsy is generally required to establish the diagnosis. Patients with scarring alopecia should be referred to a dermatologist.

KEY POINT

- Scarring alopecia is characterized by patches of hair loss with no visible follicular openings.

FIGURE 123.
Scarring alopecia with no visible follicular openings.

Bibliography

Dinh QQ, Sinclair R. Female pattern hair loss: current treatment concepts. Clin Interv Aging. 2007;2(2):189-199. [PMID: 18044135]

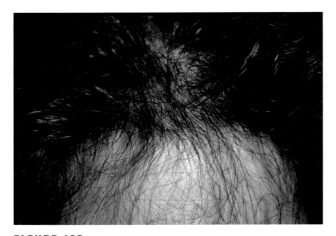

FIGURE 122.
Pattern alopecia in a female patient, characterized by a frontal hairline that is preserved and a part that is distinctly wider anteriorly.

Otberg N, Wu WY, McElwee KJ, Shapiro J. Diagnosis and management of primary cicatricial alopecia: part I. Skinmed. 2008;7(1):19-26. [PMID: 18174797]

Sperling LC. Hair and systemic disease. Dermatol Clin. 2001;19(4):711-726. [PMID: 11705356]

Leg Ulcers

Overview

Leg ulcers are common in patients with diabetes mellitus, peripheral artery disease, lymphedema, and venous stasis. Some leg ulcers have mixed causes, but the vast majority can be classified as venous (stasis), neuropathic, or arterial (ischemic).

Venous Stasis Ulcers

Venous stasis ulcers are associated with chronic venous insufficiency and typically occur on the medial aspect of the lower leg, especially near the medial malleolus overlying a perforating vein (**Figure 124**). These ulcers are irregularly shaped, tender, and shallow with a red base that may occasionally be purulent. Ulcers may be single or multiple, but they do not occur on the foot or above the knee. Accompanying signs of venous insufficiency include edema and hemosiderin staining, which results in a copper to brown coloration of the skin. Skin affected by chronic stasis dermatitis may be thickened and sclerotic, a condition known as lipodermatosclerosis. Patients with severe pain usually also suffer from segmental hyalinizing vasculopathy and demonstrate reticulated areas of white scarring (atrophie blanche).

Venous stasis ulcers respond to compression, and compression may be the essential element in healing. There are no randomized controlled trials of compression therapy, but cohort studies suggest that healing is more likely to occur and

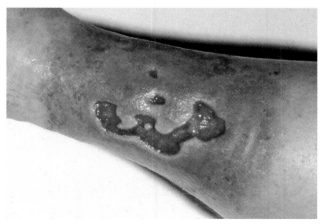

FIGURE 124.
Venous stasis ulcers are typically minimally symptomatic and occur on the medial side of the lower leg in areas of hyperpigmentation.

at a greater rate among patients compliant with compression therapy. Two types of compression devices are available, elastic (stockings) and inelastic. The zinc-oxide–impregnated paste bandage (Unna boot) is an example of an inelastic compression system. High compression is more effective than low compression, but arterial disease should be excluded prior to initiating compression therapy. Dressings are important to protect the wound and provide a moist environment for wound healing. A systematic review of multiple dressing types found no difference in healing rates among the various dressings used. Hydrocolloid or foam dressings are most often used to cover the ulcer and can be applied beneath elastic dressings and under an Unna boot, and a mid- to high-potency corticosteroid ointment can be applied to surrounding skin if there is associated stasis dermatitis. Oral, rather than topical, antibiotics should be used if there is any suggestion of infection, as there is a significant risk of developing allergic contact dermatitis to topical antibiotics used in this setting. The boot is typically changed weekly. Healing occurs over a course of weeks to months. Mechanical compression pumps can be helpful if severe edema is present. Refractory ulcers may benefit from pentoxifylline. Some patients benefit from surgical treatment of incompetent vessels, although this is not needed in the majority of patients; evaluation by a vascular surgeon is appropriate, particularly if there appears to be involvement of the deep venous system. All patients should wear elastic compression hose following healing of the ulcer. Two pairs of knee-high stockings providing at least 20 mm Hg of pressure should be supplied and should be replaced every 3 to 6 months.

KEY POINTS

- Venous stasis ulcers are associated with chronic venous insufficiency and typically occur on the medial aspect of the lower leg, especially over the medial malleolus.
- Venous stasis ulcers should be treated with compression.

Neuropathic Ulcers

Neuropathic ulcers occur in insensate limbs. The usual patient with a neuropathic ulcer has diabetes mellitus and severe peripheral neuropathy (see MKSAP 15 Endocrinology and Metabolism). As a result, the ulcers are usually asymptomatic except for associated diabetic paresthesia. Neuropathic ulcers occur primarily over the plantar aspects of the foot, especially in the region of the metatarsal heads (**Figure 125**). Thick surrounding hyperkeratosis is typically present. The ulcers are usually much deeper and wider than their surface appearance suggests. If not recognized promptly and managed properly, associated osteomyelitis can lead to amputation (see MKSAP 15 Infectious Disease).

Management usually requires assessment of infection, including the possibility of osteomyelitis, assessment of

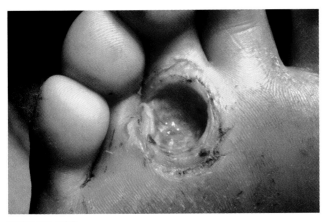

FIGURE 125.
Neuropathic ulcers have a hyperkeratotic rim and occur over pressure points such as the metatarsal heads.

vascular supply, and debridement of necrotic tissue followed by offloading of pressure, usually by means of total-contact casting.

KEY POINTS
- Neuropathic ulcers occur primarily over the plantar aspects of the foot and are common in patients with diabetes mellitus and severe peripheral neuropathy.
- Management of neuropathic ulcers requires debridement of necrotic tissue followed by offloading of pressure.

Arterial Ulcers

Arterial ulcers (also called ischemic ulcers) are the result of severe peripheral vascular disease and are typically located on the most distal portions of the extremities (**Figure 126**). They commonly overlie bony prominences that are subject to trauma or pressure. The surrounding skin is typically red, taut,

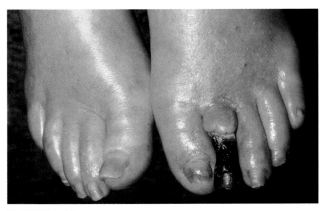

FIGURE 126.
Arterial ulcers are intensely painful and occur on the distal portions of the extremities.

and atrophic. Skin markings and hair are absent, pulses are difficult to palpate, and capillary refill is poor. The ulcer may appear punched-out or stellate, and a black or yellow eschar may be present. Pain is typically severe and worsens when the leg is elevated.

An ankle-brachial index below 0.6 suggests arterial compromise. Infarction of the toes and livedo reticularis suggest the possibility of cholesterol embolization (**Figure 127**). Renal function should be assessed in a patient with these findings, as emboli commonly involve the kidneys.

Patients with ischemic ulcers should be evaluated by a vascular surgeon. For those who are not candidates for revascularization, slow healing may be possible with gentle debridement and moist wound care. Infection should be treated if present.

KEY POINTS
- Arterial ulcers are the result of severe peripheral vascular disease and are typically located on the most distal portions of the extremities and over pressure points.
- Patients with arterial ulcers should be referred to a vascular surgeon for evaluation of their potential for revascularization.

Nonhealing Ulcers

Nonhealing ulcers suggest the possibility of invasive infection, leukocytoclastic vasculitis, or squamous cell carcinoma. Other reasons for nonhealing may be related to an incomplete treatment plan (inadequate pressure, elevation, dressings) or patient noncompliance. Refractory ulcers or those with an atypical appearance should be biopsied. Diseases as diverse as squamous cell carcinoma, pyoderma gangrenosum, rheumatoid

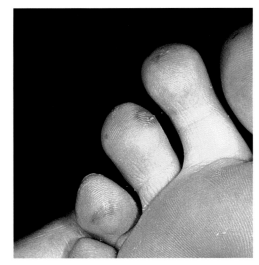

FIGURE 127.
Cholesterol embolization typically presents with distal infarctive lesions. The limb typically demonstrates livedo reticularis.

vasculitis, thrombotic disorders, and prolidase deficiency may present with nonhealing leg ulcers. Nutritional deficiency may compromise wound healing.

Systemic antibiotics are indicated only if the ulcer is clinically infected. Signs and symptoms of infection include pain or increasing tenderness, a foul smell, purulent drainage, necrosis, spreading redness, warmth, and induration. Refractory ulcers may benefit from pentoxifylline. A systematic review of 11 trials concluded that pentoxifylline was more effective for complete or partial venous ulcer healing than placebo or no treatment and was most effective when used in conjunction with compression. Several growth factors, including platelet-derived growth factor, epidermal growth factor, fibroblast growth factors, transforming growth factors, and insulin-like growth factors, have been used to treat refractory ulcers. The few randomized clinical trials that have assessed their efficacy have generally found conflicting results. The use of growth factors is expensive and not without risk. Postmarketing studies have recently identified an increased risk of cancer mortality in patients who have used three or more tubes of becaplermin gel, and caution is advised in using it in patients with known malignancy. Based on uncontrolled trials and expert opinion, skin grafting and skin substitutes can be of benefit in refractory ulcers.

KEY POINTS

- Nonhealing ulcers or those with an atypical appearance should be biopsied.

- Systemic antibiotics should be reserved for clinically infected ulcers.

- Pentoxifylline, when combined with compression, may aid in the resolution of venous ulcers.

Bibliography

Fonder MA, Lazarus GS, Cowan DA, Aronson-Cook B, Kohli AR, Mamelak AJ. Treating the chronic wound: a practical approach to the care of nonhealing wounds and wound care dressings. J Am Acad Dermatol. 2008;58(2):185-206. [PMID: 18222318]

Jones JE, Nelson EA. Skin grafting for venous leg ulcers. Cochrane Database Syst Rev. 2007;(2):CD001737. [PMID: 17443510]

Khan MN, Davies CG. Advances in the management of leg ulcers—the potential role of growth factors. Int Wound J. 2006;3(2):113-120. [PMID: 17007341]

Marston W. Evaluation and treatment of leg ulcers associated with chronic venous insufficiency. Clin Plast Surg. 2007;34(4):717-730. [PMID: 17967625]

Special Populations

Skin in Elderly Patients

As the skin ages, it thins and loses moisture and elasticity. Elderly patients tend to have dry and flaky skin, particularly on the lower extremities. Loss of elasticity coupled with a loss of subcutaneous tissues leads to sagging skin. Much of what is considered "aging" in the skin, however, is actually the result of chronic sun damage, or photoaging (**Figure 128**). Common features of aged and sun-damaged skin are listed in **Table 31**. Aged skin is less able to regulate temperature, maintain hydration, and repair damage. Sebum and sweat production decrease. Immune responsiveness declines, as does vitamin D production.

Common Clinical Problems of Aging Skin

Xerosis (dry skin) is one of the most common causes of pruritus in older persons. Because the skin is fragile, lacerations occur easily, and wound healing may be prolonged or complicated by the development of ulcers. Certain cutaneous infections occur with increased frequency in the elderly, notably varicella zoster, and many older persons have chronic onychomycosis and tinea pedis. A variety of benign and

FIGURE 128.
Photoaged skin with accentuated wrinkles, telangiectasia, and yellowish discoloration from degeneration of elastin in the skin.

TABLE 31 Common Skin Findings of Aged Versus Photoaged Skin

Intrinsic Aging	Photoaging
Thinning of skin	Accentuated wrinkling
Thinned epidermis	Coarse furrows
Loss of subcutaneous fat	Fine wrinkles
Fine wrinkles	Irregular pigmentation
Dry, flaky skin	Diffuse pigmentation; "bronzing"
Loss of elasticity	
Skin pallor	Lentigenes
Decreased skin temperature	Pebbly texture of skin (elastosis)
Loss of hair	Solar purpura
Graying of hair	Telangiectasia
Development of seborrheic keratoses, cherry angiomas	Venous lakes
	Comedones
	Actinic keratoses, skin cancers

malignant tumors appear as patients age. Nevi involute and may disappear completely by the sixth or seventh decade of life. Seborrheic keratoses, cherry angiomas, and lentigenes begin to develop in middle age and increase over time (**Figure 129**). Solar or actinic purpura occurs frequently in individuals who have extensive photodamage of the skin. Minimal trauma, which may or may not have been recognized, causes large, asymptomatic ecchymoses. Drug reactions are more common in elderly persons, likely because of increased exposure. This may also be due to decreased drug clearance or altered metabolism.

Management of Aging Skin

Gentle skin care with regular use of emollients should be recommended to all older persons to help maintain skin hydration and barrier integrity.

Sun protection is important even in older adults, because cumulative sun damage continues to accrue. Many cosmeceutical products are available to treat photodamaged skin, and their beneficial effects (and prices) vary widely. Generally, products that contain retinol or α-hydroxy or β-hydroxy acids may have some beneficial effects. Topical tretinoin reduces fine wrinkles and other evidence of sun damage and is U.S. Food and Drug Administration–approved for the treatment of wrinkling; however, insurance companies and Medicare rarely cover its use for what is considered cosmetic purposes.

Decreased estrogen levels after menopause are thought to contribute to many age-related skin changes in women. Use of hormone therapy and selective estrogen receptor modulators may improve skin elasticity and decrease wrinkling. However, the U.S. Preventive Services Task Force recommends against the use of estrogen or estrogen plus progestin for the prevention of chronic diseases after menopause because of the increase in cardiovascular disease and cancer risk. Cigarette smoking exacerbates wrinkling, particularly in women.

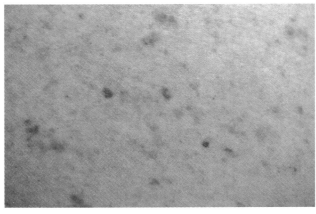

FIGURE 129.
Seborrheic keratoses (waxy tan to brown, "stuck-on"–appearing papules) and cherry angiomas (nonblanchable, pink to red, small papules) are frequently seen together on the chest and back of older patients.

Dermatologic Diseases of Immunosuppressed Patients

Skin Diseases in HIV

Since the advent of antiretroviral therapy, the incidence of many skin diseases that were once common in HIV-positive patients (such as seborrheic dermatitis, fungal infections, psoriasis, and cutaneous manifestations of opportunistic infections) has decreased. However, patients with a CD4 cell count less than 200/μL who are not on antiretroviral therapy commonly have psoriasis, photodermatitis, prurigo nodularis, molluscum contagiosum, and drug reactions. In all of these conditions, initiation of antiretroviral therapy can lead to dramatic improvement.

Psoriasis in patients with a low CD4 cell count can be severe, affect more than 50% of the body surface area, and present in an atypical fashion (more severe, explosive onset) (**Figure 130**). Treatment includes antiretroviral therapy, topical corticosteroids, and acitretin.

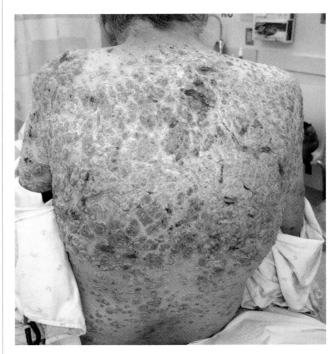

FIGURE 130.
Widespread, coalescing, erythematous plaques with overlying adherent scale of psoriasis in a patient with HIV infection.

Photodermatitis in patients with HIV infection may be caused by the virus itself and concomitant administration of photosensitizing medications. Treatment consists of sunscreen, high-potency topical corticosteroids, emollients, and antihistamines.

Pruritus in HIV infection may be the result of skin disorders common in HIV (xerosis, scabies, psoriasis), secondary to internal disease (lymphoma), or a manifestation of early infection. Eosinophilic folliculitis is also found in advanced HIV disease and is characterized by recurrent, pruritic crops of 3- to 5-mm red papules centered around hair follicles found primarily on the scalp, face, neck, and upper chest. Treatment includes high-potency topical corticosteroids and sometimes thalidomide.

Molluscum contagiosum (see Common Skin and Nail Infections) can be very severe in patients with low CD4 cell counts. First-line treatment is antiretroviral therapy. Imiquimod and cidofovir have been used off-label to treat widespread or recalcitrant disease.

Drug reactions are very common in patients with CD4 cell counts less than 50/µL.

A subset of HIV-associated skin diseases does not improve with antiretroviral therapy. These include eczema, xerosis, warts, and Kaposi sarcoma. With the use of antiretroviral therapy, the presentation of Kaposi sarcoma has changed from large violaceous or plum-colored plaques to more subtle purple patches (**Figure 131**). Despite favorable CD4 cell counts (>300/µL) and low viral loads, Kaposi sarcoma persists in the HIV-positive patient population.

KEY POINTS

- In patients with HIV infection, initiation of antiretroviral therapy can lead to dramatic improvement in psoriasis, photodermatitis, prurigo nodularis, molluscum contagiosum, and drug reactions.

- Eczema, xerosis, warts, and Kaposi sarcoma that are associated with HIV infection do not improve with antiretroviral therapy.

Skin Diseases in Hematopoietic Stem Cell Transplant and Organ Transplant Recipients

The most common skin diseases in the transplant population are infections or malignancy. Infections that are increased in patients who have undergone transplantation include herpes simplex, warts, herpes zoster, and superficial fungal infections with *Candida, Malassezia,* and dermatophytes (*Trichophyton* species). Also important to recognize are disseminated fungal infections with organisms such as *Candida, Aspergillus, Fusarium,* and fungi of the Zygomycetes class. When these infections disseminate to the skin, they most commonly present as purpuric papules and/or nodules (**Figure 132**). Disseminated fungal infection should be suspected in any febrile, neutropenic patient with purpuric skin lesions who fails to respond to broad-spectrum antibiotics and antiviral

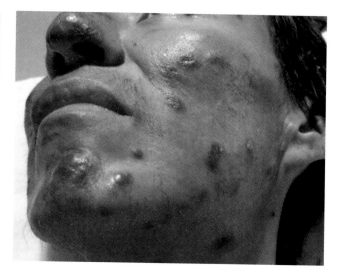

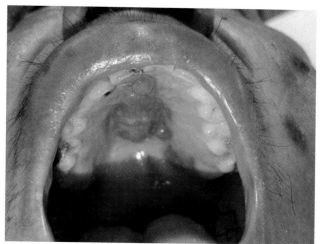

FIGURE 131.
Kaposi sarcoma, presenting as firm purple nodules in a patient with HIV infection *(top)*. Purple palatal nodules of Kaposi sarcoma in a patient with HIV infection *(bottom)*.

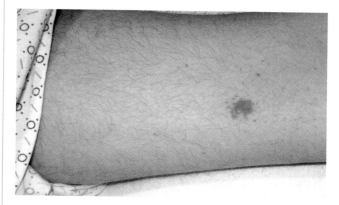

FIGURE 132.
Purpuric nodule as the presenting sign of disseminated candidiasis in a patient with acute lymphoblastic leukemia.

agents. A skin biopsy for routine histology, special stains for fungal organisms, and culture will aid in the diagnosis.

The incidence of cutaneous malignancies is increasing dramatically as patients survive longer after solid-organ transplantation. The incidence of squamous cell carcinoma, basal cell carcinoma, melanoma, and Kaposi sarcoma has increased significantly in this patient population (see MKSAP 15 Hematology and Oncology). The risk of developing skin cancers increases with time from transplantation. These skin cancers are more likely to be multiple, occur at a younger age, and behave more aggressively with a significantly increased risk of metastasis and death. Treatment for individual lesions is surgical excision. Overall risk reduction can be achieved through reduction of immunosuppression and use of oral retinoids (off label).

KEY POINTS

- The most common skin diseases in the transplant population are infections or malignancy.
- Skin cancers in organ-transplant patients are common, behave aggressively, and have a significantly increased risk of metastasis and death.

Dermatologic Diseases in Skin of Color

Patients with darker skin color are predisposed to develop a number of diseases at a higher frequency or with greater severity and impact on quality of life than those with lighter pigmentation. Abnormalities of pigmentation are common problems.

Postinflammatory Hyper- and Hypopigmentation

As the skin in patients with darker skin color recovers from an acute inflammatory disease such as an acne lesion, it may become hyperpigmented (known as postinflammatory hyperpigmentation) (**Figure 133**). The time required for the area of postinflammatory hyperpigmentation to fade to normal skin color is highly variable and relates to the patient's normal skin tone and the intensity and type of inflammation. Postinflammatory hyperpigmentation may take months or sometimes years to recover and can be psychologically distressing. Treatment with peeling agents such as glycolic or salicylic acid or with bleaching agents such as hydroquinone may help; however, they do not always result in the desired improvement.

Certain conditions may lighten the skin as they resolve. Discoid lupus erythematosus frequently causes scarring and hypopigmentation, as can seborrheic dermatitis, tinea versicolor, atopic dermatitis, and sarcoidosis. In scarred areas, the pigment alteration may be permanent; however, postinflammatory hypopigmentation generally recovers more

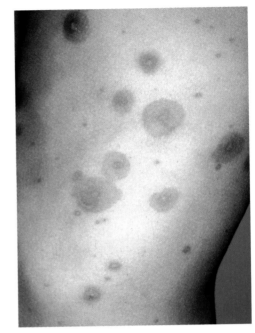

FIGURE 133.
Postinflammatory hyperpigmentation may occur in patients with darker skin color as skin recovers from an acute inflammatory disease, such as an acne lesion.

quickly without treatment than does postinflammatory hyperpigmentation.

Vitiligo

Vitiligo is characterized by depigmentation, which is a complete absence of color (**Figure 134**). White macules are most frequently found on the face, genitals, and dorsal hands and are often bilaterally symmetric in distribution. Vitiligo affects between 0.1% and 2% of the population and is most common in children or young adults. It has no racial or ethnic predisposition; however, the social and psychological impact is most devastating in patients of color. Loss of pigment results from death of melanocytes in the affected skin. It is likely due to a

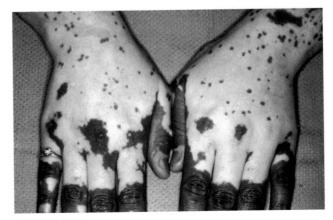

FIGURE 134.
Vitiligo in a black patient, characterized by absence of color.

cellular autoimmune response, and associations with other autoimmune diseases (particularly those of the thyroid) are common. Hashimoto thyroiditis, Graves disease, diabetes mellitus, alopecia areata, pernicious anemia, and rheumatoid arthritis are seen with increased frequency in patients with vitiligo. The skin disease often occurs before the associated endocrinopathy. Vitiligo is most commonly treated with topical corticosteroids, topical immunomodulators, or phototherapy.

KEY POINTS

- Vitiligo is characterized by depigmentation that is usually found on the face, genitals, and dorsal hands, usually in a bilaterally symmetric distribution.

- Vitiligo may precede the appearance of Hashimoto thyroiditis, Graves disease, diabetes mellitus, alopecia areata, pernicious anemia, and rheumatoid arthritis.

Disorders of Skin Appendages

Because black patients' hair may be tightly coiled, shaving may result in ingrown hairs; these can lead to inflammatory papules and pustules that may cause keloids. Abnormalities of hair, such as pseudofolliculitis barbae, acne keloidalis nuchae, and central centrifugal scarring alopecia, are particularly prevalent and distressing. Pseudofolliculitis barbae (shaving bumps) affects up to 80% of black men and is characterized by the formation of firm, skin-colored, erythematous or hyperpigmented papules. Acne keloidalis nuchae is an inflammatory folliculitis that is manifested by papules, pustules, and keloid formation at the nape of the neck (**Figure 135**). Black women have a higher prevalence of acne keloidalis nuchae in the vertex areas of the scalp. Central centrifugal scarring alopecia is a slowly progressive, permanent hair loss that begins on the crown and advances to the surrounding area.

All three diseases can be treated with topical (and sometimes intralesional) corticosteroids and oral antibiotics. Response to treatment is variable. For patients with pseudofolliculitis barbae, no shaving or shaving in the direction of hair growth (rather than "against the grain") may be recommended. For central centrifugal scarring alopecia, patients should be told to avoid tight braiding of hair and the use of hot oils for styling and straightening.

Keloids

Keloids are more common and reach a larger size in black patients than in patients of other races. Treatment with intralesional corticosteroids may decrease their size and symptoms; however, the skin rarely completely recovers (see Common Neoplasms).

Dermatosis Papulosa Nigra

Dermatosis papulosa nigra is characterized by small, hyperpigmented papules that first occur in the periorbital region and slowly increase in number on the face over time (**Figure 136**). These occur in about 35% of black patients and also are seen frequently in Asian patients. They are benign and asymptomatic and are likely related to seborrheic keratoses. They can be removed for cosmetic reasons, but they do not require treatment.

Skin Cancers

Skin cancers are relatively uncommon in darker-skinned individuals. Basal cell carcinomas occur infrequently in persons of color; patients with lighter skin tone and those exposed to high levels of ultraviolet light are at highest risk. When basal cell carcinoma does occur in darker-skinned individuals, it is almost always of the pigmented subtype. Squamous cell carcinomas are the most common skin cancer in black patients, in whom they occur most frequently on the legs and in non–sun-exposed areas. This is in contrast to squamous cell carcinomas in light-skinned persons, which usually occur on sun-damaged skin. Melanomas in persons of color also frequently occur in non–sun-exposed areas, such as the palms, soles, and mucous membranes. Because there is, in general, a

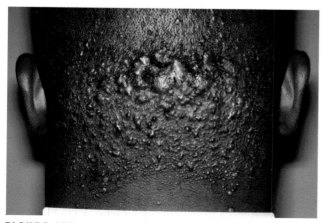

FIGURE 135.
Acne keloidalis nuchae is an inflammatory folliculitis that is manifested by keloid formation at the nape of the neck.

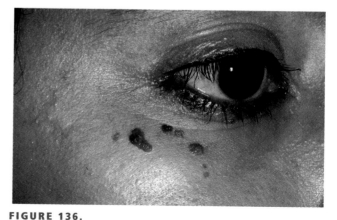

FIGURE 136.
Dermatosis papulosa nigra, characterized by small, hyperpigmented papules that first occur in the periorbital region and slowly increase in number on the face over time.

low index of suspicion for skin cancer in persons of color, the diagnosis may be delayed, leading to a worse outcome. Suspicious lesions in an individual of any skin color should be promptly and appropriately evaluated.

- Squamous cell carcinomas in black patients occur most frequently on the legs and in non–sun-exposed areas.
- Melanomas in persons of color occur frequently in non–sun-exposed areas such as the palms, soles, and mucous membranes.

Dermatologic Diseases in Obesity

Acanthosis Nigricans

Acanthosis nigricans is a velvety, dark thickening of the skin that involves primarily the flexural sites of the neck, axillae, and groin (**Figure 137**). The dorsal hands and elbows may

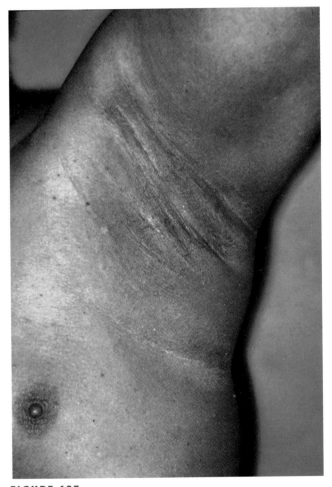

FIGURE 137.
Acanthosis nigricans, characterized by a velvety brown plaque with skin tags, in the axilla of an obese patient.

also be affected. Nearly 75% of obese patients develop acanthosis nigricans. Acrochordons (skin tags) develop in similar areas and may accompany acanthosis nigricans. All non–malignancy-associated cases of acanthosis nigricans are associated with insulin resistance. Acanthosis nigricans and insulin resistance are also associated with hyperandrogenism and such androgen-dependent conditions as acne, hidradenitis suppurativa, and androgenic alopecia. Weight loss and improved control of hyperinsulinemia are the primary interventions required.

Lymphedema and Chronic Venous Insufficiency

Lymphedema and chronic venous insufficiency are common in obese individuals. Chronic venous insufficiency results from persistent venous hypertension caused by venous incompetence or occlusion. Manifestations of chronic venous insufficiency include edema, skin hyperpigmentation, stasis dermatitis, varicose veins, lipodermatosclerosis, cellulitis, and ulceration. Lower-extremity lymphedema is initially characterized by unilateral or bilateral aching leg pain, heaviness, and pitting edema. Early in its course, lymphedema may be confused with chronic venous insufficiency. Advanced lymphedema is recognized by the characteristic nonpitting "peau d'orange" edema resulting from progressive fibrosis of cutaneous and subcutaneous tissue and by hyperkeratosis and papillomatosis. Massive localized lymphedema presenting as masses (pseudosarcoma) affecting the pendulous abdomen, upper arms, and thighs has recently been described. Massive localized lymphedema usually occurs in patients weighing over 181.4 kg (400 lb.). As with lower-extremity lymphedema, the affected area becomes firm and fibrotic over time and with increasing severity. Vesicles, bullae, and oozing of lymphatic fluid may also be seen. Surgical excision of the localized mass of lymphedema is the only reported successful therapy.

- Advanced lymphedema is characterized by nonpitting "peau d'orange" edema and by hyperkeratosis and papillomatosis.
- Lipodermatosclerosis, stasis dermatitis, and leg ulcers are common complications of chronic venous insufficiency.

Skin Infections and Intertrigo

The incidence of skin infections is increased in obese patients because the moist, warm, protected environment in skin folds is conducive to the growth of both bacteria and fungi.

Intertrigo is caused by increased moisture and friction and is not itself an infectious condition. It does, however, frequently become colonized and, at times, infected by *Candida* or, less commonly, *Staphylococcus*. The presence of satellite pustules at the periphery suggests candidiasis. Uncomplicated intertrigo responds to low-potency hydrocortisone or tacrolimus ointment, but topical antifungal medications are often required as well because of concomitant fungal infection. Combination corticosteroid-antifungal preparations should be avoided in these areas, as the corticosteroid is excessively strong and may cause striae.

Dermatophyte infection of the interdigital spaces of the feet and the toenails occurs with increased frequency in obese patients. These require topical antifungal agents, or, in patients with onychomycosis, oral antifungal agents.

> **KEY POINTS**
>
> - Intertrigo is caused by increased moisture and friction and may become colonized or overtly infected by *Candida* or *Staphylococcus*.
>
> - In patients with intertrigo, the presence of satellite pustules at the periphery suggests candidiasis.

Striae Distensae

Striae distensae are linear atrophic marks found most commonly on the abdomen, breasts, buttocks, and thighs in obese individuals. Their orientation is perpendicular to the greatest force of tension. Early lesions may be raised and pink, but over time they become white and atrophic. Similar stretch marks occur in Cushing syndrome but are wider, more atrophic, and more likely to be purple than those seen in simple obesity (**Figure 138**).

Cellulite

Gynoid lipodystrophy, or cellulite, is a dimpled, irregular contour of the skin of the thighs, buttocks, and abdomen. This is present to some degree in most postadolescent women but is more pronounced in those with increased subcutaneous fat. Weight loss has a variable effect on this appearance, and current therapies are also not reliably effective in improving the appearance. Body contouring with liposuction is the most commonly performed cosmetic surgical procedure in the United States. Obese patients may seek this procedure, but the large volumes of subcutaneous fat that must be removed significantly increase the complication rate and may be associated with an increased proportion of visceral adipose tissue. This latter effect may increase the metabolic effects of obesity.

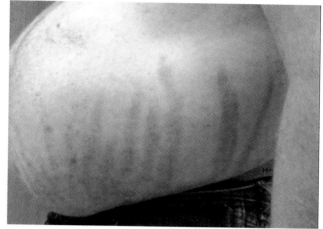

FIGURE 138.
Wide purple striae along the lateral abdomen in a patient with Cushing syndrome.

Courtesy of Rebecca L. Adochio, MD, Endocrinology Fellow, University of Colorado Health Science Center.

Bibliography

Berg D, Otley CC. Skin cancer in organ transplant recipients: epidemiology, pathogenesis, and management. J Am Acad Dermatol. 2002;47(1):1-17. [PMID: 12077575]

Grimes PE. New insights and new therapies in vitiligo. JAMA. 2005;293(6):730-735. [PMID: 15701915]

Maurer T, Ponte M, Leslie K. HIV-associated Kaposi's sarcoma with a high CD4 count and a low viral load. N Engl J Med. 2007;357(13):1352-1353. [PMID: 17898112]

Raju S, Neglén P. Chronic venous insufficiency and varicose veins. N Engl J Med. 2009;360(22):2319-2327. [PMID: 19474429]

Stevenson S, Thornton J. Effect of estrogens on skin aging and the potential role of SERMs. Clin Interv Aging. 2007;2(3):283-297. [PMID: 18044179]

Venkatesan P, Perfect JR, Myers SA. Evaluation and management of fungal infections in immunocompromised patients. Dermatol Ther. 2005;18(1):44-57. [PMID: 15842612]

Yaar M, Gilchrest BA. Skin aging: postulated mechanisms and consequent changes in structure and function. Clin Geriatr Med. 2001;17(4):617-630. [PMID: 11535419]

Yosipovitch G, DeVore A, Dawn A. Obesity and the skin: skin physiology and skin manifestations of obesity. J Am Acad Dermatol. 2007;56(6):901-916. [PMID: 17504714]

Self-Assessment Test

This self-assessment test contains one-best-answer multiple-choice questions. Please read these directions carefully before answering the questions. Answers, critiques, and bibliographies immediately follow these multiple-choice questions. The American College of Physicians is accredited by the Accreditation Council for Continuing Medical Education (ACCME) to provide continuing medical education for physicians.

The American College of Physicians designates MKSAP 15 Dermatology for a maximum of 7 *AMA PRA Category 1 Credits*™. Physicians should only claim credit commensurate with the extent of their participation in the activity. Separate answer sheets are provided for each book of the MKSAP program. Please use one of these answer sheets to complete the Dermatology self-assessment test. Indicate in Section H on the answer sheet the actual number of credits you earned, up to the maximum of 7, in ¼-credit increments. (One credit equals one hour of time spent on this educational activity.)

Use the self-addressed envelope provided with your program to mail your completed answer sheet(s) to the MKSAP Processing Center for scoring. Remember to provide your MKSAP 15 order and ACP ID numbers in the appropriate spaces on the answer sheet. The order and ACP ID numbers are printed on your mailing label. If you have *not* received these numbers with your MKSAP 15 purchase, you will need to acquire them to earn CME credits. E-mail ACP's customer service center at custserv@acponline.org. In the subject line, write "MKSAP 15 order/ACP ID numbers." In the body of the e-mail, make sure you include your e-mail address as well as your full name, address, city, state, ZIP code, country, and telephone number. Also identify where you have made your MKSAP 15 purchase. You will receive your MKSAP 15 order and ACP ID numbers by e-mail within 72 business hours.

CME credit is available from the publication date of July 31, 2009, until July 31, 2012. You may submit your answer sheets at any time during this period.

Self-Scoring Instructions: Dermatology

Compute your percent correct score as follows:

Step 1: Give yourself 1 point for each correct response to a question.

Step 2: Divide your total points by the total number of questions: 40.

The result, expressed as a percentage, is your percent correct score.

	Example	**Your Calculations**
Step 1	34	
Step 2	34 ÷ 40	÷ 40
% Correct	85%	%

*Each of the numbered items is followed by lettered answers. Select the **ONE** lettered answer that is **BEST** in each case.*

Item 1

A 62-year-old man is evaluated for an asymptomatic nodule on his shoulder that has been present for more than 1 year. Skin findings are shown.

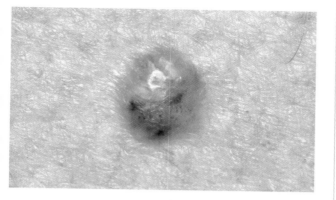

Which of the following is the most likely diagnosis?

(A) Basal cell carcinoma
(B) Pyogenic granuloma
(C) Seborrheic keratosis
(D) Squamous cell carcinoma

Item 2

A 33-year-old man is evaluated because of the recent appearance of stretch marks in his groin that extend to his thighs. He has a history of long-standing psoriasis that at times has involved much of his body, including his intertriginous areas. His topical treatments include tar-containing ointments, clobetasol propionate 0.05%, and calcipotriene 0.0005%; he has also undergone phototherapy. He is otherwise healthy.

On physical examination, scattered psoriasiform plaques are noted on the torso, elbows, knees, gluteal cleft, and scalp. There are pink, well-demarcated plaques in both axillae and in the inguinal folds. Purple striae extend from the inguinal creases onto the anterior thighs bilaterally. No moon facies or buffalo hump is present.

Which of the following treatments most likely resulted in this patient's cutaneous changes?

(A) Calcipotriene
(B) Clobetasol propionate
(C) Phototherapy
(D) Tar-containing ointment

Item 3

A 60-year-old man with a 23-year history of type 2 diabetes mellitus is evaluated for an ulcer on the bottom of his left foot that has persisted for 3 months. He does not smoke cigarettes, has no history of trauma, and denies symptoms of claudication or nocturnal foot pain. The ulcer itself is not painful. He has a 3-year history of bilateral lower-extremity paresthesia in a "stocking" distribution and a 2-year history of erectile dysfunction.

On physical examination, vital signs are normal; BMI is 31. Findings on examination of the foot are shown.

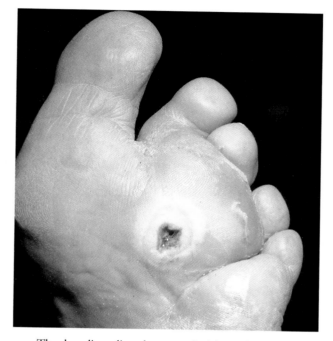

The dorsalis pedis pulses are palpable, and capillary refill is good. There is no hemosiderin staining on the ankles.

Which of the following is the most likely diagnosis?

(A) Ischemic ulcer
(B) Neuropathic ulcer
(C) Vasculitic ulcer
(D) Venous stasis ulcer

Item 4

A 51-year-old woman is evaluated for generalized rash, facial edema, fever, and severe fatigue that have developed over the past week. She was recently diagnosed with rheumatoid arthritis. She currently takes prednisone, hydroxychloroquine, and sulfasalazine. She has no previously known allergies.

On physical examination, temperature is 39.1 °C (102.3 °F), blood pressure is 110/78 mm Hg, pulse rate is 108/min, and respiration rate is 25/min. The face is edematous. Skin examination reveals a generalized morbilliform eruption. The skin is not painful, and no blisters are present. There is no ocular or mucosal involvement. Lymphadenopathy is noted in the cervical and axillary regions. Laboratory studies show a serum alanine aminotransferase level of 330 U/L and a serum aspartate aminotransferase level of 355 U/L. Results of a complete blood count are normal except for 16% eosinophils.

Which of the following is the most likely diagnosis?

(A) Drug reaction with eosinophilia and systemic symptoms (DRESS)
(B) Erythema multiforme
(C) Stevens-Johnson syndrome
(D) Toxic epidermal necrolysis

Item 5

A 60-year-old man is evaluated for a skin lesion on his right wrist. He first noted the lesion several months ago, and it has grown and bled frequently over the past 6 weeks. The patient received a cadaveric renal transplant 3 years ago because of progressive chronic glomerulonephritis. He has maintained excellent allograft function on prednisone, cyclosporine, and mycophenolate mofetil.

Physical examination is unrevealing other than the skin lesion shown.

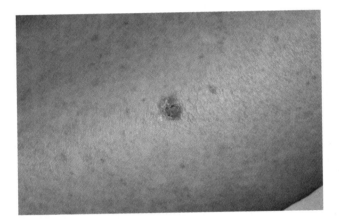

Which of the following is the most likely diagnosis?

(A) Kaposi sarcoma
(B) Melanoma
(C) Psoriasis
(D) Squamous cell carcinoma

Item 6

A 23-year-old woman from Massachusetts is evaluated for a 1-week history of mildly pruritic red papules on her lower extremities that developed after a recent camping trip in Florida.

On physical examination, vital signs are normal. Skin examination is notable for multiple 3-mm urticarial papules with excoriation along the sock line. One of the papules has a central punctum.

Which of the following is the most likely diagnosis?

(A) Bedbug bites
(B) Brown recluse spider bites
(C) Chigger bites
(D) Scabies infestation

Item 7

A 22-year-old man is evaluated for a 1-day history of a painful rash in the beard area. He has not used any ointments, creams, or other occlusive coverings on his face, and he has not had hot-tub, whirlpool, or swimming-pool exposure. He does have a history of herpes labialis and had a recurrence 3 days ago. He is otherwise healthy and takes no medications.

Skin examination findings are shown.

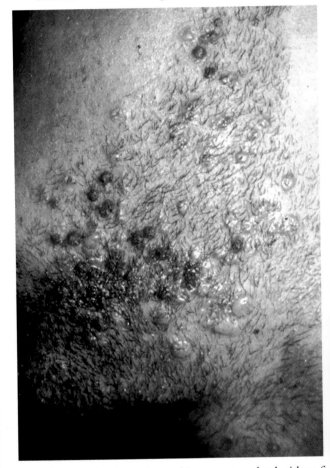

The eruption is tender and is present on both sides of the face.

Which of the following is the most likely diagnosis?

(A) Acne vulgaris
(B) Eosinophilic folliculitis
(C) Herpetic folliculitis
(D) *Pseudomonas* folliculitis
(E) Staphylococcal folliculitis

Item 8

A 38-year-old man is evaluated for an 18-month history of chronic cutaneous lupus erythematosus. He has lesions on his face and scalp. He has been using topical sunscreen, but he finds it difficult to remember to apply it before leaving for work. He is also being treated with a corticosteroid lotion, and hydroxychloroquine was recently begun. Despite 4 months of therapy, new lesions continue to develop, and the old lesions have not healed. He admits to smoking 2 packs of cigarettes per day and drinking 6 to 10 beers per day. He has hypertension and hyperlipidemia. In addition to the corticosteroid lotion and hydroxychloroquine, his current medications are amlodipine, hydrochlorothiazide, simvastatin, and a multivitamin.

On physical examination, there are multiple erythematous lesions on the face and several on the scalp consistent with the diagnosis of discoid lupus erythematosus.

Which of the following is the next step in managing this patient's skin disease?

(A) Initiate methotrexate
(B) Initiate thalidomide
(C) Recommend smoking cessation
(D) Stop amlodipine
(E) Stop hydrochlorothiazide

Item 9

A 67-year-old man is evaluated for an asymptomatic, darkly pigmented patch on his nose that has been present for 9 years.

Skin findings are shown.

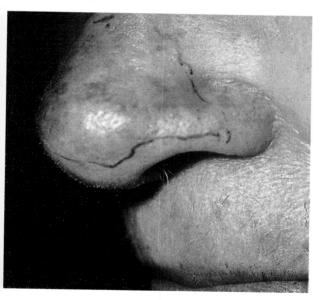

Which of the following is the most appropriate management?

(A) Broad, shallow shave biopsy
(B) Punch biopsy of the center of the lesion
(C) Punch biopsy of the edge of the lesion
(D) Reassurance

Item 10

A 42-year-old woman is evaluated for hives on her trunk and legs that are accompanied by a burning sensation. The lesions have been fixed in location for 48 hours. Her sister has systemic lupus erythematosus.

On physical examination, urticarial plaques are noted on the trunk and legs. Some of the lesions have healed, leaving a faintly bruised appearance.

Which of the following is the most appropriate diagnostic test?

(A) Chest radiograph
(B) Latex radioallergosorbent testing (RAST)
(C) Skin biopsy
(D) Stool sample for ova and parasites

Item 11

A 24-year-old woman is evaluated in the emergency department for skin blistering. Her symptoms began 3 days ago when she noted a gritty sensation in her eyes; the following day her skin all over her body became red and painful. When she awoke today, her skin was blistered and there were moist, open erosions where the skin had sloughed off. Approximately 1 week ago, she received a 3-day course of trimethoprim-sulfamethoxazole for an uncomplicated urinary tract infection. She has a history of gastroesophageal reflux disease, which is treated with omeprazole that was started 1 year ago. She also takes ibuprofen intermittently for pain.

On physical examination, temperature is 39.1 °C (102.4 °F), blood pressure is 110/75 mm Hg, pulse rate is 105/min, and respiration rate is 20/min. There is confluent erythema of the entire trunk and all extremities, with blistering and erosions affecting greater than 30% of the body surface area. Lateral pressure on erythematous, non-blistered skin causes the skin to slough. Erosions are present on the eyelids, and there is conjunctival hyperemia. The lips are crusted and bloody, and there are ragged ulcers on the buccal mucosa. There are painful ulcers on the labia minora. Laboratory studies show a slight elevation in the leukocyte count with increased polymorphonuclear cells and eosinophils, normal renal function, and a slight elevation in liver aminotransferase levels.

Which of the following is the most appropriate first step in management?

(A) Empiric acyclovir
(B) Empiric ceftazidime and vancomycin
(C) Systemic corticosteroids
(D) Stop all medications

Item 12

A 40-year-old man is evaluated for a 1-month history of painful oral erosions, which are causing difficulty in eating and drinking. He is otherwise healthy.

On physical examination, there are no skin lesions. Examination of the oral mucosa reveals widespread erosions affecting the gingiva and buccal mucosa. The remainder of the physical examination is normal. Laboratory testing, including a complete blood count and comprehensive metabolic panel, are normal. A chest radiograph is also normal.

Biopsy of a buccal mucosa blister reveals acantholytic cells. Direct immunofluorescence microscopy shows staining of the intercellular spaces with IgG. Indirect immunofluorescence microscopy shows a similar pattern and an elevation of anti-desmoglein 3 antibody.

Which of the following is the most appropriate initial treatment?

(A) Cyclophosphamide
(B) Intravenous immune globulin
(C) Mycophenolate mofetil
(D) Prednisone
(E) Rituximab

Item 13

A 45-year-old woman is evaluated in the office for a facial rash of 6 months' duration that involves the cheeks and nose. She is unsure if sun exposure worsens the rash. She does not have a rash elsewhere and does not have fatigue, ulcers, or joint pain.

Physical examination reveals a rash that is limited to the face as shown.

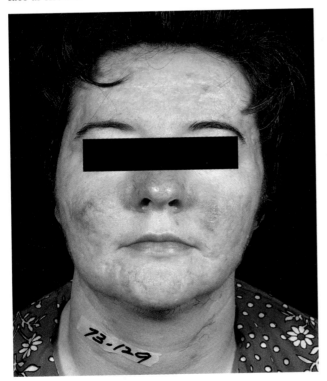

The remainder of the examination is unremarkable. Laboratory studies, including complete blood count, serum chemistry studies, and thyroid-stimulating hormone level, are normal.

Which of the following is the most likely diagnosis?

(A) Dermatomyositis
(B) Psoriasis
(C) Rosacea

(D) Seborrheic dermatitis
(E) Systemic lupus erythematosus

Item 14

A 35-year-old woman is evaluated for a 3-week history of multiple ulcers on her right leg that are associated with low-grade fever, increased fatigue, myalgia, and arthralgia. She denies paresthesias. She can recall no trauma and has never had lesions like this before. Her only medical problem is a 10-year history of rheumatoid arthritis for which she takes methotrexate and etanercept.

On physical examination, vital signs are normal. Examination of the legs discloses two punched-out–appearing ulcers with irregular borders and fibrinous bases located on the lateral calf and ankle of the right leg. Each ulcer measures approximately 1 to 1.5 cm in diameter. The borders of the ulcers are not violaceous or necrotic, there is no hemosiderin staining, and hair growth is normal. Pedal pulses are present bilaterally.

Which of the following tests is most likely to aid in the diagnosis?

(A) Ankle-brachial index measurement
(B) Sensation testing with monofilament
(C) Skin biopsy
(D) Venous duplex Doppler ultrasonography

Item 15

A 64-year-old man is evaluated in the emergency department for a rash that first developed 3 days ago and has rapidly spread to cover most of his body. His skin is painful and does not itch. He feels feverish and ill. He has a history of mild psoriasis, hypertension, asthma, and prostate cancer. His psoriasis has been well controlled with topical corticosteroids as needed. His prostate cancer was treated with radiation therapy 6 years ago and is in remission. His medications include lisinopril (started 3 weeks ago), an inhaled corticosteroid and salmeterol daily, and inhaled albuterol as needed. One week ago, he completed a 10-day tapering dose of oral corticosteroids for an acute exacerbation of asthma. He reports no known medication allergies.

On physical examination, he appears ill. Temperature is 38.9 °C (102.0 °F), blood pressure is 118/78 mm Hg, and pulse rate is 112/min. Greater than 90% of his body surface area is erythematous. There are widespread coalescing erythematous patches and plaques, many with pinpoint pustules coalescing into lakes of pus and many with fine desquamation. Erythematous plaques with overlying silvery scale are present on his occipital scalp. His conjunctival, oral, and urethral mucous membranes are normal. There is no palpable lymphadenopathy. A complete blood count reveals leukocytosis with a predominance of polymorphonuclear cells. A complete metabolic profile and serum aminotransferase levels are normal.

Which of the following is the most likely diagnosis?

(A) Drug hypersensitivity syndrome
(B) Paraneoplastic erythroderma

(C) Pustular psoriasis

(D) Sézary syndrome (cutaneous T-cell lymphoma)

(E) Staphylococcal scalded skin syndrome

Item 16

A 65-year-old woman is evaluated for a 3-month history of generalized itching. The itch is severe (she rates it 10 out of 10) and has not been adequately controlled by regular use of emollients, topical corticosteroids, or over-the-counter antihistamines. She currently takes loratadine. She has no other medical problems and takes no other medications. Screening Pap smear, mammography, and colonoscopy were all performed within the last 3 months, and all were normal.

On physical examination, linear erosions are noted on the upper back, lower back, proximal arms, and proximal thighs. There is distinct sparing of the skin overlying the scapula. No xerosis is noted, and there are no primary skin lesions. The results of her general physical examination are normal.

Which of the following is the most appropriate management option?

(A) Complete blood count, serum chemistry studies, and thyroid function tests

(B) Punch skin biopsy

(C) Skin patch testing

(D) Systemic corticosteroids

Item 17

A 35-year-old man is evaluated for an acute rash on his face. The rash is painful and somewhat itchy, and his left eye is swelling shut. He has a history of long-standing atopic dermatitis, which has been reasonably well controlled with regular use of emollients and topical corticosteroids. His current medications are triamcinolone ointment, tacrolimus ointment, and hydroxyzine. He has lately been lax in using his medications because of recent travel and therefore has been scratching more. He is allergic to sulfa.

On physical examination, vital signs are normal. The skin findings of the affected eye are shown.

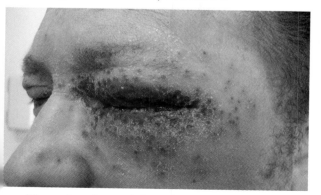

The conjunctivae are inflamed, but no purulence is noted. No gross abnormalities of the cornea are visible. Skin findings on the trunk and arm are shown (see top of next column).

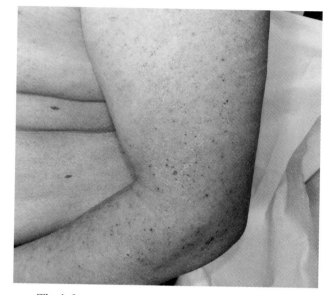

The left preauricular lymph nodes are slightly enlarged and tender.

Which of the following is the most likely diagnosis?

(A) Acute allergic contact dermatitis

(B) Acute atopic dermatitis

(C) Eczema herpeticum

(D) *Staphylococcus aureus* pyoderma

Item 18

A 62-year-old man is evaluated for a rapidly growing nodule on his face. The lesion has arisen within the past 4 to 6 weeks and is painless. He does not recall a history of trauma.

Physical examination reveals the lesion shown.

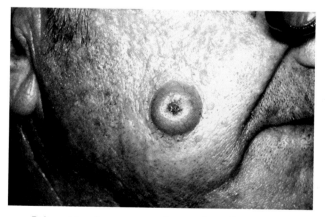

It is not tender, warm to the touch, or fluctuant. There is no associated lymphadenopathy.

Which of the following is the most likely diagnosis?

(A) Abscess

(B) Keloid

(C) Keratoacanthoma

(D) Nodular basal cell carcinoma

Item 19

A 68-year-old man is evaluated for a 6-month history of a sensation of dryness in his eyes. He notes that it feels as though there is sand in his eyes.

On physical examination, the eyes are red, and trichiasis (ingrown eyelashes) and symblepharon (adhesions of the eyelid to the globe) formation is noted.

Which of the following is the most appropriate next step in management?

(A) Conjunctival biopsy
(B) Intravenous acyclovir
(C) Prednisone and oral cyclophosphamide
(D) Topical gentamicin 0.3%

Item 20

A 24-year-old woman is evaluated for a rapidly progressive ulcer on her leg that began 3 days after she bumped her leg on a chair. The lesion began as multiple small, painful pustules that eroded and rapidly progressed over several days to form a large ulcer. She has a 6-year history of distal ulcerative colitis that is currently well controlled on mesalamine.

On physical examination, she is afebrile, and vital signs are normal. Skin findings are shown.

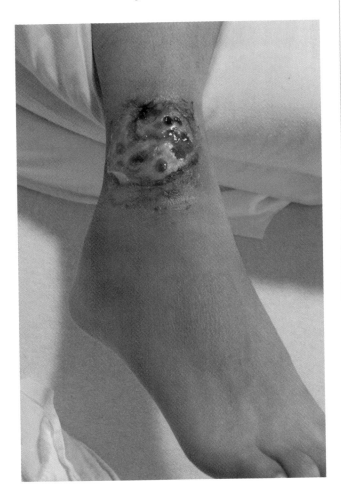

A complete blood count is normal.

Which of the following is the most appropriate treatment?

(A) Intravenous antibiotics
(B) Proctocolectomy
(C) Surgical debridement
(D) Systemic corticosteroids
(E) Wet-to-dry dressings

Item 21

A 21-year-old woman is evaluated for a marked pustular flare on the central face. She has a 1-year history of well-controlled acne vulgaris for which she takes oral tetracycline, topical tretinoin, and a benzoyl peroxide wash. She has had no recent change in therapy, and this flare of acne is uncharacteristic of her clinical course.

On physical examination, pustules are noted in the central face and around the nares. *Escherichia coli* is cultured from the nares and from a pustule on the cheek.

Which of the following is the most appropriate treatment?

(A) Ciprofloxacin
(B) Isotretinoin
(C) Minocycline
(D) Spironolactone
(E) Trimethoprim-sulfamethoxazole

Item 22

A 62-year-old woman is evaluated for an asymptomatic pigmented patch on her cheek that has been present for 15 years.

Skin findings are shown.

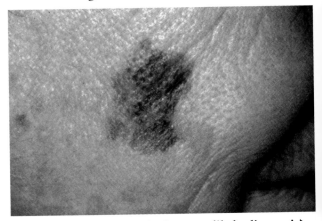

Which of the following is the most likely diagnosis?

(A) Actinic keratosis
(B) Basal cell carcinoma
(C) Benign solar lentigo
(D) Malignant melanoma
(E) Seborrheic keratosis

Item 23

A 30-year-old woman is evaluated for a pustular rash on her central face. She has a 5-year history of dandruff and a recurrent, red, scaly, itchy rash behind and in her ears and on the medial aspects of her cheeks. For several months she has been self-treating the rash with daily application of her husband's eczema cream (triamcinolone acetonide 0.1%). The rash was initially controlled using this treatment, but for the past month a new acne-like rash has appeared. She began using the triamcinolone twice daily within the last week but has noted no improvement.

On physical examination, papules and pustules on an erythematous base are observed in a perioral distribution. The remainder of the examination is normal except for seborrheic dermatitis involving the scalp.

In addition to discontinuing triamcinolone, which of the following is the most appropriate treatment?

(A) Clobetasol cream
(B) Benzoyl peroxide gel
(C) Neomycin ointment
(D) No further treatment

Item 24

A 37-year-old man is evaluated for a 6-day history of a painful eruption on his left posterior thorax. He had an episode of shingles 1 year ago that was treated with famciclovir. He has a history of alcoholism and intermittent injection drug use. He has lost approximately 3.0 kg (6.6 lb) over the past 3 months. He has had increased fatigue but denies fever, chills, lymphadenopathy, jaundice, or change in his bowel habits. He takes no medications.

On physical examination, temperature is 37.0 °C (98.6 °F), and BMI is 28. The skin findings are shown.

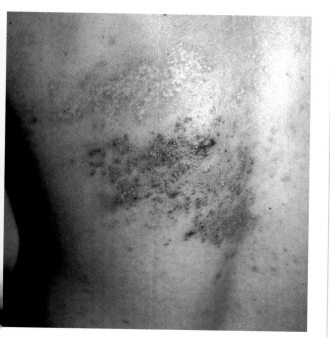

Oral mucous membranes are normal. There is no jaundice, lymphadenopathy, or hepatosplenomegaly. Direct fluorescent antibody test is positive for varicella-zoster virus.

Which of the following is the most likely underlying disease?

(A) Cirrhosis
(B) Diabetes mellitus
(C) Hepatitis B
(D) Hepatitis C
(E) HIV infection

Item 25

A 20-year-old woman is evaluated for routine health care and progressive loss of pigment on various parts of her body for the past year. Although she finds the condition distressing, she is otherwise asymptomatic. She has no other medical problems and takes no medications.

On physical examination, vital signs are normal. BMI is 23. Typical skin findings are shown.

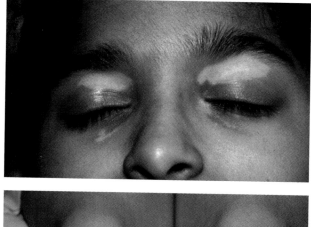

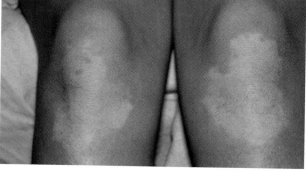

Similar skin findings are noted symmetrically on the dorsal hands, in perioral areas, and in the cleft between the buttocks. The remainder of the general physical examination and pelvic examination is normal.

Laboratory testing reveals a normal complete blood count, serum electrolytes, and lipid panel.

Which of the following screening tests is most reasonable for this patient?

(A) Fasting glucose

(B) Morning cortisol

(C) Vitamin B_{12}

(D) Thyroid-stimulating hormone

Item 26

A 65-year-old man is evaluated for a generalized, intensely pruritic eruption that has been slowly progressing over the last 6 months. He has been treated with topical corticosteroids for 4 months for widespread eczema without relief of pruritus or change in clinical appearance. He has never had a skin biopsy. He does not have a personal or family history of asthma, atopic dermatitis, allergic rhinitis, or psoriasis.

On physical examination, temperature is 37.5 °C (99.5 °F), blood pressure is 135/85 mm Hg, pulse rate is 84/min, and respiration rate is 14/min. Skin examination reveals erythema with scale affecting greater than 90% of the body surface area. Alopecia, nail dystrophy, and ectropion (turning inside out of the eyelid) are present. There is thickening and fissuring of the skin on the palms and soles. Bilateral axillary and inguinal lymphadenopathy is present. The mucous membranes are not involved.

Which of the following is the most appropriate next step in management?

(A) Antinuclear antibody assay

(B) Cyclosporine

(C) Phototherapy

(D) Rapid plasma reagin test

(E) Skin biopsy

Item 27

A 51-year-old woman is evaluated for a several-year history of persistent hand dermatitis. She has worked as a hairdresser for years, and, while she has had rashes in the past, she has never before experienced such a persistent problem. Her hands are itchy and sometimes have very painful cracks. Regular emollient use has improved the rash in the past but is not helping at this time. She wears gloves at work most of the time, but she is not sure if they are latex or vinyl. She notes improvement on weekends when she does not work, although the dermatitis does not completely clear. Symptoms improved significantly when she went on vacation. She has allergic rhinitis and hypertension and has a history of mild eczema during childhood. Her mother had asthma. She currently takes hydrochlorothiazide and nasal corticosteroids intermittently and has no known drug allergies.

On physical examination, the skin on the hands is thickened and hyperkeratotic, especially on the palms, where there are poorly defined plaques, dry scale, and fissures but no pustules. Skin on the dorsal hands is red and scaly. The surface of the nails is rough. Other areas of skin, including the soles of the feet, are not involved.

Which of the following is the most appropriate diagnostic test?

(A) Epicutaneous patch testing

(B) Lymphocyte stimulation assay

(C) Prick testing

(D) Radioallergosorbent test (RAST)

Item 28

A 70-year-old man comes to the office to ask about the skin changes on his hands, as shown.

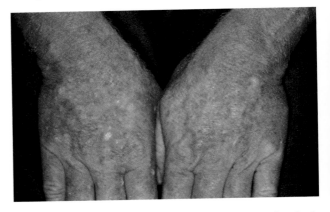

The skin changes have been present for years, but he is concerned now about the possibility of skin cancer.

Which of the following is the most likely diagnosis?

(A) Actinic keratoses

(B) Basal cell carcinoma

(C) Malignant melanoma

(D) Seborrheic keratoses

Item 29

A 60-year-old woman is evaluated for pruritic hives that have persisted for 12 weeks. The lesions appear, resolve within hours, and leave no residual mark but reappear at a later time. She does not associate the hives with any particular foods or exposures. Her medical history is significant for a 40-year history of asthma. She was diagnosed 4 months ago with peripheral vascular disease and was started on aspirin and a supervised exercise program. In addition to aspirin, her current medications are beclomethasone, salmeterol, albuterol (as needed), lisinopril, and simvastatin.

Physical examination discloses wheals on the trunk and extremities with no angioedema.

Which of the following is the most appropriate management option?

(A) Discontinue aspirin

(B) Discontinue lisinopril

(C) Initiate prednisone

(D) Radioallergosorbent test (RAST) for pollen

(E) Skin biopsy

Item 30

A 53-year-old man with a 14-year history of type 2 diabetes mellitus is evaluated for an ulcer on his left foot that has persisted for 4 months. He has numbness and tingling that involves his feet and ankles bilaterally. He currently takes aspirin, metformin, glyburide, pioglitazone, and gabapentin.

On physical examination, vital signs are normal; BMI is 28. The foot is appropriately warm and pink without evidence of erythema, warmth, swelling, tenderness, or pus. The dorsalis pedis and posterior tibial pulses are palpable, and capillary refill is good. Ankle-brachial index measurement on the left side is 0.8. There is no hemosiderin staining on the ankles. Probing the ulcer with a steel probe does not reach bone. An MRI scan of the foot is scheduled.

In addition to debridement, which of the following is most likely to accelerate healing of the ulcer?

(A) Arterial revascularization
(B) Contact casting
(C) Intravenous vancomycin
(D) Unna boot compression
(E) Whirlpool hyperthermia

Item 31

A 33-year-old woman is evaluated for a 3-day history of a rash on her palms. Several days prior to onset of the rash, she developed low-grade fever, aches, malaise, and sore throat. The rash first appeared on her palms as small red macules that increased in size over 24 to 48 hours, followed by the appearance of similar lesions on her arms and sores in her mouth. Three months ago she had a similar episode that resolved spontaneously without scarring within 2 weeks. She takes no medications or supplements. She has not been exposed to anyone with similar skin lesions, but she did recently travel to a meeting in North Carolina. She has a remote history of genital herpes, but has had no outbreaks in several years. No family members have experienced similar outbreaks.

On physical examination, she appears well. Temperature is 37.2 °C (98.9 °F), blood pressure is 118/70 mm Hg, and pulse rate is 68/min. Typical lesions are shown.

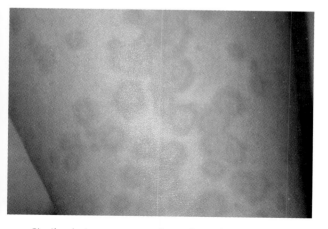

Similar lesions are noted on the palms and extensor forearms. There is a fibrinous-based, 4- to 5-mm ulcer on the palate. No conjunctival erythema and no vulvar lesions are noted.

Which of the following is most likely associated with this patient's eruption?

(A) Lyme disease
(B) Recurrent herpes simplex virus infection
(C) Rocky Mountain spotted fever
(D) Streptococcal pharyngitis

Item 32

A 40-year-old woman is evaluated for a 4-month history of symmetrically distributed, severely pruritic, grouped erosions on her elbows, knees, back, and buttocks. The skin lesions began as red spots that developed into papules and then vesicles, which broke down as she scratched them. She reports normal bowel habits. She has no other medical problems and takes no medications.

A biopsy reveals neutrophilic infiltrate at the tips of the dermal papillae causing subepidermal separation. Diffuse immunofluorescence shows granular deposition of IgA at the dermal papillae.

Which of the following is the most appropriate management option for this patient?

(A) Cyclosporine
(B) Dapsone
(C) Dapsone and a gluten-free diet
(D) Intravenous immune globulin
(E) Lactose-free diet

Item 33

A 73-year-old man is evaluated for widespread bruising on his forearms that has been recurrent for at least the past year. He occasionally gets small bruises elsewhere. The lesions are asymptomatic and last "forever." He denies significant trauma, epistaxis, bleeding of his gums, or other evident blood loss. He is generally healthy and is recovering from alcoholism. He currently takes only aspirin.

On physical examination, vital signs are normal. The facial skin is notable for hyperpigmentation and accentuation of wrinkling. There are scattered hyperpigmented macules on the cheeks. The skin appears thinned, and findings on the forearm are shown.

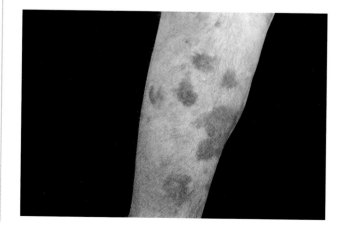

No petechiae are seen on the extremities, and there is no active bleeding. All laboratory studies, including complete blood count, aspartate aminotransferase and alanine aminotransferase levels, prothrombin time, activated partial thromboplastin time, and urinalysis, are normal.

Which of the following is the most likely diagnosis?

(A) Coagulopathy related to liver disease
(B) Immune thrombocytopenic purpura
(C) Leukocytoclastic vasculitis
(D) Porphyria cutanea tarda
(E) Solar purpura

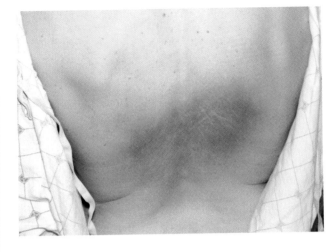

Item 34

A 28-year-old man is evaluated in the emergency department for an 8-hour history of fever, malaise, and a rash on his shoulders, lower back, arms, and palms. Ten days ago he was started on oral trimethoprim-sulfamethoxazole therapy for methicillin-resistant *Staphylococcus aureus* infection. His last dose of trimethoprim-sulfamethoxazole was taken this morning. He takes no other medications and has no known allergies.

On physical examination, temperature is 38.6 °C (101.4 °F), blood pressure is 110/70 mm Hg, pulse rate is 110/min, and respiration rate is 20/min. There are erythematous, urticarial, targetoid plaques on the shoulders that are studded with small, tense blisters. Erythematous targetoid lesions are also noted on the lower back and palms. No lesions are present on the soles or genitalia. There are small vesicles and crusts on the upper and lower lips, as well as small areas of erosion on the soft palate. His eye examination is normal. Laboratory studies reveal a normal complete blood count, comprehensive metabolic panel, and erythrocyte sedimentation rate.

Which of the following is the most likely diagnosis?

(A) Acute generalized exanthematous pustulosis
(B) Drug reaction with eosinophilia and systemic symptoms (DRESS)
(C) "Red man syndrome"
(D) Stevens-Johnson syndrome

Item 35

A 49-year-old woman is evaluated for recurrent burning and itching on her mid-back that have been present for 2 years. She is otherwise healthy, although she does have mild joint aches (neck, lower back, knees) for which she uses ibuprofen intermittently.

Physical examination discloses ill-defined hyperpigmented patches on the mid-back below the medial aspect of the scapulae as shown (see top of next column). The remainder of her physical examination, including neurologic examination, is normal.

Which of the following is the most likely diagnosis?

(A) Herpes zoster
(B) Notalgia paresthetica
(C) Nummular dermatitis
(D) Xerosis

Item 36

A 45-year-old man with poorly controlled type 2 diabetes mellitus is evaluated for the sudden onset 2 weeks ago of bumps on the elbows and knees. His medications include pioglitazone, glipizide, and metformin.

On physical examination, vital signs are normal; BMI is 32. Skin examination discloses more than 100 monomorphic, yellow-orange, 2- to 4-mm papules on the buttocks, elbows, and knees. Skin biopsy demonstrates collections of lipid-laden macrophages with extracellular lipid.

Which of the following is the most likely diagnosis?

(A) Eruptive xanthomas
(B) Plane xanthomas
(C) Tendon xanthomas
(D) Xanthelasmas

Item 37

A 35-year-old man is evaluated for a 3-month history of an asymptomatic white discoloration of his fourth and fifth nails at the proximal nailfold of both hands. He has had recent weight loss of 2.3 kg (5.0 lb) over 3 months, as well as fatigue, thrush, and a feeling of feverishness.

On physical examination, the white discoloration is subungual; it cannot be scraped off with a scalpel blade. Nail findings are shown (see next page). Fungal culture of the subungual debris yields *Trichophyton rubrum*.

Which of the following is the most likely underlying disease?

(A) Cushing disease
(B) Diabetes mellitus
(C) HIV infection
(D) Leukemia
(E) Metastatic cancer

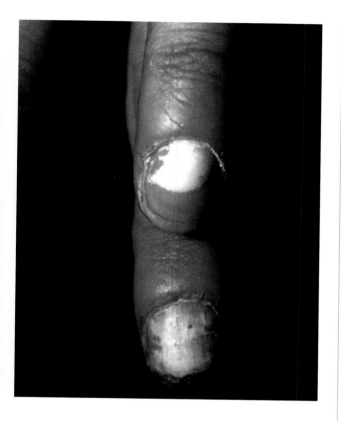

Item 38

A 39-year-old man is evaluated for a 3-day history of stinging lesions on his shins. He also notes joint pain and some numbness and tingling in his feet. He has a history of hepatitis C infection that has not required antiviral treatment.

On physical examination, vital signs are normal. Skin examination discloses 2- to 3-mm, purple, palpable, non-blanching papules on the dorsal feet, shins, and buttocks. There is no evidence of synovitis. Laboratory studies reveal a normal serum creatinine level, modestly elevated levels of serum alanine and aspartate aminotransferases, low complement levels, and circulating cryoglobulins. Skin biopsy shows leukocytoclastic vasculitis.

Which of the following is the most appropriate treatment?

(A) Pegylated interferon alfa and ribavirin
(B) Plasma exchange
(C) Systemic corticosteroids
(D) Topical corticosteroids

Item 39

A 76-year-old man is seen in the office for a routine physical examination. He is healthy and has no complaints about his health, takes no medications, and does not smoke or drink alcohol. Until he retired 5 years ago, he was a farmer.

On physical examination, several darkly pigmented lesions are noted on his trunk, as shown.

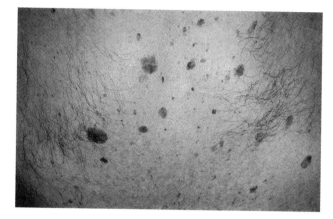

Which of the following is the most likely diagnosis?

(A) Basal cell carcinoma
(B) Malignant melanoma
(C) Seborrheic keratoses
(D) Squamous cell carcinoma

Item 40

A 55-year-old woman is seen in follow-up for a mildly pruritic eruption on and surrounding her right nipple, which developed about 5 months ago. Triamcinolone acetonide cream was begun 1 month ago, but since then there has been no improvement in the lesion. She has no personal or family history of eczema or psoriasis, and she is otherwise healthy. Her only medication is triamcinolone.

Breast findings are shown.

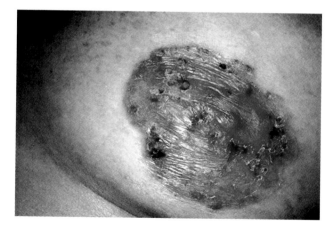

Which of the following is the most likely diagnosis?

(A) Chronic cutaneous lupus erythematosus
(B) Lichen simplex chronicus
(C) Paget disease of the breast
(D) Psoriasis

Answers and Critiques

Item 1   **Answer: A**

Educational Objective: Diagnose basal cell carcinoma.

Basal cell carcinoma (BCC) typically presents as a pearly, pink papule or nodule with telangiectatic vessels. As BCC grows, the central area often ulcerates, resulting in its characteristic rolled edge. Flecks of melanin pigment are commonly present. A biopsy is necessary, as amelanotic melanoma may have a similar appearance. Common biopsy techniques include shave or punch. Most nodular BCCs are treated with excision, whereas ill-defined lesions, high-risk histologic types, and tumors on the face and hands are treated with Mohs micrographic surgery. Selected superficial lesions can be treated with curettage, imiquimod, cryotherapy, or excision.

Pyogenic granulomas are typically bright red and friable, are commonly crusted, and develop over a few days to weeks. Removal is necessary only if the lesion is cosmetically unacceptable, painful, causes unwanted bleeding, or is otherwise bothersome.

Seborrheic keratosis is a painless, nonmalignant growth appearing as a waxy, brownish patch or plaque. Seborrheic keratoses lack a pearly appearance and typically exhibit horn cysts (epidermal cysts filled with keratin) on the surface that can best be visualized with a magnifying lens. Treatment is necessary only if lesions are symptomatic or interfere with function.

Squamous cell carcinomas are rapidly growing, hyperkeratotic, ulcerated macules, papules, or nodules that commonly appear on the scalp, neck, and pinnae. A shave or punch biopsy is used to confirm the diagnosis of suspicious lesions.

KEY POINT

- Basal cell carcinomas present as pink, pearly nodules with telangiectases and, commonly, flecks of melanin pigment.

Bibliography

Mogensen M, Jemec GB. Diagnosis of nonmelanoma skin cancer/keratinocyte carcinoma: a review of diagnostic accuracy of nonmelanoma skin cancer diagnostic tests and technologies. Dermatol Surg. 2007;33(10):1158-1174. [PMID: 17903149]

Item 2   **Answer: B**

Educational Objective: Understand the skin complications associated with the use of topical corticosteroids.

Clobetasol propionate 0.05% is an ultra–high-potency corticosteroid. Potential cutaneous complications associated with the use of topical corticosteroids include thinning of the skin, development of striae (stretch marks), development of purpura, pigmentary changes (hypo- or hyperpigmentation), acneiform eruptions, and increased risk of infections. Striae formation has been documented in 1% or more of patients using a mid-potency corticosteroid; the incidence may be higher with the use of more potent agents. The risk increases when corticosteroids are used for prolonged periods, are applied under occlusion, or are applied in skin folds where there is natural occlusion, as in this patient.

Calcipotriene, a vitamin D analog, inhibits proliferation of keratinocytes, normalizes keratinization, and inhibits accumulation of inflammatory cells (neutrophils and T-lymphocytes). Calcipotriene's efficacy is comparable to that of medium-strength topical corticosteroids, but the drug is not associated with the cutaneous side effects seen in this patient.

Phototherapy induces T-lymphocyte apoptosis and therefore decreases proinflammatory cytokines. The most commonly reported side effects include photoaging, cataracts, and skin cancer. Severe cutaneous atrophy with striae formation is not a side effect of phototherapy.

Topical tar compounds are frequently used as corticosteroid-sparing drugs for patients with refractory psoriasis and are associated with excellent results when combined with ultraviolet B phototherapy. Coal tar products do not result in thinning of the skin.

KEY POINT

- Potential side effects of topical corticosteroids include development of striae and atrophy of the skin.

Bibliography

Hengge UR, Ruzicka T, Schwartz RA, Cork MJ. Adverse effects of topical glucocorticosteroids. J Am Acad Dermatol. 2006;54(1):1-15; quiz 16-8. [PMID: 16384751]

Item 3   **Answer: B**

Educational Objective: Diagnose a neuropathic ulcer.

This patient has a neuropathic ulcer. Neuropathic ulcers are common in patients with diabetes mellitus who have severe peripheral neuropathy. Neuropathic ulcers occur at pressure points such as the plantar aspect of the foot in the region of the metatarsal heads. The ulcers characteristically have a thick surrounding zone of hyperkeratosis, and accompanying deformities of the foot, including hammer toes and a flattened foot arch, are common.

A comprehensive foot examination should be performed annually in all patients with diabetes to identify high-risk foot problems. Early detection of sensory deficits in the foot alerts the patient to take extra care in compulsive visual inspection to detect early changes. Meticulous self-care, including daily washing, rehydration with emollient creams, and the use of comfortable, protective, and well-fitting shoes and plain cotton socks, is recommended. Patients should also avoid walking barefoot. Particular attention should be paid to the feet after purchasing new footwear so that evidence of new pressure points may be ascertained. Callus formation, evidence of irritation from improperly fitting shoes, and unrecognized foreign bodies on the foot are of particular importance.

Ischemic ulcers are typically distal and are not associated with surrounding hyperkeratosis. The skin is thin and atrophic. Pulses and capillary refill are poor.

Vasculitic ulcers are irregular in shape and have a punched-out appearance. They lack surrounding hyperkeratosis and rarely occur over pressure points.

Venous stasis ulcers are associated with chronic venous insufficiency and typically occur on the medial aspect of the lower leg, especially over the medial malleolus. Hemosiderin staining is typically prominent.

KEY POINT

- **Neuropathic ulcers occur over pressure points, usually on the plantar surface of the foot, and commonly have surrounding hyperkeratosis.**

Bibliography

Dalla Paola L, Faglia E. Treatment of diabetic foot ulcer: an overview strategies for clinical approach. Curr Diabetes Rev. 2006;2(4):431-447. [PMID: 18220646]

Item 4   Answer: A

Educational Objective: Diagnose drug reaction with eosinophilia and systemic symptoms (DRESS).

This patient has a drug reaction characterized by a generalized papular eruption, eosinophilia, and systemic symptoms and is consistent with drug reaction with eosinophilia and systemic symptoms (DRESS). With cessation of the causative drug, most likely sulfasalazine, the skin reaction rapidly subsides along with lymphadenopathy, fever, elevated aminotransferase levels, and eosinophilia. Patients with DRESS may develop severe hepatitis, and fulminant hepatic necrosis may occur if the condition is unrecognized.

Erythema multiforme (EM) is an acute, often recurrent mucocutaneous eruption that usually follows an acute infection, most frequently recurrent herpes simplex virus infection, but it may also be drug related or idiopathic. Lesions range in size from several millimeters to several centimeters and consist of erythematous plaques with concentric rings of color. Patients may have low-grade fever during an EM outbreak. However, this patient's skin lesions are not consistent with EM, and EM does not cause lymphadenopathy, aminotransferase elevations, or eosinophilia.

The reactions that are generally classified within the spectrum of severe cutaneous adverse reactions include acute generalized exanthematous pustulosis, Stevens-Johnson syndrome/toxic epidermal necrolysis, DRESS, and vasculitis. Stevens-Johnson syndrome (SJS) and toxic epidermal necrolysis (TEN) are characterized by fever, skin pain, and mucocutaneous lesions resulting in epidermal death and sloughing. The clinical difference between SJS and TEN is the severity and percentage of body surface involved. SJS involves less than 10% of body surface area, SJS/TEN overlap involves 10% to 30%, and TEN involves greater than 30%. This patient's skin lesions are not compatible with SJS or TEN, and these conditions cannot explain the patient's other systemic findings.

KEY POINT

- **Drug reaction with eosinophilia and systemic symptoms (DRESS) is a serious cutaneous adverse reaction characterized by a generalized papular eruption, facial edema, fever, arthralgia, and generalized lymphadenopathy and is commonly associated with elevated aminotransferase levels, eosinophilia, and lymphocytosis.**

Bibliography

Knowles SR, Shapiro LE, Shear NH. Anticonvulsant hypersensitivity syndrome: incidence, prevention and management. Drug Saf. 1999;21(6):489-501. [PMID: 10612272]

Item 5   Answer: D

Educational Objective: Diagnose squamous cell carcinoma in a renal transplant recipient.

Long-term immunosuppression to prevent allograft rejection increases the risk of malignancy about 100 times that of the general population. The most common posttransplant cancers involve the skin, including the lips. Skin cancers in transplant recipients differ from those in the general population. Squamous cell carcinoma is more common than basal cell carcinoma in transplant recipients; transplant recipients develop lesions at an earlier age and at multiple sites; squamous cell carcinomas are usually associated with multiple warts and premalignant keratoses, such that their appearance may be misleading; and tumors in transplant recipients are more aggressive and are more likely to recur after resection. Superficial tumors can be managed with excision, and, in select instances, destructive methods including cryotherapy or electrodesiccation and curettage. Invasive cancers require excision with margin evaluation.

Kaposi sarcoma usually manifests as a purple nodule or plaque predominantly affecting the legs in persons of Mediterranean, Jewish, Arabic, Caribbean, or African descent, possibly related to the geographic distribution of human herpesvirus 8.

Melanoma may account for up to 6% of posttransplant skin cancers in adults, but the clinical features in this patient are not consistent with melanoma.

Psoriasis may occur in transplant recipients, but this patient's lesion is not typical of psoriasis, which typically presents as a thick, silvery scale on an erythematous plaque.

KEY POINT

- The most common cancers in transplant recipients involve the skin, particularly squamous cell carcinoma; these cancers are more aggressive than those in the general population.

Bibliography

Zafar SY, Howell DN, Gockerman JP. Malignancy after solid organ transplantation: an overview. Oncologist. 2008;13(7):769-778. [PMID: 18614590]

Item 6   Answer: C

Educational Objective: Diagnose chigger bites.

The correct diagnosis is chigger bites. The history of outdoor activity and the finding of erythematous excoriated papules along clothing lines, occasionally with a central punctum, are consistent with the diagnosis of chigger bites. Appropriate therapy consists of a mid-strength topical corticosteroid. Camphor and menthol lotion is helpful for the symptomatic relief of pruritus associated with insect bites.

If a patient asked the pharmacist for a camphor and menthol lotion, it is likely he or she would receive Sarna® lotion, as it is the most common brand of camphor and menthol lotion available. "Sarna" is also a Spanish word for scabies. In fact, the product is widely used in Latin countries for the symptomatic relief of pruritus associated with scabies. For Spanish-speaking patients, forewarning the patient about the possibility of receiving a product labeled "Sarna" can prevent concerned revisits or office telephone calls in this situation.

Bedbug bites occur most frequently on exposed sites such as the face, neck, arms, and hands and present as pruritic, urticaria-like papules arranged in a row with a central hemorrhagic punctum. The patient's outdoor activities and the distribution of the bites along the sock line make this diagnosis unlikely.

Brown recluse spider bites are rare and are most likely to present as rapidly progressive, necrotic skin lesions. Furthermore, brown recluse spiders are not found in Florida, the Southeast coast, the mid-Atlantic or northern states, or the far West. In the United States, brown recluse spiders are located in the central and south central regions.

Scabies infestation causes intense itching, a papular or vesicular rash, and subcutaneous burrows that are most often found in the interdigital webs, flexure surface of the wrists, penis, axillae, nipples, umbilicus, scrotum, and buttocks. This patient's lesions do not have these characteristics.

KEY POINT

- A history of outdoor activity and a finding of erythematous, excoriated papules along clothing lines, occasionally with a central punctum, are consistent with the diagnosis of chigger bites.

Bibliography

Schexnayder SM, Schexnayder RE. Bites, stings, and other painful things. Pediatr Ann. 2000;29(6):354-358. [PMID: 10868431]

Item 7   Answer: C

Educational Objective: Diagnose herpes simplex infection (herpetic folliculitis).

Folliculitis is a superficial or deep infection or inflammation limited to the hair follicles. This patient has herpetic folliculitis. The figure reveals multiple, clear, fluid-filled vesicles, which are the characteristic primary lesions of herpetic skin infections. This patient most likely shaved through the active lesion of his recurrent herpes labialis, spreading the infection across his beard area. These vesicular lesions will erode and crust over. Treatment options include a course of antiviral drugs such acyclovir, valacyclovir, or famciclovir.

There are no comedones present, as one would expect in acne vulgaris. Furthermore, acne is not generally tender, and an extensive eruption appearing in 1 day would be unusual for acne vulgaris.

Pseudomonas folliculitis primarily affects the trunk. The papules and pustules characteristically have a small, pink flare and are pruritic, and there is usually a history of hot-tub, whirlpool, or swimming-pool exposure. The distribution, appearance, and lack of water exposure make *Pseudomonas* folliculitis unlikely.

Staphylococcal folliculitis may occur as a beard folliculitis, but the lesions are typically raised, pruritic, erythematous, and less than 5 mm in diameter, with apical pustules. Lesions of staphylococcal folliculitis are not vesicular.

Eosinophilic folliculitis is an intensely pruritic, nonvesicular eruption of 3- to 5-mm papules or pustules found mainly on the scalp, face, neck, and upper chest. In the United States, eosinophilic folliculitis is found primarily in adults with advanced HIV infection but also has been reported in infants and patients with hematologic diseases and as a side effect of medication. Excoriation of the lesions is quite common and alters the primary morphology. This patient has no history of HIV infection, hematologic disease, or medication use, which makes eosinophilic folliculitis unlikely.

KEY POINT

- The vesicle is the primary lesion of herpes simplex infection and may cause folliculitis in the beard area.

Bibliography

Fatahzadeh M, Schwartz RA. Human herpes simplex virus infections: epidemiology, pathogenesis, symptomatology, diagnosis, and management. J Am Acad Dermatol. 2007;57(5):737-763. [PMID: 17939933]

Item 8   Answer: C

Educational Objective: Manage cutaneous lupus erythematosus.

Smoking is known to adversely affect the efficacy of therapy with antimalarial agents in patients with cutaneous lesions of lupus erythematosus. The mechanism of this phenomenon is not understood, but the products of cigarette smoking may interfere with antimalarial agents, lupus may be worsened by these chemicals, or both. Smoking cessation is therefore the most appropriate choice prior to initiating more aggressive and potentially toxic therapy.

Both methotrexate and thalidomide are treatments for cutaneous lupus erythematosus that is resistant to antimalarial agents, but smoking-cessation efforts should occur prior to the initiation of either of these more toxic alternatives.

Both amlodipine and hydrochlorothiazide are known to cause or exacerbate subacute cutaneous lupus erythematosus, but they have not been implicated as a cause of chronic cutaneous lupus erythematosus.

KEY POINT

- **Smoking interferes with therapy of cutaneous lupus erythematosus.**

Bibliography

Hügel R, Schwarz T, Gläser R. Resistance to hydroxychloroquine due to smoking in a patient with lupus erythematosus tumidus. Br J Dermatol. 2007;157(5):1081-1083. [PMID: 17854374]

Item 9   Answer: A

Educational Objective: Manage lentigo maligna.

This patient's lesion is large and irregular with uneven pigmentation. The most likely diagnosis is malignant melanoma in situ (lentigo maligna type). Lesions may have black as well as light-tan pigmentation. Lentigo maligna grows slowly and is commonly present for many years before the diagnosis is established. In early stages, the lesion is confined to the epidermis; however, once it invades the dermis, it is just as lethal as any other melanoma. Lentigo maligna is the most important exception to the general rule that pigmented lesions should never receive shave biopsy. The atypical melanocytes grow at the dermal-epidermal junction, and a broad, shallow shave biopsy allows accurate diagnosis without disfiguring the patient. This sampling technique is different from the complete excision recommended in other forms of melanoma.

Punch biopsies should never include normal skin, as this only increases the risk of sampling error. In the setting of lentigo maligna, even a punch biopsy from the center of

the lesion has a false-negative rate of up to 80% and is not preferred to shave biopsy.

Even though this skin lesion is asymptomatic and has been present for many years, reassurance is inappropriate in this setting because lentigo maligna melanoma is slow growing, may be present for many years before the diagnosis is made, and can be lethal if not diagnosed and treated properly.

KEY POINT

- **A broad, shallow shave biopsy is the preferred method for diagnosis of lentigo maligna.**

Bibliography

Cockerell CJ. Biopsy technique for pigmented lesions. Semin Cutan Med Surg. 1997;16(2):108-112. [PMID: 9220549]

Item 10   Answer: C

Educational Objective: Diagnose urticarial vasculitis.

Urticarial plaques that are fixed in location for more than 24 hours should be biopsied to rule out urticarial vasculitis. Patients often report that the lesions burn rather than itch. Lesions commonly heal with bruising. Most cases of urticarial vasculitis are idiopathic, but it can also be associated with autoimmune diseases (most commonly systemic lupus erythematosus), drug reactions, infections, or cancer. If urticarial vasculitis is diagnosed on skin biopsy, the next diagnostic step is measurement of serum complement levels. The presence of hypocomplementemia predicts the presence of systemic vasculitis.

Laboratory testing and imaging studies are appropriate for patients with urticaria when prompted by additional signs or symptoms. A chest radiograph is not appropriate in the absence of respiratory symptoms. Latex radioallergosorbent testing (RAST) would be appropriate for a patient with a history of hives that develop at the site of contact with latex. A stool sample for ova and parasites would be appropriate for a patient with peripheral eosinophilia, diarrhea, or other gastrointestinal symptoms.

KEY POINT

- **Urticarial plaques that remain fixed in position for longer than 24 hours should be biopsied to rule out urticarial vasculitis.**

Bibliography

Brodell LA, Beck LA. Differential diagnosis of chronic urticaria. Ann Allergy Asthma Immunol. 2008;100(3):181-188. [PMID: 18426134]

Item 11   Answer: D

Educational Objective: Manage toxic epidermal necrolysis.

This patient has toxic epidermal necrolysis (TEN), which is characterized by mucous membrane involvement (eyes, oral mucosa, and genitalia in this patient), epidermal detachment affecting greater than 30% of the body surface area, and a positive Nikolsky sign (lateral pressure on non-blistered skin leads to denudation). TEN is almost always caused by a medication. The medications most closely associated with TEN are allopurinol, aromatic anticonvulsants (carbamazepine, phenytoin, phenobarbital), lamotrigine, sulfasalazine, sulfonamide antibiotics, NSAIDs, and nevirapine. In patients with TEN, survival and severity of disease are improved when the suspected causative medication and all unnecessary medications are immediately stopped.

The two most important determinants of outcome in patients with TEN are stopping all unnecessary medications and management in a burn unit.

Empiric treatment with acyclovir is not indicated because there is no evidence of an active herpes simplex infection; TEN is rarely caused by infection (including viral infections), and starting acyclovir would add an unnecessary medication.

Empiric antibiotics are not indicated in the initial management of TEN because they expose the patient to unnecessary drugs when the goal is to minimize medication exposures. However, because TEN typically results in loss of epidermis over a significant portion of the body surface area, patients are at risk for life-threatening infections during the course of the disease.

Systemic corticosteroids may be useful in the management of severe allergic drug reactions, particularly early in the course; however, clinical trials do not support the use of corticosteroids once the diagnosis of TEN is established, as their use predisposes the patient to serious side effects, including superinfection.

KEY POINT

- The most important initial step in managing patients with toxic epidermal necrolysis is stopping the suspected causative medication, as well as stopping all unnecessary medications.

Bibliography

Mockenhaupt M, Viboud C, Dunant A, et al. Stevens-Johnson syndrome and toxic epidermal necrolysis: assessment of medication risks with emphasis on recently marketed drugs. The EuroSCAR-study. J Invest Dermatol. 2008;128(1):35-44. [PMID: 17805350]

Item 12   Answer: D

Educational Objective: Treat pemphigus vulgaris.

Painful oral erosions are a common presenting manifestation of pemphigus vulgaris, which then may spread to the skin, usually the scalp, chest, face, axillae, and groin. Referral to a dermatologist who is skilled in treating pemphigus is recommended. Oral corticosteroids (1 to 2 mg/kg/d of prednisone) have the most rapid onset and are therefore indicated for initial therapy of pemphigus vulgaris. Once patients are on prednisone, immunosuppressive agents such as azathioprine should be added to limit the corticosteroid toxicity.

Cyclophosphamide, mycophenolate mofetil, rituximab, and intravenous immune globulin are viable corticosteroid-sparing agents in the treatment of pemphigus, and one of them might be initiated early in the course of the disease; however, they are not first-line treatments.

Cyclophosphamide is an excellent immunosuppressive/cytotoxic agent; however, it is a third choice for pemphigus therapy due to long-term consequences associated with its use.

A few studies involving a small number of patients suggest that intravenous immune globulin may improve disease in patients with pemphigus. Treatment is generally recommended for disease that is recalcitrant to corticosteroid therapy.

Mycophenolate mofetil has been used in patients with pemphigus vulgaris, but it is usually reserved for the patient who is either intolerant to azathioprine or in whom azathioprine is contraindicated.

Rituximab is approved for use in patients with B-cell lymphomas and rheumatoid arthritis, and its usefulness in treating pemphigus has been documented in open label trials.

KEY POINT

- The initial therapy for pemphigus vulgaris is prednisone with the later addition of an immunosuppressive agent to limit corticosteroid toxicity.

Bibliography

Prajapati V, Mydlarski PR. Advances in pemphigus therapy. Skin Therapy Lett. 2008;13(3):4-7. [PMID: 18506357]

Item 13   Answer: C

Educational Objective: Diagnose rosacea.

This patient has rosacea, which is an inflammatory dermatitis characterized by erythema, telangiectasias, papules, pustules, and sebaceous hyperplasia that develops on the central face, including the nasolabial folds. Rhinophyma, or the presence of a bulbous, red nose, is a variant of this condition.

Dermatomyositis may be associated with various skin manifestations. Periungual erythema and malar erythema, consisting of a light purple (heliotrope) edematous discoloration of the upper eyelids and periorbital tissues, are the most common presentations. Dermatomyositis also may cause an erythematous, papular eruption that develops in a V-shaped pattern along the neck and upper torso; in a shawl-shaped pattern along the upper arms; and on the elbows, knees, ankles, and other sun-exposed areas. Involvement of the hands may include scaly, slightly raised, purplish papules and plaques that develop in periarticular areas of the metacarpal and interphalangeal joints and other bony prominences (Gottron sign) and scaly, rough, dry, darkened, cracked, horizontal lines on the palmar and lateral aspects of the fingers (mechanic's hands).

Psoriasis usually involves the scalp, elbows, or other areas but does not typically manifest as an isolated facial rash. Characteristic findings of psoriasis include an erythematous plaque with an adherent, variably thick, silvery scale.

Seborrheic dermatitis causes white, scaling macules and papules that are sharply demarcated on yellowish-red skin and may be greasy or dry. Sticky crusts and fissures often develop behind the ears, and significant dandruff or scaling of the scalp frequently occurs. Seborrheic dermatitis may develop in a "butterfly"-shaped pattern but also may involve the nasolabial folds, eyebrows, and forehead. This condition usually improves during the summer and worsens in the fall and winter.

Distinguishing rosacea from systemic lupus erythematosus can be difficult and is frequently a reason that patients are referred to a dermatologist. Systemic lupus erythematosus is unlikely in this patient because the malar rash associated with this condition is usually photosensitive and often spares the nasolabial folds and the areas below the nares and lower lip (areas relatively protected from the sun).

KEY POINT

- **Rosacea is an inflammatory dermatitis characterized by erythema, telangiectasias, papules, pustules, and sebaceous hyperplasia that affects the central face, including the nasolabial folds.**

Bibliography

Powell FC. Clinical practice. Rosacea. N Engl J Med. 2005;352(8):793-803. [PMID: 15728812]

Item 14   Answer: C

Educational Objective: Diagnose vasculitic ulcers.

The patient has atypical-appearing ulcers. The presence of irregular, punched-out–appearing ulcers with fibrinous bases in a patient with known rheumatoid arthritis suggests the possibility of vasculitis. The appropriate diagnostic test is a punch biopsy. Biopsy should also be considered for nonhealing ulcers.

Ulcers on the medial leg are most commonly due to venous insufficiency and are often associated with the hyperpigmentation of venous stasis. This patient's ulcers are located on the lateral aspect of the leg and are not associated with hyperpigmentation. Neuropathic ulcers are often associated with peripheral neuropathy, appear over pressure points such as the metacarpal joints, and may have a hyperkeratotic border. Arterial ulcers are typically found at the end of digits or over pressure points and are found in association with other chronic findings of ischemic disease, such as a history of claudication; atrophic, shiny, and hairless skin; and thickened toenails. Pulses are often absent, the skin is cool, and capillary refill is slow. Arterial ulcers are not commonly located on the leg unless this happens to be a point of pressure (as might occur with a cast, brace, or prosthesis).

Measurement of the ankle-brachial index is useful when arterial ulcers are suspected, but this patient's physical findings do not support arterial disease.

Testing with a monofilament is useful in assessing risk for neuropathic ulcers but is not useful in diagnosing the etiology of ulcers.

Venous duplex Doppler ultrasonography is useful in assessing the presence of venous incompetence and planning surgery for deep venous disease; however, it is unlikely to be helpful in a patient who lacks physical examination findings typical of venous insufficiency.

KEY POINT

- **The diagnostic test of choice for atypical-appearing or nonhealing ulcers is biopsy.**

Bibliography

Fonder MA, Lazarus GS, Cowan DA, Aronson-Cook B, Kohli AR, Mamelak AJ. Treating the chronic wound: a practical approach to the care of nonhealing wounds and wound care dressings. J Am Acad Dermatol. 2008;58(2):185-206. [PMID: 18222318]

Item 15   Answer: C

Educational Objective: Diagnose pustular psoriasis.

An erythematous eruption that involves greater than 90% of the body surface area is indicative of erythroderma. The most common causes of erythroderma are drug eruptions, psoriasis, atopic dermatitis, and cutaneous T-cell lymphoma; however, the erythroderma may also be idiopathic. Patients such as this, who have a history of psoriasis and are treated with systemic corticosteroids, are particularly prone to developing an acute pustular erythrodermic flare days to weeks after discontinuation of the corticosteroids. The appropriate management is to treat the underlying disease (psoriasis in this patient), provide general supportive care for the erythrodermic skin, and treat complications such as temperature dysregulation, fluid and electrolyte shifts, and superinfections.

Drug hypersensitivity syndromes are classically associated with anticonvulsants, allopurinol, dapsone, and NSAIDs. They begin 3 to 6 weeks after the initiation of therapy. Angiotensin-converting enzyme inhibitors (lisinopril) are not commonly associated with hypersensitivity drug eruptions. In addition, patients with hypersensitivity drug eruptions typically present with widespread erythema that evolves over weeks rather than days and skin that is itchy more than painful, as well as facial swelling, lymphadenopathy, eosinophilia, atypical lymphocytosis, and elevated aminotransferases.

Because of this patient's history of prostate cancer, paraneoplastic erythroderma may be a consideration. However, paraneoplastic erythroderma evolves slowly over months to years rather than in a few days.

Sézary syndrome is a leukemic form of cutaneous T-cell lymphoma that evolves slowly and is intensely pruritic. A severe, fissured keratoderma and lymphadenopathy are often present. This patient's symptoms are not consistent with the diagnosis of Sézary syndrome.

Staphylococcal scalded skin syndrome (SSSS) may be difficult to differentiate from pustular psoriasis, as it also presents with widespread erythroderma and skin pain. It is most common in children less than 6 years of age, but adults with underlying immunosuppression or renal failure may be affected. This patient is an adult with normal renal function who is without significant immunosuppression. Clinical features that are characteristic of SSSS include perioral crusting and fissuring and early involvement of the intertriginous areas. The diagnosis is made clinically, but it can be confirmed by isolation of *Staphylococcus aureus* with bacterial culture of any suspected source of infection, blood, and mucous membranes.

KEY POINT

- **Patients with a history of psoriasis who are treated with systemic corticosteroids may develop an acute pustular erythrodermic flare days to weeks after the systemic corticosteroids are discontinued.**

Bibliography

Rothe MJ, Bernstein ML, Grant-Kels JM. Life-threatening erythroderma: diagnosing and treating the "red man." Clin Dermatol. 2005;23(2):206-217. [PMID: 15802214]

Item 16   Answer: A

Educational Objective: Manage a patient with neurogenic pruritus.

This patient has subacute, severe, and generalized pruritus. In addition, only secondary erosions are present, with no identifiable primary dermatologic lesions (for example, papule, vesicle, pustule). These characteristics suggest neurogenic pruritus. Neurogenic pruritus is itch caused by a systemic disease or circulating pruritogens and requires an investigation into the underlying etiology. Important underlying causes of neurogenic pruritus include cholestasis, end-stage renal disease, thyroid disease (hypo- or hyperthyroidism), iron deficiency anemia, malignancy (usually hematologic or lymphoma), medications (opiates), and HIV infection. Laboratory studies in patients who have pruritus without obvious cause might include a complete blood count, erythrocyte sedimentation rate, serum creatinine level, serum thyroid-stimulating hormone level, and liver chemistry tests. Patients should also be evaluated with age- and sex-appropriate cancer screening tests, and additional tests should be guided by the presence of symptoms.

Because this patient has no identifiable primary skin lesions, a skin biopsy is unlikely to reveal the etiology of her pruritus. Patch testing is useful in the diagnosis of contact dermatitis, but this diagnosis is unlikely in the absence of an eczematous dermatitis. The use of systemic corticosteroids is not indicated to treat pruritus prior to establishing a diagnosis, and it exposes the patient to unnecessary side effects.

KEY POINT

- **Neurogenic pruritus should prompt a thorough evaluation for systemic causes.**

Bibliography

Greaves MW. Itch in systemic disease: therapeutic options. Dermatol Ther. 2005;18(4):323-327. [PMID: 16297004]

Item 17   Answer: C

Educational Objective: Diagnose locally disseminated herpes simplex virus infection as a complication of atopic dermatitis.

The skin around the left eye has multiple coalescing, crusted vesicles on an erythematous base and is red and edematous. The presence of discrete and coalescing vesicles should immediately suggest the diagnosis of herpesvirus infection. There are also widespread, symmetrical, eczematous patches on the trunk and extremities, supporting the diagnosis of atopic dermatitis. Herpesvirus infection can locally disseminate in abnormal skin, such as that of patients with atopic dermatitis, in which the normal barrier function is lost.

Patients with eczema herpeticum may feel ill, be febrile, and have regional lymphadenopathy. The diagnosis can be confirmed by direct fluorescent antibody testing or herpes viral culture. Emergent ophthalmologic consultation should be obtained in this patient to evaluate for herpes keratitis. Primary herpes keratoconjunctivitis is treated with topical trifluorothymidine, vidarabine ointment, or acyclovir gel. Systemic antiviral therapy is typically prescribed for primary herpesvirus infection of the skin, but evidence for its efficacy is unclear. Because eczema herpeticum is considered to be a locally disseminated disease, treatment with systemic antiviral agents is appropriate. A more prolonged course may be needed for treatment of immunosuppressed patients. In some cases, hospitalization is needed for management of acutely ill patients.

Allergic contact dermatitis can cause edema and small papulovesicles in affected skin, but it does not cause the discrete vesicles that are characteristic of herpes simplex virus infection. Vesicles are not seen in atopic dermatitis. The presence of serum and crusting may suggest staphylococcal infection, and, indeed, a secondary infection is possible; however, the finding of vesicles and, later in the course of infection, punched-out–appearing ulcers or erosions is characteristic of herpes simplex virus infection.

KEY POINT

- **Patients with atopic dermatitis are more susceptible to disseminated cutaneous herpesvirus infection (eczema herpeticum).**

Bibliography

Peng WM, Jenneck C, Bussmann C, et al. Risk factors of atopic dermatitis patients for eczema herpeticum. J Invest Dermatol. 2007;127(5):1261-1263. [PMID: 17170734]

Item 18   Answer: C

Educational Objective: Diagnose keratoacanthoma.

Keratoacanthoma is an epithelial neoplasm that is characterized by rapid growth over 2 to 6 weeks and by a crater-like configuration. Early lesions are frequently misdiagnosed as skin infections. The typical early lesion is a hard, erythematous nodule with a keratotic (horny) center. Keratoacanthomas typically occur on heavily sun-damaged skin, usually in older persons, with a peak age of 60 years. As the lesion enlarges, the center of the crater becomes more prominent. Unlike typical squamous cell carcinomas, keratoacanthomas are capable of spontaneous resolution by terminal differentiation, in which the tumor "keratinizes itself to death." The clinical presentation and characteristic histologic features establish the diagnosis.

Keratoacanthomas occurring together with sebaceous adenomas suggest a diagnosis of Muir-Torre syndrome, an autosomal dominant syndrome associated with colon cancer. Muir-Torre syndrome is allelic to the hereditary nonpolyposis colorectal cancer syndrome.

Because keratoacanthomas may cause significant local tissue destruction, simple observation is generally not recommended despite the tendency for spontaneous involution. Prompt surgical excision is recommended for solitary lesions on the trunk or extremities. Intralesional 5-fluorouracil or methotrexate, topical imiquimod, and radiation therapy have also been used to treat large lesions or those in areas where surgical excision would be anatomically difficult.

Abscesses are warm, red, and tender and may be fluctuant if the lesion is palpated.

Keloids present as slow-growing, hard nodules, often with a dumbbell shape. They occur at sites of prior trauma.

Nodular basal cell carcinoma is often found on the face and is characterized by slow growth, the presence of a skin-toned to pink, pearly, translucent papule with telangiectasia, rolled borders, and central depression, often with ulceration.

KEY POINT

- **Keratoacanthomas are rapidly growing, non-tender, firm nodules with depressed keratotic centers that are often misdiagnosed as cutaneous infections.**

Bibliography

Sarabi K, Selim A, Khachemoune A. Sporadic and syndromic keratoacanthomas: diagnosis and management. Dermatol Nurs. 2007; 19(2):166-170. [PMID: 17526304]

Item 19   Answer: A

Educational Objective: Manage scarring ocular cicatricial pemphigoid.

This patient probably has ocular cicatricial pemphigoid based upon the history of dryness of the eyes and evidence of conjunctival scarring (trichiasis and symblepharon).

Ocular pemphigoid can result from several immunologic phenomena, including linear IgA deposition, linear IgG deposition resembling bullous pemphigoid, or linear IgG deposition resembling epidermolysis bullosa acquisita. This disorder can be sight-threatening and, therefore, warrants accurate diagnosis with biopsy and appropriate histopathologic studies. Biopsy of the conjunctiva will reveal subepithelial separation below the basement membrane, and direct immunofluorescence will reveal linear deposition of IgG and C3 at the basement membrane zone. Once the diagnosis is confirmed, aggressive management with corticosteroids and cyclophosphamide is indicated. However, treatment with prednisone and cyclophosphamide should wait until confirmation of the diagnosis.

Herpes zoster ophthalmicus is a complication of varicella-zoster virus infection involving the ophthalmic division of the fifth cranial nerve. Most patients with herpes zoster ophthalmicus will experience headache and fever associated with pain or hypesthesia in the affected eye and forehead. With outbreak of the characteristic cutaneous vesicles, patients typically develop hyperemic conjunctivitis. Severely ill patients are often treated with intravenous acyclovir, but less-ill patients may be successfully treated with oral valacyclovir or famciclovir. In the absence of the typical vesicular eruption of herpes zoster, there is no indication for intravenous acyclovir.

Bacterial conjunctivitis is caused by a range of gram-positive and gram-negative organisms and is characterized by presentation in one eye, but this condition often spreads to involve the other eye and is associated with purulent discharge. Empiric treatment with broad-spectrum topical antibiotics is indicated in patients with bacterial conjunctivitis. The patient's 6-month history of ocular symptoms is not compatible with an acute bacterial conjunctivitis, and treatment with a topical antibiotic should not take precedence over a conjunctival biopsy.

KEY POINT

- **Ocular cicatricial pemphigoid is sight-threatening and warrants accurate diagnosis with biopsy and appropriate histopathologic studies, as well as aggressive management with corticosteroids and cyclophosphamide.**

Bibliography

Chang JH, McCluskey PJ. Ocular cicatricial pemphigoid: manifestations and management. Curr Allergy Asthma Rep. 2005;5(4):333-338. [PMID: 15967079]

Item 20   Answer: D

Educational Objective: Treat pyoderma gangrenosum.

This patient has pyoderma gangrenosum (PG). PG typically begins as tender papules, papulopustules, or vesicles that spontaneously ulcerate and progress to painful ulcers with a purulent base and undermined, ragged, violaceous borders. Active lesions often show a gunmetal-gray border surrounded by an erythematous halo. Pathergy, a phenomenon characterized by exacerbation of disease after trauma, is observed in 20% to 30% of patients and can initiate or aggravate PG. PG is associated with an underlying systemic disease in 50% to 78% of patients, and it can present before, concurrently with, or after the development of the associated underlying condition. Diseases most commonly associated with PG are inflammatory bowel disease (either ulcerative colitis or Crohn disease), rheumatoid arthritis, seronegative spondyloarthropathy, and hematologic disease or malignancy, specifically acute myeloid leukemia. PG reflects the activity of the bowel disease in about 50% of patients with inflammatory bowel disease. Treatment of PG is immunosuppression, most often with systemic corticosteroids.

The diagnosis of PG requires ruling out other entities that can mimic PG, including infection. This patient's normal leukocyte count and lack of fever argue against infection and, therefore, do not support empiric treatment with antibiotics. Wet-to-dry dressings and surgical debridement are contraindicated, because both are traumatic to the skin and may worsen the PG. In patients with extensive, poorly controlled colitis, proctocolectomy has been suggested as a treatment option for those with severe, refractory PG. However, there are case reports of PG first appearing after proctocolectomy. Nevertheless, proctocolectomy is an inappropriate treatment for a patient with well-controlled colitis prior to initiation of first-line treatment with systemic corticosteroids.

KEY POINT

- **Systemic corticosteroids are the initial treatment of choice for pyoderma gangrenosum.**

Bibliography

Reichrath J, Bens G, Bonowitz A, Tilgen W. Treatment recommendations for pyoderma gangrenosum: an evidence-based review of the literature based on more than 350 patients. J Am Acad Dermatol. 2005;53(2):273-283. [PMID: 16021123]

Item 21   Answer: B

Educational Objective: Treat gram-negative folliculitis as a complication of acne vulgaris.

Gram-negative folliculitis is a complication of long-term oral antibiotic therapy for acne vulgaris. The typical history is an acute pustular exacerbation of preexisting common acne or nodular acne. Physical examination reveals many inflamed pustules, most often on the central face. The diagnosis is confirmed by a culture positive for gram-negative bacteria, usually *Escherichia coli,* in the nares and/or from a pustule. The broad-spectrum antibiotic allows overgrowth of gram-negative organisms in the anterior nares. Nearly 85% of patients treated with an oral antibiotic for longer than 6 months have a dominant gram-negative organism present in the nares. This organism can then secondarily infect acne lesions, causing the flare of pustules. Isotretinoin is not an antibiotic, but it is the treatment of choice for gram-negative folliculitis. Isotretinoin modulates epidermal proliferation; induces orthokeratosis; and inhibits comedo formation and comedolysis via disruption of desmosomes, inhibition of inflammation, shrinkage of sebaceous glands, and inhibition of sebum secretion. Common side effects include dry skin, chapped lips, dry eyes, nosebleeds, and hair shedding. It also dries the anterior nares, ridding the mucosa of the colonized organisms, and it treats the underlying acne effectively. Isotretinoin is a pregnancy risk category X drug. All prescribers, patients, wholesalers, and dispensing pharmacies must be registered in the U.S. Food and Drug Administration–approved iPLEDGE program (1-866-495-0654).

The antibiotics ciprofloxacin, minocycline, and trimethoprim-sulfamethoxazole would likely result in a temporary improvement of the pustules, but they would not eliminate the gram-negative overgrowth from the nares. Recurrence would rapidly follow discontinuation of the antibiotic.

Spironolactone may improve this patient's acne but would not address the underlying gram-negative overgrowth.

KEY POINT

- **Gram-negative folliculitis is a complication of long-term oral antibiotic therapy for acne vulgaris; isotretinoin is the treatment of choice.**

Bibliography

James WD. Clinical practice. Acne. N Engl J Med. 2005;352(14): 1463-1472. [PMID: 15814882]

Item 22   Answer: D

Educational Objective: Diagnose lentigo maligna.

This patient's lesion is large and irregular with mottled pigmentation. The most likely diagnosis is malignant melanoma in situ (lentigo maligna type), which is confined to the epidermis. Lentigo maligna grows slowly and is commonly present for many years before the diagnosis is established. Once it invades the dermis (lentigo maligna melanoma), it is just as lethal as any other melanoma. The patient should be sent to an experienced dermatologist for a broad, paper-thin shave biopsy to sample the lesion. This biopsy technique is specific to lentigo maligna and is different from techniques used in other melanomas.

Pigmented actinic keratosis is usually 4 mm or less; has a keratotic, rough surface; and appears on sun-exposed skin. It ranges in clinical presentation from macular erythematous patches to large hyperkeratotic excrescences. The erythema surrounding the base of the lesion and its rough, prickly surface texture help differentiate this lesion from other skin conditions.

Pigmented basal cell carcinoma typically presents as a firm, pearly papule with telangiectasia and flecks of brown pigment. With time, the center may umbilicate and ulcerate to produce the characteristic rolled borders.

Benign solar lentigo is tan to light brown and evenly pigmented, which helps distinguish it from lentigo maligna. However, like lentigo maligna, it may have irregular borders. Typical lesions range in size from a few millimeters to over 1 cm in diameter. Like lentigo maligna, these lesions are typically found in older individuals on sun-exposed skin.

Seborrheic keratosis is a painless, nonmalignant growth that appears as a waxy, brownish patch or plaque. Seborrheic keratoses typically exhibit horn cysts (epidermal cysts filled with keratin) on the surface that can best be visualized with a magnifying lens. Treatment is necessary only if lesions are symptomatic or interfere with function.

KEY POINT
- **Lentigo maligna melanoma begins as a tan-brown macule on sun-exposed skin of older individuals and may be present for many years before it invades the dermis.**

Bibliography
Cockerell CJ. Biopsy technique for pigmented lesions. Semin Cutan Med Surg. 1997;16(2):108-112. [PMID: 9220549]

Item 23   Answer: D
Educational Objective: Treat a patient with perioral dermatitis caused by fluorinated corticosteroid use.

This young woman has perioral dermatitis, which resulted from the use of a fluorinated topical corticosteroid to control seborrheic dermatitis. Perioral dermatitis is a papular and pustular eruption that appears around the mouth and is usually caused by the use of topical or inhaled corticosteroids. This patient initially had seborrheic dermatitis, which is itchy, recurrent, red, and scaly and responds well to fluorinated topical corticosteroids. However, fluorinated topical corticosteroids should be avoided on the facial skin. If used chronically, they may produce atrophy, telangiectasia, or a rosacea- or perioral dermatitis–type papular and pustular rash. Facial seborrheic dermatitis should instead be treated with nonsteroidal preparations such as ketoconazole cream. If this patient's seborrheic dermatitis flares upon discontinuation of the triamcinolone, ketoconazole cream is the treatment of choice.

Topical corticosteroid therapy should be avoided in this patient. Increasing the corticosteroid potency, as with clobetasol, will only worsen the perioral dermatitis.

Benzoyl peroxide is an excellent treatment for acne; however, it is known to be quite irritating and drying. It is likely to exacerbate this patient's seborrheic dermatitis. Additionally, this patient's perioral dermatitis will resolve spontaneously after discontinuation of the topical corticosteroid.

Neomycin ointment is not known to improve acne, rosacea, or perioral dermatitis. It is, however, one of the top culprits in causing allergic contact dermatitis reactions. There is no role for this medication in the treatment of perioral dermatitis.

KEY POINT
- **Perioral dermatitis is a papular and pustular eruption that appears around the mouth and is usually caused by the use of topical or inhaled corticosteroids.**

Bibliography
Weber K, Thurmayr R. Critical appraisal of reports on the treatment of perioral dermatitis. Dermatology. 2005;210(4):300-307. [PMID: 15942216]

Item 24   Answer: E
Educational Objective: Understand the association between recurrent herpes zoster and HIV infection.

This patient most likely has HIV infection. Herpes zoster infection is the reactivation of the varicella virus in a single cutaneous nerve. Recurrence of herpes zoster infection in the immunocompetent host is uncommon but does occur. When recurrent disease is present, the underlying cause is overwhelmingly HIV infection. In this patient, there is a band of crusts and blisters on an erythematous base along a dermatomal distribution on the left thorax. There is evidence of scarring in a dermatome several centimeters above the currently involved site, representing a previous herpes zoster infection. Almost half of all herpes zoster episodes diagnosed in patients with HIV are recurrences. The advent of highly active antiretroviral therapy has not lessened the incidence of recurrent herpes zoster infection in patients with HIV infection. Patients on chemotherapy and patients who have undergone organ transplant may also develop recurrent herpes zoster. All patients with HIV infection and herpes zoster infection are treated with antiviral therapy regardless of the age of the zoster lesions. Most patients with HIV infection can be treated with an oral antiviral drug with good bioavailability, such as valacyclovir, but patients with severe disease, evidence of dissemination, or ophthalmologic involvement may have better outcomes if treated with intravenous acyclovir.

A patient with unexplained weight loss and fatigue may have an underlying metabolic disease like diabetes mellitus, but diabetes is not associated with recurrent herpes zoster. Because of this patient's injection drug use, he is at risk for hepatitis B and hepatitis C, and screening for these infections is recommended. However, neither of these infections is associated with recurrent herpes zoster. This patient's alcoholism is a risk factor for cirrhosis but not for recurrent herpes zoster infection.

KEY POINT
- **Recurrent herpes zoster infection should trigger testing for possible associated HIV infection.**

Bibliography

Gebo KA, Kalyani R, Moore RD, Polydefkis MJ. The incidence of, risk factors for, and sequelae of herpes zoster among HIV patients in the highly active antiretroviral therapy era. J Acquir Immune Defic Syndr. 2005;40(2):169-174. [PMID: 16186734]

Item 25   Answer: D

Educational Objective: Understand the association between vitiligo and autoimmune diseases.

This patient has vitiligo. Vitiligo is primarily a clinical diagnosis based on characteristic skin findings of depigmented, "chalk"-white, clearly demarcated, round or oval macules that may present in a variety of distributions. Thyroid screening with measurement of the thyroid-stimulating hormone level is the single most reasonable screening test for this patient. Vitiligo has been significantly associated with various autoimmune diseases, which should lower the clinician's threshold for evaluating such diseases. A survey study of 2624 patients with vitiligo revealed a statistically significant association between vitiligo and several autoimmune diseases when compared with population frequencies of these diseases. The study found that 19.4% of all white patients aged ≥20 years had autoimmune thyroid disease; 1.78% had pernicious anemia; 0.67% had inflammatory bowel disease; 0.38% had Addison disease; and 0.19% had systemic lupus erythematosus. No statistically significant association with diabetes mellitus was found in this study. Variants of the gene *NALP1*, a regulator of the innate immune system, have been shown to be associated with the risk of developing vitiligo, as well as other epidemiologically associated autoimmune diseases, including autoimmune thyroid disease, diabetes, rheumatoid arthritis, psoriasis, pernicious anemia, systemic lupus erythematosus, and Addison disease.

Although there is a statistically significant association between vitiligo and pernicious anemia, the absolute prevalence is quite small. Because this patient has a normal complete blood count, pernicious anemia is unlikely, and measurement of the serum vitamin B_{12} level is not indicated. Similarly, the likelihood of Addison disease in a patient with normal vital signs and normal serum electrolytes is quite small, and a morning cortisol measurement is not needed. This patient has a normal BMI and no symptoms, and the vitiligo probably does not increase her risk of diabetes enough to warrant screening with a fasting glucose measurement.

KEY POINT

- **The most common systemic condition associated with vitiligo is autoimmune thyroid disease.**

Bibliography

Daneshpazhooh M, Mostofizadeh GM, Behjati J, Akhyani M, Robati RM. Anti-thyroid peroxidase antibody and vitiligo: a controlled study. BMC Dermatol. 2006;6:3. [PMID: 16526964]

Item 26   Answer: E

Educational Objective: Manage a patient with erythroderma.

This patient's signs and symptoms are consistent with a slowly evolving erythroderma. An underlying cause for erythroderma should always be sought in order to guide therapy and determine prognosis. The diagnosis of idiopathic erythroderma is one of exclusion and should only be made after all other potential causes have been ruled out. Skin biopsy with routine hematoxylin and eosin staining should be performed in every patient with erythroderma; however, histopathologic findings diagnostic of the underlying cause are present in only 50% of patients. If the initial biopsy is nondiagnostic, additional biopsies may be useful and are recommended. This patient's disease, previously diagnosed as eczema, began in adulthood and has not responded to therapy (topical corticosteroids) that is typically effective in the treatment of atopic dermatitis. In addition, he had no personal or family history of atopy (asthma, atopic dermatitis, allergic rhinitis). Atopic dermatitis rarely presents in adulthood in patients without a personal or family history of atopy and is most commonly confused in this setting with cutaneous T-cell lymphoma. Therefore, the most important next step in the management of this patient is a skin biopsy to rule out cutaneous T-cell lymphoma/Sézary syndrome.

Cyclosporine and phototherapy are potential treatments for erythroderma, either idiopathic or related to a particular cause. However, before treating erythroderma with a systemic agent or phototherapy, the cause of the erythroderma should be sought.

Antinuclear antibody and rapid plasma reagin are tests for autoimmune connective tissue disease and syphilis, respectively. Neither autoimmune connective tissue disease nor syphilis commonly causes erythroderma, making these options incorrect.

KEY POINT

- **A skin biopsy is always required in the evaluation of a patient with erythroderma.**

Bibliography

Rothe MJ, Bernstein ML, Grant-Kels JM. Life-threatening erythroderma: diagnosing and treating the "red man." Clin Dermatol. 2005;23(2):206-217. [PMID: 15802214]

Item 27   Answer: A

Educational Objective: Diagnose allergic contact dermatitis.

This patient has chronic hand dermatitis, the differential diagnosis of which includes allergic contact dermatitis (ACD) and irritant contact dermatitis. Several features of this patient's dermatitis suggest ACD, including the relatively recent onset of her condition (as opposed to lifelong), pruritus, and improvement when she is away from work. Epicutaneous patch testing is the appropriate test to evaluate for ACD and may help distinguish this from other types of chronic eczematous dermatitis, including irritant dermatitis and atopic dermatitis. This patient has a history of childhood eczema and, with her history of allergic rhinitis and family history of asthma, may also have atopic dermatitis. Hairdressers are exposed to several allergens that not infrequently cause occupational ACD. Accelerants and other chemicals can also cause allergies. Gloves may not protect a sensitized individual from reactions to all allergens, because some chemicals are able to penetrate natural rubber latex and synthetic rubber gloves.

Lymphocyte stimulation or proliferation assays are used primarily in the laboratory setting; their clinical utility in the evaluation of allergy remains uncertain. Prick testing and radioallergosorbent testing (RAST) are useful in diagnosing immediate-type hypersensitivity reactions; however, these tests are less appropriate in the setting of ACD, which is a delayed-type hypersensitivity reaction.

KEY POINT

- Epicutaneous patch testing is the gold standard for diagnosis of allergic contact dermatitis in patients with persistent eczematous dermatitis.

Bibliography

Templet JT, Hall S, Belsito DV. Etiology of hand dermatitis among patients referred for patch testing. Dermatitis. 2004;15(1):25-32. [PMID: 15573645]

Item 28   Answer: A

Educational Objective: Diagnose actinic keratoses.

This patient has actinic keratoses, common lesions that occur on sun-exposed skin of older white-skinned persons. Actinic keratoses are believed to be the earliest clinically recognized step in a biologic continuum that may result in invasive squamous cell carcinoma. Actinic keratoses are 1- to 3-mm, elevated, flesh-colored or red papules surrounded by a whitish scale. They are often easier to feel as "rough spots" on the skin than they are to see. Most patients will have, on average, 6 to 8 lesions. Most remain stable and some regress, but others enlarge to become invasive squamous cell carcinomas.

A basal cell carcinoma classically presents as a pink, pearly or translucent, dome-shaped papule with telangiectasias. The papule may have central umbilication.

A melanoma is classically a pigmented macule or plaque that is asymmetric and has irregular, scalloped, notched, or indistinct borders. It is black or dark brown or has variegated (multiple) coloration, including shades of black, red, and blue. Melanomas may also have depigmented or white areas, which represent regression of the lesion. Rarely, melanomas are not pigmented and can resemble basal cell carcinomas.

Seborrheic keratoses can be brown or black, but have discrete borders, are elevated above the surface of the skin, and have a "stuck-on" warty or waxy appearance.

KEY POINT

- Actinic keratoses are precancerous lesions that can develop into invasive squamous cell carcinoma and that typically appear as erythematous lesions with overlying hyperkeratosis.

Bibliography

Schwartz RA, Bridges TM, Butani AK, Ehrlich A. Actinic keratosis: an occupational and environmental disorder. J Eur Acad Dermatol Venereol. 2008;22(5):606-615. [PMID: 18410618]

Item 29   Answer: A

Educational Objective: Manage urticaria in a patient with salicylate sensitivity.

Individuals with the triad of asthma, nasal polyps, and aspirin sensitivity may experience hives with exposure to aspirin. Although this patient has no history of nasal polyps, they may have been missed, and an examination at this time might be revealing. This patient was recently diagnosed with peripheral vascular disease and was started on aspirin. Patients who are sensitive to aspirin may also react to benzoic acid derivatives, tartrazine, or natural salicylates. In such patients, elimination of aspirin or dietary triggers may result in resolution of the hives without the need for medication. Sodium benzoate is commonly added to foods as a preservative. Tartrazine (FD&C yellow number 5) also cross-reacts with aspirin but has largely been eliminated from food products and medications in the United States. It could still be found in products manufactured overseas, however.

Prednisone can be helpful in patients with acute urticaria refractory to antihistamines, but it plays no role in the management of chronic urticaria. Laboratory testing and imaging studies should be directed by signs or symptoms. Radioallergosorbent testing (RAST) for pollen would be appropriate in a patient with a history that suggests seasonal allergy and hives in response to pollen exposure. Skin biopsy is indicated if urticarial vasculitis is suspected by the presence of urticarial plaques that are fixed in location for more than 24 hours. This patient's hives last a few hours and then resolve, making the diagnosis of urticarial vasculitis unlikely and a skin biopsy unnecessary. Although angiotensin-converting enzyme inhibitors such as lisinopril may cause angioedema, they are rarely a cause of urticaria.

KEY POINT

- Patients with asthma and nasal polyps may experience hives due to aspirin sensitivity.

Bibliography

Namazy JA, Simon RA. Sensitivity to nonsteroidal anti-inflammatory drugs. Ann Allergy Asthma Immunol. 2002;89(6):542-550. [PMID: 12487218]

Item 30　　Answer: B

Educational Objective: Manage a neuropathic ulcer.

This patient with long-standing diabetes mellitus and evidence of peripheral neuropathy has a neuropathic ulcer. In addition to ensuring adequate vascular supply, removing devitalized tissue, and treating infection, removing pressure from the ulcer aids in healing. This can typically be accomplished by prolonged bed rest or the application of a total-contact cast. Most patients prefer the contact cast with its attendant freedom of mobility.

Neuropathic ulcers are recognized by their location at pressure points such as over the metatarsal heads. The ulcers characteristically have a thick surrounding zone of hyperkeratosis, and hammer toes and a flattened foot arch are commonly found. The presence of foot pulses, good color and warmth, and a near-normal ankle-brachial index strongly suggests that revascularization is not necessary for this patient. Antibiotics should not be used in the absence of infection. The patient's ulcer appears clean, and the absence of erythema, warmth, tenderness, and swelling also suggests that infection is absent. The ability to probe to bone is a highly sensitive test for the presence of an underlying osteomyelitis; however, the inability to probe to bone does not rule out infection. This patient should probably have an MRI of the foot to assess for underlying bone infection.

Empiric antibiotics are not indicated. Furthermore, vancomycin would be a poor choice for empiric antibiotic treatment because of the necessity to cover streptococci, methicillin-resistant *Staphylococcus aureus*, aerobic gram-negative bacilli, and anaerobes.

An Unna boot is appropriate compression therapy for venous ulcers, which are typically found on the medial ankle around the malleolus. An Unna boot is inappropriate therapy for a neuropathic ulcer because the pressure that may be applied over the ulcer may inhibit healing.

Whirlpool hyperthermia is of no proven benefit in the treatment of neuropathic ulcers.

KEY POINT

- **Offloading, usually with contact casting, can accelerate the healing of a neuropathic ulcer.**

Bibliography

Dalla Paola L, Faglia E. Treatment of diabetic foot ulcer: an overview strategies for clinical approach. Curr Diabetes Rev. 2006;2(4):431-447. [PMID: 18220646]

Item 31　　Answer: B

Educational Objective: Understand the association between erythema multiforme and recurrent herpes simplex virus infection.

Erythema multiforme is a mucocutaneous reaction characterized by targetoid lesions and, in most cases, both skin and mucosal involvement. The majority (up to 90%) of recurrent cases of erythema multiforme have been associated with infections, the most common of which is herpes simplex virus (both HSV-1 and HSV-2). No virus is routinely recovered with culture, and treatment with antiviral agents does not affect the outcome of an acute outbreak. Suppressive antiviral therapy, however, may minimize the number of erythema multiforme recurrences. It is important to recognize that recurrences of erythema multiforme can occur in the absence of apparent clinical reactivation of HSV; patients may not be aware that they are infected with HSV.

Erythema migrans (also called erythema chronicum migrans) is the hallmark cutaneous lesion of early Lyme disease. A centrifugally spreading ring of erythema that resembles a bull's eye usually develops at the site of infection 3 to 30 days after a tick bite. Erythema migrans lesions are most typically found near the axilla, inguinal region, popliteal fossa, or at the belt line, and palmar involvement is rare, if it occurs at all. Lesions slowly expand over days or weeks, with central clearing producing a target or bull's-eye appearance, and increase in size to 20 cm or more. Erythema migrans is distinguished from erythema multiforme by the lesion size, its location, and lack of associated mucosal involvement. This patient's findings are not consistent with erythema migrans, and neither current nor past infection with *Borrelia burgdorferi* predisposes the patient to recurrent episodes of erythema multiforme.

Rocky Mountain spotted fever (RMSF) is a tick-borne disease caused by *Rickettsia rickettsii*. RMSF may present with subtle, fine, pink, blanching macules and papules on the wrists and ankles that then spread centripetally and to the palms and soles. As the rash spreads, the characteristic petechial and purpuric "spots" appear. Most patients have fever, severe headache, and myalgia. This patient's findings are not consistent with RMSF, and neither current nor past infection with *R. rickettsii* predisposes the patient to recurrent episodes of erythema multiforme.

Streptococcal infections have been associated with erythema nodosum, flares of psoriasis, and several skin infections, including perianal cellulitis and blistering distal dactylitis; however, they are not commonly associated with erythema multiforme.

KEY POINT

- **Up to 90% of cases of recurrent erythema multiforme are associated with infections, the most common of which is herpes simplex virus.**

Bibliography

Aurelian L, Ono F, Burnett J. Herpes simplex virus (HSV)-associated erythema multiforme (HAEM): a viral disease with an autoimmune component. Dermatol Online J. 2003;9(1):1. [PMID: 12639459]

Item 32　　Answer: C

Educational Objective: Manage dermatitis herpetiformis using a gluten-free diet.

Most, if not all, patients with dermatitis herpetiformis have gluten sensitivity, even when they have no evidence of enteropathy. Treatment with a gluten-free diet is successful in greater than 70% of patients with dermatitis herpetiformis, but excellent adherence to the diet is required for a minimum of 3 to 12 months. In the interim, initial suppression of symptoms with dapsone is usually necessary for more rapid relief of symptoms. Continued compliance with the gluten-free diet will allow a decrease in the dapsone, and it can often be discontinued. A gluten-free diet treats the cause, rather than the symptoms, of the disease. Dapsone treatment requires careful monitoring. Hemolysis is the most common side effect of treatment and may be severe in patients with glucose-6-phosphate dehydrogenase (G6PD) deficiency. Pretesting for G6PD deficiency prior to initiating therapy with dapsone is generally recommended. Additional adverse reactions include toxic hepatitis, cholestatic jaundice, psychosis, and both motor and sensory neuropathy. Patients with dermatitis herpetiformis and their first-degree relatives are at increased risk for other autoimmune diseases, including thyroid disease, rheumatoid arthritis, and lupus erythematosus.

There is no role for cyclosporine, a lactose-free diet, or intravenous immune globulin in the treatment of dermatitis herpetiformis.

KEY POINT

- **Treatment with a gluten-free diet is successful in greater than 70% of patients with dermatitis herpetiformis, even in the absence of symptomatic enteropathy.**

Bibliography

Viljamaa M, Kaukinen K, Pukkala E, Hervonen K, Reunala T, Collin P. Malignancies and mortality in patients with coeliac disease and dermatitis herpetiformis: 30-year population-based study. Dig Liver Dis. 2006;38(6):374-380. [PMID: 16627018]

Item 33   Answer: E

Educational Objective: Diagnose solar (senile) purpura in a patient with aged and photodamaged skin.

Solar or actinic purpura occurs frequently in individuals who have extensive photodamage of the skin. Minimal trauma, which may or may not have been recognized, causes large, asymptomatic ecchymoses. The surrounding skin is fragile and tears easily; in some cases, it heals with stellate scars. The forearms are most frequently involved, but other extremities and the face can develop similar lesions. Chronic sun damage weakens the blood vessel walls and surrounding stroma, allowing minimal trauma to cause extravasation of blood and a large bruise. Use of topical or systemic corticosteroids can exacerbate fragility.

Ecchymoses in this setting should not suggest an underlying coagulopathy; however, this can be ruled out by performing appropriate coagulation studies. This patient's normal coagulation studies rule out a liver-related coagulopathy.

Defects in platelets, either quantitative or qualitative, can cause purpura, but most commonly cause small (<4 mm) petechiae. These are most frequently located on dependent parts of the body, including the legs in ambulatory patients and the back and buttocks in those who are bedridden. Immune thrombocytopenic purpura is therefore unlikely based upon the appearance of the skin lesions and the normal platelet count.

Cutaneous vasculitis is characterized by palpable purpura, necrotic papules, or ulcerative lesions and occasionally urticaria. The disease process may be limited entirely to the skin as an isolated cutaneous vasculitis. This patient does not have palpable purpura and therefore leukocytoclastic vasculitis is unlikely.

The classic cutaneous findings of porphyria cutanea tarda (PCT) include tense blisters and resultant erosions on sun-exposed areas of skin, particularly the hands, scalp, and face. These blisters may heal with scarring and formation of milia, which appear as firm, white, 1- to 2-mm "pearls" in the skin. The skin is fragile and tears easily. Hyperpigmentation and hypertrichosis are also common. Purpura is itself not characteristic of PCT, making this diagnosis unlikely in this patient. However, since PCT can be associated with a number of diseases or conditions that cause thrombocytopenia or a coagulopathy (including chronic liver diseases, renal failure, and hematologic malignancies), the presence of petechiae or purpura warrants appropriate evaluation.

KEY POINT

- **Solar or actinic purpura is characterized by large, asymptomatic ecchymoses that occur with minimal trauma; it occurs frequently in individuals who have extensive photodamage of the skin.**

Bibliography

Carlson JA, Chen KR. Cutaneous pseudovasculitis. Am J Dermatopathol. 2007;29(1):44-55. [PMID: 17284961]

Item 34   Answer: D

Educational Objective: Diagnose Stevens-Johnson syndrome.

This patient has Stevens-Johnson syndrome (SJS). SJS is characterized by fever followed by the onset of erythematous macules and plaques that progress to epidermal necrosis and sloughing limited to less than 10% of the body surface area. Mucous membranes are affected in most patients, and ocular, oral, and genital surfaces may be involved. A sulfonamide is the most likely causative drug. Treatment in a burn unit is preferable for patients with extensive blistering and erosions.

Acute generalized exanthematous pustulosis (AGEP) is an exanthem that follows an infection or drug ingestion. It is characterized by the acute onset of widespread pustules that may resemble pustular psoriasis, along with fever, leukocytosis, and possibly eosinophilia. AGEP is usually self-limiting and clears without residual skin changes approximately 2 weeks after drug cessation.

Drug reaction with eosinophilia and systemic symptoms (DRESS) is characterized by a generalized papular eruption, fever, arthralgia, and generalized lymphadenopathy. Associated laboratory findings may include elevated aminotransferase levels, eosinophilia, and lymphocytosis. This patient's cutaneous and laboratory findings are not compatible with DRESS.

The "red man syndrome" (RMS) is the most common adverse reaction to vancomycin. This reaction appears not to be antibody related and is characterized by flushing, erythema, and pruritus involving primarily the upper body, neck, and face. In a few individuals, it may be associated with back and chest pain, dyspnea, and hypotension. This patient has none of the clinical findings characteristic of RMS and was not exposed to vancomycin, making RMS an unlikely diagnosis.

KEY POINT

- Stevens-Johnson syndrome is an acute severe cutaneus reaction that is characterized by fever followed by the onset of erythematous macules and plaques that progress to epidermal necrosis and sloughing.

Bibliography

Greenberger PA. 8. Drug allergy. J Allergy Clin Immunol. 2006;117(2 Suppl Mini-Primer):S464-S470. [PMID: 16455348]

Item 35   Answer: B

Educational Objective: Diagnose localized neuropathic pruritus (notalgia paresthetica).

This patient has notalgia paresthetica, which is characterized by recurrent pruritus, burning, or stinging on the mid-back. On physical examination, signs of chronic scratching or rubbing such as hyperpigmentation or lichenification (thickened skin with increased and exaggerated skin markings due to scratching) may be present, but there are no primary skin abnormalities that cause the itching. The skin may appear entirely normal. Notalgia paresthetica and brachioradial pruritus, a similar type of recurrent itching on the forearms, are examples of neuropathic pruritus—itch caused by an anatomic lesion in the peripheral or central nervous system. Some cases of notalgia paresthetica or brachioradial pruritus are associated with disease in the cervical and/or thoracic spine (frequently degenerative changes, such as osteophytes), and radiographic imaging may be appropriate; however, it is unusual to find a cause that would benefit from surgical management. Most patients have a normal neurologic examination despite their intense pruritus. These localized forms of neuropathic itch are difficult to treat; because they are noninflammatory and are not histamine mediated, corticosteroids are generally ineffective, as are

antihistamines. Topical anesthetics (such as pramoxine) and topical capsaicin may provide some relief. Successful use of gabapentin, as well as tricyclic antidepressants including amitriptyline, has also been reported. For some patients, clarifying the diagnosis alone can be beneficial.

Herpes zoster presents as pruritic or painful vesicles in a dermatomal distribution. Itching or burning can precede the onset of vesicles; however, this patient's symptoms have persisted for years.

Nummular dermatitis is a pruritic eczematous condition that presents as annular, coin-shaped, erythematous plaques with pinpoint vesicles, overlying oozing scale, and honey-colored, serous crusting. This patient does not have a presentation consistent with nummular dermatitis.

Xerosis is the medical term for dry skin. While dry skin can be itchy, it presents with diffuse flaking of the skin without localized areas of hyperpigmentation. It is most common on the extremities and flanks.

KEY POINT

- Neuropathic pruritus should be considered in patients with localized itching without associated skin lesions; it can be associated with disease in the cervical and/or thoracic spine.

Bibliography

Goodkin R, Wingard E, Bernhard JD. Brachioradial pruritus: cervical spine disease and neurogenic/neuropathic [corrected] pruritus. J Am Acad Dermatol. 2003;48(4):521-524. [PMID: 12664013]

Item 36   Answer: A

Educational Objective: Diagnose eruptive xanthomas.

This patient has eruptive xanthomas, a specific subtype of xanthoma. Xanthomas are yellow, orange, or reddish papules, plaques, or nodules that are associated with underlying primary or secondary hyperlipidemias. Eruptive xanthomas present suddenly as crops of 1- to 4-mm, erythematous, yellow papules on extensor surfaces. They are specifically associated with marked elevations in serum triglyceride levels, often greater than 3000 mg/dL (33.9 mmol/L). Eruptive xanthomas and the associated hypertriglyceridemia may be caused by underlying diseases such as lipoprotein lipase deficiency, dysfunctional apoprotein CII, impaired insulin activity, familial hypercholesterolemia, and medications (isotretinoin, ritonavir). Treatment of hypertriglyceridemia leads to clinical improvement.

Plane xanthomas are yellow-red, slightly elevated plaques located in the skin folds of the neck and upper trunk. They may be associated with homozygous familial hypercholesterolemia, dysbetalipoproteinemia, or no lipid disorder. Nonlipid disease associations include multiple myeloma, paraproteinemia, leukemia, and lymphoma. This patient's findings are not consistent with plane xanthomas.

Tendon xanthomas are flesh-colored, smooth, firm, and lobulated subcutaneous nodules that move with the underlying extensor tendon. Tendon xanthoma is associated with familial hypercholesterolemia caused by a defect in the LDL cholesterol receptors on the cell membrane. This patient's sudden eruption of multiple small, colored papules is not consistent with tendon xanthoma.

Xanthelasmas are soft, yellow-orange, polygonal papules and plaques that are localized to the eyelids. They are the most common of all xanthomas and may be an isolated finding unrelated to hyperlipidemia or may be associated with familial hypercholesterolemia or familial dyslipoproteinemia.

KEY POINT

- Eruptive xanthomas present suddenly as crops of 1- to 4-mm, erythematous, yellow papules on extensor surfaces.

Bibliography

Pitambe HV, Schulz EJ. Life-threatening dermatoses due to metabolic and endocrine disorders. Clin Dermatol. 2005;23(3):258-266. [PMID: 15896541]

Item 37   Answer: C

Educational Objective: Understand the association between proximal white subungual onychomycosis and HIV infection.

This patient has proximal white subungual onychomycosis (PWSO), a rare form of onychomycosis. Onychomycosis usually presents as distal subungual debris; the infection rarely begins proximally in patients who are not immunocompromised. Studies show PWSO to be a common presentation of onychomycosis in patients with HIV infection. It can also be found in patients with other causes of immunodeficiency. If a patient presents with PWSO, HIV infection should be suspected as a predisposing factor.

In some studies, diabetes mellitus has been shown to be independently associated with an increase in onychomycosis, but the onychomycosis is not specifically of the PWSO type. Cushing disease, leukemia, and metastatic cancer, while often associated with opportunistic infections, have not been reported to be associated with an increased incidence of onychomycosis of any type.

KEY POINT

- Proximal white subungual onychomycosis is a common presentation of onychomycosis in patients with HIV infection.

Bibliography

Surjushe A, Kamath R, Oberai C, et al. A clinical and mycological study of onychomycosis in HIV infection. Indian J Dermatol Venereol Leprol. 2007;73(6):397-401. [PMID: 18032858]

Item 38   Answer: A

Educational Objective: Treat mixed cryoglobulinemia associated with hepatitis C infection.

This patient's clinical signs and symptoms are most consistent with a diagnosis of mixed cryoglobulinemia associated with hepatitis C virus (HCV) infection. Mixed cryoglobulinemia, which is associated with HCV infection in greater than 90% of cases, is one cause of palpable purpura, the histologic correlate of which is leukocytoclastic vasculitis. Although a skin biopsy showing leukocytoclastic vasculitis does not distinguish between the different etiologies for cutaneous small vessel vasculitis, the HCV infection, low complement levels, and presence of circulating cryoglobulins point to mixed cryoglobulinemia as the cause of his signs and symptoms.

Indications for treatment of mixed cryoglobulinemia include evidence of progressive systemic disease affecting the small blood vessels (such as cutaneous vasculitis), kidneys, liver, or peripheral nerves. The first-line therapy for mixed cryoglobulinemia associated with HCV is treatment of the underlying infection with pegylated interferon alfa and ribavirin.

There is no evidence that treatment with systemic corticosteroids is beneficial in patients with mixed cryoglobulinemia, and there is a theoretical concern that immunosuppression may lead to enhanced replication of HCV. Plasma exchange can lower circulating levels of cryoglobulins, and this therapy is typically reserved for patients with very aggressive disease, including advanced renal failure, distal necroses requiring amputation, or advanced neuropathy. These clinical findings are absent, and plasma exchange is therefore not indicated. Topical corticosteroids will have no effect on the systemic manifestations of circulating cryoglobulins and minimal, if any, effect on the cutaneous lesions.

KEY POINT

- The therapy of choice for mixed cryoglobulinemia associated with hepatitis C virus is treatment of the underlying infection with pegylated interferon alfa and ribavirin.

Bibliography

Saadoun D, Delluc A, Piette JC, Cacoub P. Treatment of hepatitis C-associated mixed cryoglobulinemia vasculitis. Curr Opin Rheumatol. 2008;20(1):23-28. [PMID: 18281853]

Item 39   Answer: C

Educational Objective: Diagnose seborrheic keratoses.

This patient has seborrheic keratoses, a benign skin condition. These lesions are common in adults and increase in number with age. They are characterized by sharply demarcated, tan to dark brown, warty papules, plaques, and nodules that have a waxy texture and appear to be "stuck on" the skin. While they can arise on any area of the skin, they are frequently located in the scalp and on the back and chest.

Skin cancers tend to occur on the sun-exposed parts of the body. Basal cell carcinoma is a pearly or translucent papule or nodule with associated telangiectasias. Melanomas, like seborrheic keratoses, are pigmented, but do not classically have a waxy, warty surface. Melanomas often have irregular borders, whereas seborrheic keratoses are usually well demarcated. Distinguishing between the two can be difficult, however, and a biopsy may be necessary if the diagnosis is in question. Squamous cell carcinoma presents as a scaly, hyperkeratotic, red or pink papule, patch, or plaque. It is not brown, tan, or black and does not have a warty appearance like seborrheic keratoses.

> **KEY POINT**
>
> - Seborrheic keratoses are common, benign neoplasms that present as brown to black, well-demarcated, "stuck-on"–appearing papules with waxy surfaces.

Bibliography
Luba MC, Bangs SA, Mohler AM, Stulberg DL. Common benign skin tumors. Am Fam Physician. 2003;67(4):729-738. [PMID: 12613727]

Item 40   Answer: C

Educational Objective: Diagnose Paget disease of the breast.

This patient has Paget disease of the breast, defined as a persistent, scaling, eczematous, or ulcerated lesion involving the nipple/areolar complex. This disease is actually an extension of an underlying ductal adenocarcinoma of the breast that may be present even in the absence of abnormal physical examination findings or mammogram. It is often misdiagnosed on the first presentation as either eczema or psoriasis, but when there is a lack of response to appropriate therapy a biopsy should be performed.

The most characteristic lesions of chronic cutaneous lupus erythematosus are discoid lesions (erythematous, infiltrated plaques that are covered with scale and are associated with follicular plugging). These lesions are most often found on the face, neck, and scalp. As they expand, they develop depressed central scars. This patient's lesion is not clinically compatible with chronic cutaneous lupus.

Lichen simplex chronicus is a localized disorder characterized by intense pruritus, which leads to a localized area of lichenified skin (thickened skin with increased and exaggerated skin markings due to scratching). This patient has no evidence of lichenification.

The most common form of psoriasis is plaque psoriasis. The skin lesions of this disorder are sharply demarcated, erythematous plaques covered by silvery-white scales that affect the scalp and extensor surfaces (elbows and knees) as well as the nails. A single patch of psoriasis located on the nipple would be a very rare presentation.

> **KEY POINT**
>
> - Paget disease of the breast presents as a persistent, scaling, eczematous, or ulcerated lesion involving the nipple/areolar complex and may be mistaken for more benign conditions such as eczema.

Bibliography
Caliskan M, Gatti G, Sosnovskikh I, et al. Paget's disease of the breast: the experience of the European Institute of Oncology and review of the literature. Breast Cancer Res Treat. 2008;112(3):513-521. [PMID: 18240020]

Index